YOUCAT

Youth Catechism of
the Catholic Church

YOUCAT

ENGLISH

YOUTH CATECHISM
OF THE CATHOLIC CHURCH

With a Foreword
by Pope Benedict XVI

Translated by Michael J. Miller

IGNATIUS PRESS   SAN FRANCISCO

Original German edition: YOUCAT deutsch
Jugendkatechismus der Katholischen Kirche
© 2010 by Pattloch Verlag GmbH & Co. KG, Munich, Germany

Nihil Obstat, March 3, 2010 by the Austrian Bishops' Conference Imprimatur, Austrian
Bishops' Conference with the approval of the German Bishops' Conference, November
29, 2010; the Swiss Bishops' Conference, December 6, 2010 with the prior approval of
the Congregation for the Doctrine of the Faith, the Congregation for the Clergy, and the
Pontifical Council for the Laity.

Nihil Obstat: Reverend Monsignor J. Warren Holleran, S.T.D.
Imprimatur: † Most Reverend George Niederauer, Archbishop of San Francisco
August 8, 2011

Instructions for Use

The Youth Catechism, which is written in language suitable for young people,
deals with the entire Catholic faith as it was presented in the Catechism of
the Catholic Church (CCC of 1997), without aiming, however, at the com-
pleteness provided in that volume. The work is structured in **Question-and-
Answer** format, and **numbers** after each answer refer the reader to the more
extensive and in-depth treatments in the CCC. A **commentary** following the
answer is meant to give the young person additional help in understanding
the questions that are discussed and their significance in his life. Furthermore, the Youth Catechism offers in the margin a continuous series of supple-
mentary elements, such as **pictures,** summary **definitions,** citations from
Sacred Scripture, quotations from **saints** and reliable **teachers of the faith**
but also from non-religious authors. At the conclusion of the book, there is
an **index of subjects and persons** to facilitate finding specific topics.

Symbols and Their Meaning:

 Citation from Sacred Scripture

 Quotations from various authors, including saints
and other Christian authors

 Definitions   See definition given for the term

 Cross reference to additional texts in YOUCAT

Layout, Design, Illustrations by Alexander von Lengerke, Cologne, Germany
© 2011 by Ignatius Press, San Francisco
All rights reserved
ISBN 978-1-58617-516-0
Library of Congress Control Number 2010931314
Printed in the United States of America
20 19 18 17 16 15 14 13

CONTENTS

Dear young friends!

Today I recommend for your reading an unusual book. It is unusual both because of its content and because of the way it came to be. I would like to tell you a little about how it was written, because then it will be clear why it is so unusual.

You could say that it came to be from another work, whose origins go back to the 1980s. It was a difficult time for the Church and for society worldwide. New guidance was needed to find the path to the future. After the Second Vatican Council (1962–1965) and in a changed cultural situation, many people were confused about what Christians actually believe, what the Church teaches, whether in fact she can teach anything at all, and how everything can find its place in a culture that had changed from its very foundations. Is it still reasonable today to be a believer? These were the questions that even good Christians were asking.

At that time Pope John Paul II made a bold decision. He decided that bishops from all over the world should together write a book in which they would answer these questions. He gave me the task of coordinating the work of the bishops and seeing to it that from the contributions of the bishops a book would result—a real book, not just a haphazard collection of all sorts of documents. This book would have the old-fashioned title *Catechism of the Catholic Church* but would be something entirely new and exciting. It would show what the Catholic Church believes today and how one can with good reason believe.

I was alarmed by this task. I must admit that I doubted whether something like this could succeed. For how was it possible that authors scattered all over the world could together produce a readable book? How could men who not only geographically but also intellectually and spiritually lived on different continents create a text with an inner unity, one that would also be understandable throughout all those continents? And there was the further difficulty that these bishops would not be writing as individual authors but would be in contact with their brother bishops and with the people in their dioceses. I must admit that even today it still seems to me to be a miracle that this project finally succeeded.

We met for a week three or four times a year and vigorously discussed the different individual sections that had taken shape in between meetings. First, of course, we had to determine the structure of the book. It had to be simple so that the individual groups of authors that we established would have a clear task and would not have to force their work into a complicated system. It is the same structure you will find in this book. It is simply taken from centuries of catechetical experience: What we believe—How we should celebrate the Christian mysteries—How we have life in Christ—How we should pray. I will not describe now how we slowly made our way through so many and varied questions until finally a book came from it all. One can, of course, criticize some things or even many things in such a work: Everything that man makes is inadequate and can be improved. Still it is a marvelous book: a witness to unity in diversity. We were able to form a single choir from many voices because we had the same score, the faith that the Church has borne through the centuries from the apostles onward.

Why am I telling you all this? We realized at the time we were working on the book that not only are the continents and cultures diverse, but that even within individual communities there are again diverse "continents": The worker thinks differently from the farmer; a physicist differently from a philologist; an executive differently from a journalist; a young man differently from an old man. So we had to find a way of thinking and speaking that was in some way above all these differences, a common space, so to speak, between different worlds of thought. In doing this it became ever more apparent to us that the text needed to be "translated" for different cultural worlds in order to reach people in those worlds in ways that correspond to their own questions and ways of thinking.

In the World Youth Days since the introduction of the Catechism of the Catholic Church—Rome, Toronto, Cologne, Sydney— young people from all over the world have come together, young people who want to believe, who are seeking God, who love Christ, and who want fellowship on their journey. In this context the question arose: Should we not attempt to translate the *Catechism of the Catholic Church* into the language of young people? Should we not bring its great riches into the world of today's youth? Of course, there are many differences even among the youth of today's world. And so now, under the capable direction of the Archbishop of Vienna, Christoph Cardinal Schönborn, YOUCAT has been produced for young people. I hope that many young people will let themselves be fascinated by this book.

Many people say to me: The youth of today are not interested in this. I disagree, and I am certain that I am right. The youth of today are not as superficial as some think. They want to know what life is really all about. A detective story is exciting because it draws us into the destiny of other men, a destiny that could be ours. This book is exciting because it speaks of our own destiny and so deeply engages every one of us.

So I invite you: Study this Catechism! That is my heartfelt desire. This Catechism was not written to please you. It will not make life easy for you, because it demands of you a new life. It places before you the Gospel message as the "pearl of great value" (Mt 13:46) for which you must give everything. So I beg you: Study this Catechism with passion and perseverance. Make a sacrifice of your time for it! Study it in the quiet of your room; read it with a friend; form study groups and networks; share with each other on the Internet. By all means continue to talk with each other about your faith.

You need to know what you believe. You need to know your faith with that same precision with which an IT specialist knows the inner workings of a computer. You need to understand it like a good musician knows the piece he is playing. Yes, you need to be more deeply rooted in the faith than the generation of your parents so that you can engage the challenges and temptations of this time with strength and determination. You need God's help if your faith is not going to dry up like a dewdrop in the sun, if you want to resist the blandishments of consumerism, if your love is not to drown in pornography, if you are not going to betray the weak and leave the vulnerable helpless.

If you are now going to apply yourselves zealously to the study of the Catechism, I want to give you one last thing to accompany you: You all know how deeply the community of faith has been wounded recently through the attacks of the evil one, through the penetration of sin itself into the interior, yes, into the heart of the Church. Do not make that an excuse to flee from the face of God! You yourselves are the Body of Christ, the Church! Bring the undiminished fire of your love into this Church whose countenance has so often been disfigured by man. "Never flag in zeal, be aglow with the

Spirit, serve the Lord!" (Rom 12:11). When Israel was at the lowest point in her history, God called for help, not from the great and honored ones of Israel, but from a young man by the name of Jeremiah. Jeremiah felt overwhelmed: "Ah, Lord God! Behold, I do not know how to speak, for I am only a youth" (Jer 1:6). But God was not to be deterred : "Do not say, 'I am only a youth'; for to all to whom I send you you shall go, and whatever I command you you shall speak" (Jer 1:7).

I bless you and pray each day for all of you.

Benedictus PP XVI

Benedictus P.P. XVI

What We Believe

[God] desires all men to be saved and to come to the knowledge of the truth.

1 Tim 2:4

You cannot imagine at all how much you interest God; he is interested in you as if there were no one else on earth.

JULIEN GREEN
(1900–1998, French writer)

One must know man and human things in order to love them. One must love God and divine things in order to know them.

BLAISE PASCAL,
(1623–1662, French mathematician and philosopher)

God is love.

1 Jn 4:16b

The measure of love is love without measure.

ST. FRANCIS OF SALES
(1567–1622, distinguished bishop, brilliant spiritual guide, founder of a religious community, and Doctor of the Church)

❧ SECTION ONE ❧
Why We Are Able to Believe

1 *For what purpose are we here on earth?*

We are here on earth in order to know and to love God, to do good according to his will, and to go someday to heaven. [1–3, 358]

To be a human being means to come from God and to go to God. Our origin goes back farther than our parents. We come from God, in whom all the happiness of heaven and earth is at home, and we are expected in his everlasting, infinite blessedness. Meanwhile we live on this earth. Sometimes we feel that our Creator is near; often we feel nothing at all. So that we might find the way home, God sent us his Son, who freed us from sin, delivers us from all evil, and leads us unerringly into true life. He is "the way, and the truth, and the life" (Jn 14:6). → 285

2 *Why did God create us?*

God created us out of free and unselfish love. [1–3]

When a man loves, his heart overflows. He would like to share his joy with others. He gets this from his Creator. Although God is a mystery, we can still think about him in a human way and say: Out of the "surplus" of his love he created us. He wanted to share his endless joy with us, who are creatures of his love.

❧ CHAPTER ONE ❧
Man Is Receptive to God

3 *Why do we seek God?*

God has placed in our hearts a longing to seek and find him. St. Augustine says, "You have made us for yourself, and our heart is restless until it rests in you." We call this longing for God → RELIGION. [27–30]

It is natural for man to seek God. All of our striving for truth and happiness is ultimately a search for the one

RELIGION

We can understand religion generally to mean a relationship to what is divine. A religious person acknowledges something divine as the power that created him and the world, on which he is dependent and to which he is ordered. He wants to please and honor the Divinity by his way of life.

> The noblest power of man is reason. The highest goal of reason is the knowledge of God.

ST. ALBERT THE GREAT (ca. 1200–1280, Dominican priest, scientist, and scholar, Doctor of the Church, and one of the greatest theologians of the Church)

who supports us *absolutely,* satisfies us *absolutely,* and employs us *absolutely* in his service. A person is not completely himself until he has found God. "Anyone who seeks truth seeks God, whether or not he realizes it" (St. Edith Stein). → 5, 281–285

4 *Can we know the existence of God by our reason?*

Yes. Human reason can know God with certainty. [31–36, 44–47]

The world cannot have its origin and its destination within itself. In everything that exists, there is more than we see. The order, the beauty, and the development of the world point beyond themselves toward God. Every man is receptive to what is true, good, and beautiful. He hears within himself the voice

> They [men] should seek God, in the hope that they might feel after him and find him. Yet he is not far from each one of us, for "In him we live and move and have our being."

Acts 17:27–28a

of conscience, which urges him to what is good and warns him against what is evil. Anyone who follows this path reasonably finds God.

5 *Why do people deny that God exists, if they can know him by reason?*

To know the invisible God is a great challenge for the human mind. Many are scared off by it. Another reason why some do not want to know God is because they would then have to change their life. Anyone who says that the question about God is meaningless because it cannot be answered is making things too easy for himself. [37–38] → 357

6 *Can we grasp God at all in concepts? Is it possible to speak about him meaningfully?*

Although we men are limited and the infinite greatness of God never fits into finite human concepts, we can nevertheless speak rightly about God. [39–43, 48]

In order to express something about God, we use imperfect images and limited notions. And so everything we say about God is subject to the reservation that our language is not equal to God's greatness. Therefore we must constantly purify and improve our speech about God.

◇ CHAPTER TWO ◇
God Approaches Us Men

7 *Why did God have to show himself in order for us to be able to know what he is like?*

Man can know by reason that God exists, but not what God is really like. Yet because God would very much like to be known, he has revealed himself. [50–53, 68–69]

God did not have to reveal himself to us. But he did it—out of love. Just as in human love one can know something about the beloved person only if he opens his heart to us, so too we know something about

God's inmost thoughts only because the eternal and mysterious God has opened himself to us out of love. From creation on, through the patriarchs and the prophets down to the definitive → REVELATION in his Son Jesus Christ, God has spoken again and again to mankind. In him he has poured out his heart to us and made his inmost being visible for us.

REVELATION
Revelation means that God opens himself, shows himself, and speaks to the world voluntarily.

8 *How does God reveal himself in the Old Testament?*

God shows himself in the → OLD TESTAMENT as God, who created the world out of love and remains faithful to men even when they have fallen away from him into sin. [54–64, 70–72]

God makes it possible to experience him in history: With Noah he establishes a covenant to save all living things. He calls Abraham so as to make him "the father of a multitude of nations" (Gen 17:5b) and to bless "all the families of the earth" in him (Gen 12:3b). The people Israel, sprung from Abraham, becomes his special possession. To Moses he introduces himself by name. His mysterious name יהוה → YHWH, usually transcribed Yahweh, means "I AM WHO I AM" (Ex 3:14). He frees Israel from slavery in Egypt, establishes a covenant with them on Sinai, and through Moses gives them the Law. Again and again, God sends prophets to his people to call them to conversion and to the renewal of the covenant. The prophets proclaim that God will establish a new and everlasting covenant, which will bring about a radical renewal and definitive redemption. This covenant will be open to all human beings.

9 *What does God show us about himself when he sends his Son to us?*

God shows us in Jesus Christ the full depth of his merciful love. [65–66, 73]

Through Jesus Christ the invisible God becomes visible. He becomes a man like us. This shows us how far God's love goes: He bears our whole burden. He walks every

> We cannot talk about God, but woe to the one who remains silent about him.

ST. AUGUSTINE
(354–430, Doctor of the Church, the most important writer and theologian of the early Church)

> This is his [the theologian's] mission: in the loquacity of our day and of other times, in the plethora of words, to make the essential words heard. Through words, it means making present the Word, the Word who comes from God, the Word who is God.

POPE BENEDICT XVI,
October 6, 2006

> All that is said about God presupposes something said by God.

ST. EDITH STEIN
(1891–1942, Jewish Christian, philosopher, and Carmelite nun, concentration camp victim)

? INCARNATION
(from the Latin *caro, carnis* = flesh, "becoming flesh"): God's act of becoming man in Jesus Christ. This is the foundation of Christian faith and of hope for the redemption of mankind.

path with us. He is there in our abandonment, our sufferings, our fear of death. He is there when we can go no farther, so as to open up for us the door leading into life. → 314

10 With Jesus Christ, has everything been said, or does revelation continue even after him?

In Jesus Christ, God himself came to earth. He is God's last Word. By listening to him, all men of all times can know who God is and what is necessary for their salvation. [66–67]

With the Gospel of Jesus Christ, the → REVELATION of God is perfect and complete. To make it comprehensible to us, the Holy Spirit leads us ever deeper into the truth. God's light breaks so forcefully into the lives of many individuals that they "see the heavens opened" (Acts 7:56). That is how the great places of pilgrimage such as Guadalupe in Mexico or Lourdes in France came about. The "private revelations" of visionaries cannot improve on the Gospel of Jesus Christ. No one is obliged to believe in them. But they can help us understand the Gospel better. Their authenticity is tested by the → CHURCH.

11 Why do we hand on the faith?

We hand on the faith because Jesus commands us: "Go therefore and make disciples of all nations" (Mt 28:19). [91]

No genuine Christian leaves the transmission of the faith exclusively to specialists (teachers, pastors, missionaries). We are Christ for others. This means that every genuine Christian would like God to come to other people, too. He says to himself, "The Lord needs me! I have been baptized and confirmed and am responsible for helping the people around me to learn about God and 'to come to the knowledge of the truth' (1 Tim 2:4b)." Mother Teresa used a good comparison: "Often you can see power lines running alongside the street. Unless current is flowing through them, there is no light. The power line is you and I! The current is God! We have the power to allow the current to flow

> The happiness you are seeking, the happiness you have a right to enjoy, has a name and a face: it is Jesus of Nazareth.

POPE BENEDICT XVI,
August 18, 2005

> There is an urgent need for the emergence of a new generation of apostles anchored firmly in the word of Christ, capable of responding to the challenges of our times and prepared to spread the Gospel far and wide.

POPE BENEDICT XVI,
February 22, 2006

through us and thus to generate the light of the world: JESUS—or to refuse to be used and, thus, allow the darkness to spread." → 123

12 *How can we tell what belongs to the true faith?*

We find the true faith in Sacred Scripture and in the living Tradition of the Church.
[76, 80–82, 85–87, 97, 100]

The → NEW TESTAMENT developed out of the faith of the Church. Scripture and Tradition belong together. Handing on the faith does not occur primarily through documents. In the early Church it was said that Sacred Scripture was "written on the heart of the Church rather than on parchment". The disciples and the → APOSTLES experienced their new life above all through a living fellowship with Jesus. The early Church invited people into this fellowship, which continued in a different way after the Resurrection. The first Christians held fast "to the apostles' teaching and fellowship, to the breaking of the bread and to

MISSION
(from Latin *missio* = sending): Mission is the essence of the Church and Jesus' mandate to all Christians to proclaim the Gospel in word and deed, so that all men can freely make a decision for Christ.

the prayers" (Acts 2:42). They were united with one another and yet had room for others. This is part of our faith to this day: Christians invite other individuals to come to know a fellowship with God that has been preserved unaltered since the times of the apostles in the Catholic Church.

13 Can the Church err in questions of faith?

The faithful as a whole cannot err in faith, because Jesus promised his disciples that he would send them the Spirit of truth and keep them in the truth (Jn 14:17). [80–82, 85–87, 92, 100]

Just as the disciples believed Jesus with their whole heart, a Christian can rely completely on the Church when he asks about the way to life. Since Jesus Christ himself gave his apostles the commission to teach, the Church has a teaching authority (the → MAGISTERIUM) and must not remain silent. Although individual members of the Church can err and even make serious mistakes, the Church as a whole can never fall away from God's truth. The Church carries through the ages a living truth that is greater than herself. We speak about a *depositum fidei,* a deposit of faith that is to be preserved. If such a truth is publicly disputed or distorted, the Church is called upon to clarify again "what has always and everywhere been believed by all" (St. Vincent of Lerins, d. 450).

14 Is Sacred Scripture true?

"The books of Scripture firmly, faithfully, and without error teach [the] truth. ... Written under the inspiration of the Holy Spirit, they have God as their author" (Second Vatican Council, DV 11). [103–107]

The → BIBLE did not fall from heaven in its final form, nor did God dictate it to human scribes who copied it down mechanically. Rather "God chose certain men who ... made full use of their own faculties and powers so that, though he acted in them and by them, it was as true authors that they consigned to writing whatever he wanted written, and no more" (Second Vatican

Council, DV 11). One factor in recognizing particular texts as Sacred Scripture was their general acceptance in the Church. In the Christian communities there had to be a consensus: "Yes, through this text God himself speaks to us—this is inspired by the Holy Spirit!" Which of the many original Christian writings are really inspired by the Holy Spirit has been defined since the fourth century in the so-called → CANON of Sacred Scriptures.

15 *How can Sacred Scripture be "truth" if not everything in it is right?*

The → Bible is not meant to convey precise historical information or scientific findings to us. Moreover, the authors were children of their time. Their forms of expression are influenced by the sometimes inadequate cultural images of the world around them. Nevertheless, everything that man must know about God and the way of his salvation is found with infallible certainty in Sacred Scripture. [106–107, 109]

16 *What is the right way to read the Bible?*

The right way to read Sacred Scripture is to read it prayerfully, in other words, with the help of the Holy Spirit, under whose influence it came into being. It is God's Word and contains God's essential communication to us. [109–119, 137]

The → BIBLE is like a long letter written by God to each one of us. For this reason I should accept the Sacred Scriptures with great love and reverence. First of all, it is important really to read God's letter, in other words, not to pick out details while paying no attention to the whole message. Then I must interpret the whole message with a view to its heart and mystery: Jesus Christ, of whom the whole Bible speaks, even the Old Testament. Therefore I should read the Sacred Scriptures in the faith that gave rise to them, the same living faith of the Church. ➔ 491

INSPIRATION
(Latin: *inspiratio* = inbreathing): God's influence on the human writers of the Bible, so that he himself should be regarded as the author of the Sacred Scriptures.

CANON
(Greek: *kanon* = measuring rod, rule, norm): the authoritative collection of Sacred Scriptures in the Old and New Testaments of the Bible.

BIBLE
"Bible" (Latin *biblia* = scrolls, books) is what Jews and Christians call a collection of Sacred Scriptures that came into being over a period of more than one thousand years and is for them the charter of their faith. The Christian Bible is considerably more extensive than the Jewish Bible, because besides their Scriptures it also contains the four Gospels, the letters of St. Paul, and other writings of the early Church.

The Books of the Bible (→ CANON)

OLD TESTAMENT (46 Books)

The Historical Books

Genesis (Gen), Exodus (Ex), Leviticus (Lev), Numbers
(Num), Deuteronomy (Deut), Joshua (Josh), Judges
(Judg), Ruth (Ruth), 1 Samuel (1 Sam), 2 Samuel (2
Sam), 1 Kings (1 Kings), 2 Kings (2 Kings), 1 Chronicles
(1 Chron), 2 Chronicles (2 Chron), Ezra (Ezra),
Nehemiah (Neh), Tobit (Tob), Judith (Jud), Esther
(Esther), 1 Maccabees (1 Mac), 2 Maccabees (2 Mac)

The Wisdom Books

Job (Job), Psalms (Ps), Proverbs (Prov), Ecclesiastes
(Eccles), Song of Solomon (Song), Wisdom (Wis),
Sirach/Ecclesiasticus (Sir)

The Prophets

Isaiah (Is), Jeremiah (Jer), Lamentations (Lam),
Baruch (Bar), Ezekiel (Ezek), Daniel (Dan), Hosea
(Hos), Joel (Joel), Amos (Amos), Obadiah (Obad),
Jonah (Jon), Micah (Mic), Nahum (Nahum), Habakkuk
(Hab), Zephaniah (Zeph), Haggai (Hag), Zechariah
(Zech), Malachi (Mal)

NEW TESTAMENT (27 Books)

The Gospels

Matthew (Mt), Mark (Mk), Luke (Lk), John (Jn)

The Acts of the Apostles (Acts)

The Letters of St. Paul

Romans (Rom), 1 Corinthians (1 Cor), 2 Corinthians
(2 Cor), Galatians (Gal), Ephesians (Eph),
Philippians (Phil), Colossians (Col), 1
Thessalonians (1 Thess), 2 Thessalonians (2
Thess), 1 Timothy (1 Tim), 2 Timothy (2 Tim), Titus
(Tit), Philemon (Philem), Hebrews (Heb)

The Catholic Letters

James (Jas), 1 Peter (1 Pet), 2 Peter (2 Pet), 1 John (1 Jn), 2 John (2 Jn), 3 John (3 Jn), Jude (Jude)

Revelation/Apocalypse (Rev)

17 What significance does the Old Testament have for Christians?

In the → OLD TESTAMENT God reveals himself as the Creator and preserver of the world and as the leader and instructor of mankind. The Old Testament books are also God's Word and Sacred Scripture. Without the Old Testament, we cannot understand Jesus. [121–123, 128–130, 140]

In the → OLD TESTAMENT a great history of learning the faith begins, which takes a decisive turn in the → NEW TESTAMENT and arrives at its destination with the end of the world and Christ's second coming. The Old Testament is far more than a mere prelude for the New. The commandments and prophecies for the people of the Old Covenant and the promises that are contained in it for all men were never revoked. In the books of the Old Covenant we find an irreplaceable treasure of prayers and wisdom; in particular, the Psalms are part of the Church's daily prayer.

18 What significance does the New Testament have for Christians?

In the → NEW TESTAMENT God's → REVELATION is completed. The four Gospels according to Matthew, Mark, Luke, and John are the centerpiece of Sacred Scripture and the most precious treasure of the Church. In them the Son of God shows himself as he is and encounters us. In the Acts of the Apostles we learn about the beginnings of the Church and the working of the Holy Spirit. In the letters written by the apostles, all facets of human life are set in the light of Christ. In the Book of Revelation we foresee the end of the ages. [124–127, 128–130, 140]

Jesus is everything that God would like to tell us. The entire Old Testament prepares for the Incarnation of

The God of Abraham, the God of Isaac, the God of Jacob— not of the philosophers and scholars! The God of Jesus Christ. One finds and keeps him only on the paths that are taught in the Gospel.

The French philosopher BLAISE PASCAL (1588–1651), after having an experience of God

Ignorance of Scripture is ignorance of Christ.

ST. JEROME (347–419, Father of the Church, Doctor of the Church, interpreter and translator of the Bible)

Only when we meet the living God in Christ do we know what life is. ... There is nothing more beautiful than to be surprised by the Gospel, by the encounter with Christ.

POPE BENEDICT XVI, April 24, 2005

The Bible is God's love letter to us.

SØREN KIERKEGAARD

God's Son. All of God's promises find their fulfillment in Jesus. To be a Christian means to unite oneself ever more deeply with the life of Christ. To do that, one must read and live the Gospels. Madeleine Delbrêl says, "Through his Word God tells us what he is and what he wants; he says it definitively and says it for each individual day. When we hold our Gospel book in our hands, we should reflect that in it dwells the Word that wants to become flesh in us, desires to take hold of us, so that we might begin his life anew in a new place, at a new time, in a new human setting."

19 *What role does Sacred Scripture play in the Church?*

The Church draws her life and strength from Sacred Scripture. [103–104, 131–133, 141]

Besides the presence of Christ in the Holy → EUCHARIST, there is nothing that the Church honors more reverently than Christ's presence in Sacred Scripture. At Holy Mass we receive the Gospel standing, because in the human words we hear, God himself speaks to us. → 128

CHAPTER THREE

Man Responds to God

20 *How can we respond to God when he speaks to us?*

To respond to God means to believe him. [142–149]

Anyone who wants to believe needs a heart that is ready to listen (see 1 Kings 3:9). In many ways God seeks contact with us. In every human encounter, in every moving experience of nature, in every apparent coincidence, in every challenge, every suffering, there is a hidden message from God to us. He speaks even more clearly to us when he turns to us in his Word or in the voice of our conscience. He addresses us as friends. Therefore we, too, should respond as friends and believe him, trust him completely, learn to understand him better and better, and accept his will without reservation.

21 *Faith – what is it?*

Faith is knowledge *and* trust. It has seven characteristics:

- **Faith is a *sheer gift* of God, which we receive when we fervently ask for it.**
- **Faith is the supernatural power that is absolutely *necessary* if we are to attain salvation.**
- **Faith requires the *free will and clear understanding of a person* when he accepts the divine invitation.**
- **Faith is *absolutely certain,* because Jesus guarantees it.**
- **Faith is incomplete unless it leads to active love.**
- **Faith *grows* when we listen more and more carefully to God's Word and enter a lively exchange with him in prayer.**
- **Faith gives us even now a *foretaste of the joy of heaven*.**

[153–165, 179–180, 183–184]

Many people say that to believe is not enough for them; they want to know. The word "believe", however, has two completely different meanings. If a parachutist asks the clerk at the airport, "Is the parachute

---

Behold, I am the handmaid of the Lord; let it be to me according to your word.

Lk 1:38

"If you have faith as a grain of mustard seed, you will say to this mountain, 'Move from here to there,' and it will move; and nothing will be impossible to you."

Mt 17:20

❞ Faith means putting up with God's incomprehensibility for a lifetime.

KARL RAHNER
(1904-1984, German theologian)

Faith is the substance of things hoped for, the proof of things not seen.

Heb 11:1 (new translation by Pope Benedict XVI in the Encyclical *Spe salvi 7*)

packed safely?" and the other man answers casually, "Hmm, I believe so", then that will not be enough for him; he would like to know it for sure. But if he has asked a friend to pack the parachute, then the friend will answer the same question by saying, "Yes, I did it personally. You can trust me!" And to that the parachutist will reply, "Yes, I believe you." This belief is much more than knowing; it means assurance. And that is the kind of belief that prompted Abraham to travel to the Promised Land; that is the faith that caused the → MARTYRS to stand fast till death; that is the faith that still today upholds Christians in persecution. A faith that encompasses the whole person.

22 *How does one go about believing?*

Someone who believes is seeking a personal union with God and is ready to believe God in everything that he shows (reveals) about himself. [150–152]

At the beginning of faith, there is often an emotional disturbance or uneasiness. The person senses that the visible world and the normal course of things cannot be all there is. He feels touched by a mystery and follows the traces that point to the existence of God and gradually finds the confidence to speak to God and finally to unite himself to him in freedom. In John's Gospel it says, "No one has ever seen God; the only-begotten Son, who is in the bosom of the Father, he has made him known" (Jn 1:18). That is why we must believe Jesus, the Son of God, if we want to know what God would like to communicate to us. Believing, therefore, means accepting Jesus and staking one's whole life on him.

23 *Is there a contradiction between faith and science?*

There is no insoluble contradiction between faith and science, because there cannot be two kinds of truth. [159]

There is not one truth of faith that is in competition with another truth of science. There is only one truth, to which both faith and scientific reason refer. God intended reason, with which we can recognize the rational structures of the world, just as he intended faith. That is why the Christian faith demands and promotes the (natural) sciences. Faith exists so that we might know things that are not apparent to reason yet are real *above and beyond* reason. Faith reminds science that it is supposed to serve creation and not set itself up in place of God. Science must respect human dignity instead of violating it.

24 What does my faith have to do with the Church?

No one can believe alone and by himself, just as no one can live alone and by himself. We receive the faith from the Church and live it out in fellowship with the people with whom we share our faith. [166–169, 181]

Faith is the most personal thing a person has, yet it is not a private matter. Anyone who wants to believe must be able to say both "I" and "we", because a faith you cannot share and communicate would be irrational. The individual believer gives his free assent to the "we believe" of the Church. From her he received the faith. She was the one who handed it down through the centuries and then to him, preserved it from falsifications, and caused it to shine forth again and again. Believing is therefore participation in a common conviction. The faith of others supports me, just as the fervor of my faith enkindles and strengthens others. The Church emphasizes the "I" and the "we" of faith by using two professions of faith in her liturgies: the Apostles' Creed, the → CREED that begins with "I believe" (Credo), and the Great Creed of Nicaea-Constantinople, which in its original form starts with the words "We believe" (Credimus).

" No one can arrive at the knowledge of divine and human things unless he has previously and thoroughly learned mathematics.

ST. AUGUSTINE (354–430)

" Mathematics is the alphabet with which God wrote the world.

GALILEO GALILEI
(1564–1642, Italian mathematician, philosopher, and physicist)

? CREED
(from the Latin *credo* = I believe): The first word of the Apostles' Creed became the name for various formulas of the Church's profession of faith, in which the essential contents of the faith are authoritatively summarized.

"Where two or three are gathered in my name, there am I in the midst of them."

Mt 18:20

The Christian Profession of Faith

25 *Why does the faith require definitions and formulas?*

Faith is not about empty words but about reality. In the →CHURCH, condensed formulas of faith developed over the course of time; with their help we can contemplate, express, learn, hand on, celebrate, and live out this reality. [170–174]

Without fixed forms, the content of the faith would dissipate. That is why the Church attaches great importance to definite sentences, the precise wording of which was usually achieved painstakingly, so as to protect the message of Christ from misunderstandings and falsifications. Furthermore, creeds are important when the Church's faith has to be translated into different cultures while being preserved in its essentials, because a common faith is the foundation for the Church's unity.

26 *What are creeds?*

→CREEDS are brief formulas of faith that make it possible for all believers to make a common profession. [185–188, 192–197]

Brief formulas of this kind can be found already in the letters of St. Paul. The early Christian *Apostles' Creed* has a special dignity, because it is thought to be a summary of the faith of the →APOSTLES. The *Nicene Creed* is highly esteemed because it resulted from the great councils of the Church when Christendom was still undivided (Nicaea, 325; Constantinople, 381) and is to this day the common basis for the Christian in the East and the West.

27 *How did the creeds come about?*

The →CREEDS go back to Jesus, who commanded his disciples to baptize. In doing so, they were to require

of the people seeking Baptism the profession of a *definite* faith, namely, faith in the Father, the Son, and the Holy Spirit (→TRINITY). [188–191]

The original cell from which all later →CREEDS grew is the profession of faith in Jesus the Lord and in his missionary mandate. He told his apostles, "Go therefore and make disciples of all nations, baptizing them in the name of the Father and of the Son and of the Holy Spirit" (Mt 28:19). All the creeds of the Church are elaborations of the faith in this Triune God. Each of them begins with a profession of faith in the *Father,* the Creator and preserver of the world, then refers to the *Son,* through whom the world and we ourselves have found redemption, and concludes with a profession of faith in the *Holy Spirit,* who is the presence of God in the Church and in the world.

28 *What does the Apostles' Creed say?*

I believe in God, the Father almighty,
Creator of heaven and earth,
and in Jesus Christ, his only Son,
our Lord,
who was conceived by the Holy Spirit,
born of the Virgin Mary,
suffered under Pontius Pilate,
was crucified, died and was buried;
he descended into hell;
on the third day he rose again from the dead;
he ascended into heaven,
and is seated at the right hand of God the Father almighty;
from there he will come to judge the living and the dead.
I believe in the Holy Spirit,
the holy catholic Church,
the communion of saints,
the forgiveness of sins,
the resurrection of the body,
and life everlasting. Amen.

The Church … guards [this preaching and faith] with care, as dwelling in but a single house, and similarly believes as if having but one soul and a single heart, and preaches, teaches, and hands on this faith with a unanimous voice, as if possessing only one mouth.

ST. IRENAEUS OF LYON
(ca. 135–202, Father of the Church)

Let the Creed be like a mirror for you. Look at yourself in it to see whether you really believe all that you claim to believe. And rejoice every day in your faith.

ST. AUGUSTINE
(354–430)

No man lives alone, no man believes alone. God speaks his word to us and in speaking it calls us together, creates a community, his people, his Church. After the return of Jesus to his Father the Church is the sign of his presence in the world.

ST. BASIL THE GREAT
(Bishop, 5th century)

What does the Nicene (Nicene-Constantinopolitan) Creed say?

I believe in one God,
the Father almighty,
maker of heaven and earth,
of all things visible and invisible.

I believe in one Lord Jesus Christ,
the Only Begotten Son of God,
born of the Father before all ages.
God from God, Light from Light,
true God from true God,
begotten, not made,
consubstantial with the Father;
through him all things were made.
For us men and for our salvation
he came down from heaven,
and by the Holy Spirit was incarnate
of the Virgin Mary,
and became man.
For our sake he was crucified under Pontius Pilate,
he suffered death and was buried,
and rose again on the third day
in accordance with the Scriptures.
He ascended into heaven
and is seated at the right hand of the Father.
He will come again in glory
to judge the living and the dead
and his kingdom will have no end.

I believe in the Holy Spirit,
the Lord, the giver of life,
who proceeds from the Father and the Son,
who with the Father and the Son is adored and glorified,
who has spoken through the prophets.
I believe in one, holy, catholic and apostolic Church.
I confess one baptism for the forgiveness of sins
and I look forward to the resurrection of the dead
and the life of the world to come.
Amen.

✦ CHAPTER ONE ✦
I Believe in God the Father

30 *Why do we believe in only <u>one</u> God?*

We believe in only one God because, according to the testimony of Sacred Scripture, there is only one God and, according to the laws of logic, there can be only one. [200–202, 228]

If there were two gods, then the one god would be a limit on the other; neither of the two would be infinite, neither one perfect; in these respects neither of the two would be God. Israel's fundamental experience of God is: "Hear, O Israel: The Lord our God is one Lord" (Deut 6:4). Again and again the prophets exhort the people to abandon their false gods and to convert to the one God: "For I am God, and there is no other" (Is 45:22).

31 *Why does God give himself a name?*

God gives himself a name so as to make it possible to address him. [203–213, 230–231]

God does not wish to remain incognito. He does not want to be revered as a "higher being" that is merely sensed or surmised. God wishes to be known and to be called upon as someone real and active. In the burning bush God reveals to Moses his holy name: → Yhwh (Ex 3:14). God makes it possible for his people to address him, but he still remains the hidden God, the present mystery. Out of reverence for God, the name of God was not (and is not) spoken in Israel; the title *Adonai* (Lord) is substituted. This same word is used by the → New Testament when it glorifies Jesus as true God: "Jesus is Lord!" (Rom 10:9).

32 *What does it mean to say that God is truth?*

"God is light and in him is no darkness" (1 Jn 1:5). His Word is truth (Prov 8:7; 2 Sam 7:28), and his Law is truth (Ps 119:142). Jesus himself vouches for God's truth by declaring before Pilate, "For this I was born, and for this I have come into the world, to bear witness to the truth" (Jn 18:37). [214–217]

The Lord our God, the Lord is one; and you shall love the Lord your God with all your heart, and with all your soul, and with all your mind, and with all your strength.

Mk 12:29–30

MONOTHEISM
(from Greek *monos* = only and *theos* = God, doctrine about the existence of only one God): the teaching that God is a unique, absolute, and personal being, the ultimate ground of everything. Monotheistic religions are Judaism, Christianity, and Islam.

YHWH/YAHWEH
The most important name of God in the Old Testament (Ex 3:14). It can be translated "I am who I am." For Jews as well as for Christians, it designates the one God of the whole world, their creator, preserver, covenant partner, liberator from slavery in Egypt, judge, and savior.

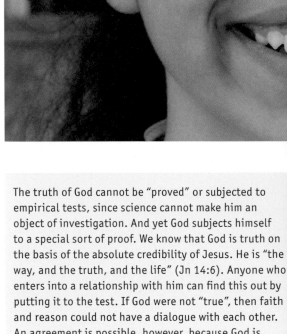

Then Moses said to God, "If I come to the sons of Israel and say to them, 'The God of your fathers has sent me to you,' and they ask me, 'What is his name?' what shall I say to them?" God said to Moses, "I am who I am." And he said, "Say this to the sons of Israel, 'I am has sent me to you.'" God also said to Moses, "Say this to the sons of Israel, 'The Lord, the God of your fathers, the God of Abraham, the God of Isaac, and the God of Jacob, has sent me to you': this is my name forever, and thus I am to be remembered throughout all generations."

Ex 3:13–15

> If God's point of view does not exist, there is no truth beyond our subjective perspectives.
>
> ROBERT SPAEMANN (b. 1927, German philosopher)

> After I discovered that there is a God, it was impossible for me not to live for him alone.
>
> BL. CHARLES DE FOUCAULD (1858–1916, Christian hermit in the Sahara Desert)

The truth of God cannot be "proved" or subjected to empirical tests, since science cannot make him an object of investigation. And yet God subjects himself to a special sort of proof. We know that God is truth on the basis of the absolute credibility of Jesus. He is "the way, and the truth, and the life" (Jn 14:6). Anyone who enters into a relationship with him can find this out by putting it to the test. If God were not "true", then faith and reason could not have a dialogue with each other. An agreement is possible, however, because God is truth, and the truth is divine.

33 *What does it mean to say that God is love?*

If God is love, then there is nothing created that is not carried and surrounded by his infinite benevolence. God not only declares that he is love, he also proves it: "Greater love has no man than this, that a man lay down his life for his friends" (Jn 15:13). [218, 221]

No other → RELIGION says what Christianity says: "God is love" (1 Jn 4:8, 16). Faith holds fast to this promise, although the experience of suffering and evil in the world may make people wonder whether God is really loving. Already in the → OLD TESTAMENT God communicates to his people through the words of the prophet Isaiah: "Because you are precious in my eyes, and honored, and I love you, I give men in return for you, peoples in exchange for your life. Fear not, for I am with you" (Is 43:4–5a) and has him say, "Can a woman forget her sucking child, that she should have no compassion on the son of her womb? Even these may forget, yet I will not forget you. Behold, I have graven you on the palms of my hands" (Is 49:15–16a). This talk about divine love does not consist of empty words; Jesus proves this on the Cross, where he gives up his life for his friends.

34 What should you do once you have come to know God?

Once you have come to know God, you must put him in the first place in your life. And with that a new life begins. You should be able to recognize Christians by the fact that they love even their enemies. [222–227, 229]

After all, to know God means to know that he who created and willed me, who looks at me every moment with love, who blesses and upholds my life, who has the world and the people I love in his hand, who waits longingly for me, who wishes to fulfill and perfect me and to make me dwell forever with him—is there. To nod with your head at this is not enough. Christians must adopt Jesus' way of life.

35 Do we believe in one God or in three Gods?

We believe in one God in three persons (→TRINITY). "God is not solitude but perfect communion." (Pope Benedict XVI, May 22, 2005). [232–236, 249–256, 261, 265–266]

> Question from a journalist: "What has to change in the Church?"
> BL. TERESA OF CALCUTTA (1910–1997): "You and I."

> True love hurts. It always must hurt. It has to be painful to love someone; painful to leave him, you would like to die for him. When people marry, they have to give up everything in order to love each other. A mother who gives life to a child suffers much. The word "love" is misunderstood and misused so much.
>
> BL. TERESA OF CALCUTTA (1910–1997)

> My Lord and my God, take from me everything that distances me from you. My Lord and my God, give me everything that brings me closer to you. My Lord and my God, detach me from myself and give my all to you.
>
> ST. NICHOLAS OF FLÜE (1417–1487, Swiss mystic and hermit)

? TRINITY

(Latin *trinitas* = the state of being threefold): God is only one, but he exists in three persons. The fact that in English we have two terms, *the Triune God* and *the Trinity* for the same reality (one emphasizes God's unity, the other the distinction of persons in him) is an indication of the unfathomable mystery of the Trinity.

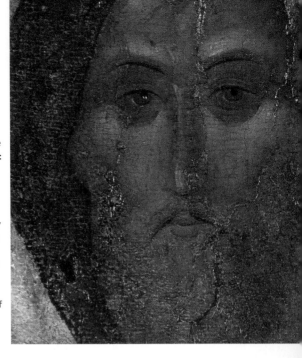

Christians do not worship three different Gods, but one single Being that is threefold and yet remains one. We know that God is triune from Jesus Christ: He, the Son, speaks about his *Father in heaven* ("I and the Father are one", Jn 10:30). He prays to him and sends us the *Holy Spirit,* who is the love of the Father and the Son. That is why we are baptized "in the name of the Father and of the Son and of the Holy Spirit" (Mt 28:19).

36 *Can we deduce logically that God is triune?*

No. The fact that there are three persons (→ TRINITY) in one God is a mystery. We know only through Jesus Christ that God is Trinitarian. [237]

Men cannot deduce the fact that God is a Trinity by means of their own reason. They acknowledge, however, that this mystery is reasonable when they accept God's → REVELATION in Jesus Christ. If God were alone and solitary, he could not love from all eternity. In the light of Jesus we find already in the → OLD TESTAMENT (for example, Gen 1:2; 18:2; 2 Sam 23:2), indeed, even in all of creation, traces of God's Trinitarian Being.

37 Why is God "Father"?

We revere God as Father first of all because he is the Creator and cares lovingly for his creatures. Jesus, the Son of God, has taught us, furthermore, to regard his Father as our Father and to address him as "our Father". [238–240]

Several pre-Christian religions had the divine title "Father". Even before Jesus, the Israelites addressed God as their Father (Deut 32:6; Mal 2:10), realizing that he is also like a mother (Is 66:13). In human experience, father and mother stand for origin and authority, for what is protective and supportive. Jesus Christ shows us what God the Father is really like: "He who has seen me has seen the Father" (Jn 14:9). In the parable of the prodigal son, Jesus addresses the most profound human longings for a merciful father.

→ 511–527

38 Who is the "Holy Spirit"?

The Holy Spirit is the third person of the Holy →TRINITY and has the same divine majesty as the Father and the Son. [243–248, 263–264]

When we discover the reality of God *in us,* we are dealing with the working of the Holy Spirit. God sent "the Spirit of his Son into our hearts" (Gal 4:6), so that he might fill us completely. In the Holy Spirit a Christian finds profound joy, inner peace, and freedom. "For you did not receive the spirit of slavery to fall back into fear, but you have received the spirit of sonship [in whom] we cry, 'Abba! Father!'" (Rom 8:15b). In the Holy Spirit, whom we receive in Baptism and → CONFIRMATION we are permitted to call God "Father".

→ 113–120, 203–207, 310–311

Can a woman forget her sucking child, that she should have no compassion on the son of her womb? Even these may forget, yet I will not forget you.

Is 49:15

> The memory of this Father sheds light on our deepest human identity: where we come from, who we are, and how great is our dignity. Certainly we come from our parents, and we are their children, but we also come from God, who has created us in his image and called us to be his children. Consequently, at the origin of every human being there is not something haphazard or chance, but a loving plan of God. This was revealed to us by Jesus Christ, the true Son of God and a perfect man. He knew whence he came and whence all of us have come: from the love of his Father and our Father.

POPE BENEDICT XVI,
July 9, 2006

39 *Is Jesus God? Does he belong to the Trinity?*

Jesus of Nazareth is the Son, the second divine person mentioned when we pray, "In the name of the Father and of the Son and of the Holy Spirit" (Mt 28:19). [243–260]

Jesus was either an imposter who made himself Lord of the → Sabbath and allowed himself to be addressed with the divine title "Lord"—or else he was really God. The scandal came when he forgave sins. In the eyes of his contemporaries, that was a crime deserving death. Through signs and miracles, but especially through the Resurrection, his disciples recognized who Jesus is and worshipped him *as Lord*. That is the faith of the → Church.

40 *Can God do anything? Is he almighty?*

"For God nothing is impossible" (see Lk 1:37). He is almighty. [268–278]

Anyone who calls on God in need believes that he is all-powerful. God created the world out of nothing. He is the Lord of history. He guides all things and can do everything. How he uses his omnipotence is of course a mystery. Not infrequently people ask, Where was God then? Through the prophet Isaiah he tells us, "My thoughts are not your thoughts, neither are your ways my ways" (Is 55:8). Often God's omnipotence is displayed in a situation where men no longer expect anything from it. The powerlessness of Good Friday was the prerequisite for the Resurrection.
→ 51, 478, 506–507

41 *Does science make the Creator superfluous?*

No. The sentence "God created the world" is not an outmoded scientific statement. We are dealing here with a theo-logical statement, therefore a statement about the divine meaning (*theos* = God, *logos* = meaning) and origin of things. [282–289]

The creation account is not a scientific model for explaining the beginning of the world. "God created the world" is a theological statement that is concerned with the relation of the world to God. God willed the world; he sustains it and will perfect it. *Being created* is a lasting quality *in* things and an fundamental truth *about* them.

42 *Can someone accept the theory of evolution and still believe in the Creator?*

Yes. Although it is a different kind of knowledge, faith is open to the findings and hypotheses of the sciences. [282–289]

Theology has no scientific competence, and natural science has no theological competence. Natural science cannot dogmatically rule out the possibility that there are purposeful processes in creation; conversely, faith cannot define specifically how these processes take place in the course of nature's development. A Christian can accept the theory of evolution as a helpful explanatory model, provided he does not fall into the heresy of evolutionism, which views man as the random product of biological processes. → EVOLUTION presupposes the existence of something that can develop. The theory says nothing about where this "something" came from. Furthermore, questions about the being, essence, dignity, mission, meaning, and wherefore of the world and man cannot be answered in biological terms. Just as "evolutionism" oversteps a boundary on the one side, so does → CREATIONISM on the other. Creationists naively take biblical data literally (for example, to calculate the earth's age, they cite the six days of work in Genesis 1).

43 *Is the world a product of chance?*

No. God, not chance, is the cause of the world. Neither in its origin nor with respect to its intrinsic order and purposefulness is it the product of factors working "aimlessly". [295–301, 317–318, 320]

Christians believe that they can read God's handwriting in his creation. To scientists who talk about the whole world as a random, meaningless, and aimless process, Pope John Paul II pointed out in reply in 1985, "Given a

EVOLUTION
(Latin *evolutio* = unfolding, development): the growth of the final form of organisms over millions of years. Viewed from a Christian perspective, evolution takes place as God's continuous creation in natural processes.

CREATIONISM
(From Latin *creatio* = making, producing): the idea that God himself by his direct action created the world all at once, as if the book of Genesis were an eyewitness account.

Jesus Christ is the center of all things and the foundation for all things; he who does not know him knows nothing about the world and nothing about himself.

BLAISE PASCAL
(1588–1651)

For you created all things, and by your will they existed and were created.

Rev 4:11

universe in which there is such a complex organization of its elements and such a wonderful purposefulness in its life, talking about chance would be equivalent to giving up the search for an explanation of the world as it appears to us. In fact it would be tantamount to accepting effects without cause. It would be an abdication of human reason, which in this way would be refusing to think and to search for a solution to problems." → 49

44 *Who created the world?*

God alone, who is beyond time and space, created the world out of nothing and called all things into being. Everything that exists depends on God and continues in being only because God wills it to be. [290–292, 316]

The creation of the world is, so to speak, a "community project" of the Trinitarian God. The *Father* is the Creator, the Almighty. The *Son* is the meaning and heart of the world: "All things were created through him and for him" (Col 1:16). We find out what the world is good for only when we come to know Christ and understand that the world is heading for a destination: the truth, goodness, and beauty of the Lord. The *Holy Spirit* holds everything together; he is the one "that gives life" (Jn 6:63).

45 *Do natural laws and natural systems come from God also?*

Yes. The laws of nature and natural systems are also part of God's creation. [339, 346, 354]

Man is not a blank slate. He is shaped by the order and the natural laws that God has inscribed in his creation. A Christian does not simply do "whatever he wants". He knows that he harms himself and damages his environment when he denies natural laws, uses things in ways contrary to their intrinsic order, and tries to be wiser than God, who created them. It demands too much of a person when he tries to design himself from start to finish.

46 *Why does the Book of Genesis depict creation as "the work of six days"?*

The symbol of the work week, which is crowned by a day of rest (Gen 1:1—2:3), is an expression of how good, beautiful, and wisely ordered creation is. [337–342]

From the symbolism of "the work of six days" we can derive important principles: (1) Nothing exists that was not called into being by the Creator. (2) Everything that exists is good in its own way. (3) Something that has become bad still has a good core. (4) Created beings and things are interrelated and interdependent. (5) Creation in its order and harmony reflects the surpassing goodness and beauty of God. (6) In creation there is an order of complexity: man is superior to an animal, an animal is superior to a plant, a plant is superior to inanimate matter. (7) Creation is heading for the great celebration when Christ will bring the world home and God will be everything to everyone.

→ 362

> Wood and stones will teach you what you can never hear from teachers.
>
> ST. BERNHARD OF CLAIRVAUX
> (1090-1153, second founder of the Cistercian Order)

> Who could fail to be led by observation and thoughtful familiarity with the magnificent order of the cosmic system, which is derived from divine wisdom, to marvel at the almighty Architect!
>
> NICHOLAS COPERNICUS
> (1473–1543, naturalist and astronomer)

> And God saw everything that he had made, and behold, it was very good.
>
> Gen 1:31

GENESIS
(Greek = origin, beginning): the first book of the Bible, which describes, among other things, the creation of the world and of man.

47 Why did God rest on the seventh day?

God's rest from his work points toward the completion of creation, which is beyond all human efforts. [349]

Although man in his work is the junior partner of his Creator (Gen 2:15), he can by no means redeem the world by his toil. The goal of creation is "new heavens and a new earth" (Is 65:17) through a redemption that is given to us as a *gift*. Thus the Sunday rest, which is a foretaste of heavenly rest, is superior to the work that prepares us for it.

48 Why did God create the world?

"The world was made for the glory of God" (First Vatican Council). [293–294, 319]

There is no other reason for creation than love. In it God's glory and honor appears. To praise God, therefore, does not mean applauding the Creator. After all, man is not a spectator to the work of creation. For him, "praising" God means being grateful for his own existence together with all creation. → 489

Divine Providence

49 Does God guide the world and my life?

Yes, but in a mysterious way; God guides everything along paths that only he knows, leading it to its perfection. At no point in time does something that he has created fall out of his hands. [302–305]

God influences both the great events of history and also the little events of our personal life, without reducing our freedom or making us mere marionettes in his eternal plans. In God "we live and move and have our being" (Acts 17:28). God is in everything we meet in all the changes in our life, even in the painful events and the seemingly meaningless coincidences. God wants to write straight even with the crooked lines of our life. What he takes away from us and what he gives us, the ways in which he strengthens us and the ways in which he tests us—all these are arrangements and signs of his will. → 43

→ 43

50 *What role does man play in God's providence?*

The completion of creation through divine providence is not something that happens above and beyond us. God invites us to collaborate in the completion of creation. [307–308]

Man can reject God's will. He does better, though, to become an instrument of God's love. Mother Teresa during her lifetime strove to think in this way: "I am only a little pencil in the hand of our Lord. He may cut or sharpen the pencil. He may write or draw whatever and whenever he wants. If the writing or drawing is good, we do not honor the pencil or the material that is used, but rather the one who used it." Although God works with us and through us also, nevertheless we must never mistake our own thinking, planning, and doing for the working of God. God does not need our work, as though he would lack something without it.

51 *If God is all-knowing and all-powerful, why does he not prevent evil?*

"God allows evil only so as to make something better result from it" (St. Thomas Aquinas). [309–314, 324]

Evil in the world is an obscure and painful mystery. Even the Crucified asked his Father, "My God, why have you forsaken me?" (Mt 27:46). Much about it is incomprehensible. One thing, though, we know for sure: God is 100 percent good. He can never be the originator of something evil. God created the world to be good, but it is not yet complete. In violent upheavals and painful processes it is being shaped and moved toward its final perfection. There is what is called *physical evil,* for example, a birth defect, or a natural catastrophe and these remain puzzling with respect to God's goodness. *Moral evils,* in contrast, come about through the misuse of freedom in the world. "Hell on earth"—child soldiers, suicide bombings, concentration camps—is usually man-made. The decisive question is

> Lord, make me an instrument of your peace:
> Where there is hatred, let me sow love,
> Where there is injury—pardon,
> Where there is strife—unity,
> Where there is error—truth,
> Where there is doubt—faith,
> Where there is despair—hope,
> Where there is darkness—light,
> Where there is sadness—joy.
> O Master, grant that I may seek not so much to be consoled as to console;
> to be understood as to understand;
> to be loved as to love.

FRANCISCAN MOVEMENT, France 1913

> What did not lie in my plan lay in God's plan. And the more often something like this happens to me, the livelier becomes the conviction of my faith that—from God's perspective—nothing is accidental.

ST. EDITH STEIN (1891–1942)

God whispers to us in our pleasures; speaks to us in our conscience, but shouts in our pain: it is His megaphone to rouse a deaf world.

CLIVE STAPLES LEWIS
(1898–1963, English writer, author of *The Chronicles of Narnia*)

Walk with your feet on earth, but in your heart be in heaven.

ST. JOHN BOSCO (1815–1888, patron saint of youth)

Jesus came to tell us that he wants us all to be in Paradise, and that Hell—of which one speaks little in our time—exists and is eternal for all who close their hearts to his love.

BENEDICT XVI,
May 8, 2007

We long for the joy of heaven, where God is. It is within our power to be with him in heaven even now, to be happy with him in this very moment. But to be happy with him now means to help as he helps, →

therefore not, "How can anyone believe in a good God when there is so much evil?" but rather, "How could a person with a heart and understanding endure life in this world if God did *not* exist?" Christ's death and Resurrection show us that evil did not have the first word, nor does it have the last. God made absolute good result from the worst evil. We believe that in the Last Judgment God will put an end to all injustice. In the life of the world to come, evil no longer has any place and suffering ends. → 40, 286–287

Heaven and Heavenly Creatures

52   What is heaven?

Heaven is God's milieu, the dwelling place of the angels and saints, and the goal of creation. With the words "heaven and earth" we designate the whole of created reality. [325–327]

Heaven is not a place in the universe. It is a condition in the next life. Heaven is where God's will is done without any resistance. Heaven happens when life is present in its greatest intensity and blessedness—a kind of life that we do not find on earth. If with God's help we arrive someday in heaven, then waiting for us will be "what no eye has seen, nor ear heard, nor the heart of man conceived, what God has prepared for those who love him" (1 Cor 2:9). → 158, 285

53   What is hell?

Our faith calls "hell" the condition of final separation from God, the absolute "No" to love. [1033–1036]

Jesus, who knows what hell is like, speaks about it as the "outer darkness" (Mt 8:12). Expressed in our terms, it is cold rather than hot. It is horrible to contemplate a condition of complete rigidity and hopeless isolation from everything that could bring aid, relief, joy, and consolation into one's life. → 161–162

→ to give as he gives, to serve as he serves, to save as he saves, to love as he loves. To be with him twenty-four hours a day, to encounter him in his most frightening disguise. For he said so: "What you did to the least of my brethren, you did to me."

BL. TERESA OF CALCUTTA (1910–1997)

99 All that is not eternal is eternally out of date.

C.S. LEWIS (1898–1963)

For he will give his angels charge of you to guard you in all your ways. On their hands they will bear you up, lest you dash your foot against a stone.

Ps 91:11–12

99 Beside each believer stands an angel as protector and shepherd leading him to life.

ST. BASIL THE GREAT (ca. 330–379, Father of the Church)

---

54 *What are angels?*

Angels are pure spiritual creatures of God who have understanding and will. They have no bodies, cannot die, and are usually not visible. They live constantly in God's presence and convey God's will and God's protection to men. [328–333, 350–351]

An angel, wrote Cardinal Joseph Ratzinger, is "so to speak the personal thought with which God is turned toward me". At the same time the angels are turned completely toward their Creator. They burn with love for him and serve him day and night. Their song of praise is never-ending. In Sacred Scripture the angels who have fallen away from God are called devils or demons.

55 *Can we interact with angels?*

Yes. We can call on angels for help and ask them to intercede with God. [334–336, 352]

Every person receives from God a guardian angel. It is good and sensible to pray to one's guardian angel for oneself and for others. Angels can also make themselves noticeable in the life of a Christian, for example, as bearers of a message or as helpful guides. Our faith has nothing to do with the false angels of New Age spirituality and other forms of esotericism.

Man the Creature

56 *Does man have a special place in creation?*

Yes. Man is the summit of creation, because God created him in his image (Gen 1:27). [343–344, 353]

The creation of man is clearly distinguished from the creation of other living things. Man is a *person,* which means that through his understanding and will he can decide for or against love.

57 *How should man treat animals and other fellow creatures?*

Man should honor the Creator in other creatures and treat them carefully and responsibly. Man, animals, and plants have the same Creator who called them into being out of love. Therefore a love of animals is profoundly human. [344, 354]

Although man is allowed to use and to eat plants and animals, he is nevertheless not allowed to torture animals or to keep them in inhumane conditions. That contradicts the dignity of creation just as much as exploiting the earth thoughtlessly out of greed.

58 What does it mean to say that man was created "in God's image"?

Unlike inanimate objects, plants, and animals, man is a person endowed with a spirit. This characteristic unites him with God more than with his visible fellow creatures. [355–357, 380]

Man is not a *something* but rather a *someone*. Just as we say about God that he is *person,* so too we say this about man. Man can think beyond his immediate horizon and measure the whole breadth of being; he can even know himself with critical objectivity and work to improve himself; he can perceive others as persons, understand them in their dignity, and love them. Of all the visible creatures, man alone is "able to know and love his creator" (Second Vatican Council, *Gaudium et spes* [GS] 12, 3). Man is destined to live with him in friendship (Jn 15:15).

59 Why did God make man?

God made everything for man. Man, however, who is "the only creature on earth that God has willed for its own sake" (GS 24, 3), was created in order to be blessed. This happens when he knows, loves, and serves God and lives in gratitude toward his Creator. [358]

Gratitude is love that has been acknowledged. Someone who is grateful turns freely to the giver of the good and enters into a new, deeper relationship with him. God wishes us to acknowledge his love and even now to live our whole life in relation with him. This relationship lasts forever.

60 Why is Jesus the greatest example in the world?

Jesus Christ is unique because he shows us not only God's true nature but also the true ideal of man. [358–359, 381]

Jesus was more than an ideal man. Even seemingly ideal men are sinners. That is why no man can be the

Love is of God, and he who loves is born of God and knows God.

1 Jn 4:7

❝ If the only prayer you said in your life was "I thank you", that would be enough.

MEISTER ECKHART
(ca. 1260–1328, Dominican, mystic)

❝ Man is God's image and likeness, in which God wants to be honored for his own sake.

ST. FRANCIS OF ASSISI
(1182–1226)

❝ God loved men. For their sake he created the cosmos; he subjected everything on earth to them; he gave them the ability to speak and understand; he permitted them alone to look up to heaven; he formed them after his likeness; he sent his Son to them; he promised them the kingdom of heaven, and he will give it to those who love him.

Letter to Diognetus, second century

measure of humanity. Jesus, however, was without sin. We cannot know what it means to be a man, and what makes man *infinitely loveable* in the truest sense of the word, except in Jesus Christ, who "in every respect has been tempted as we are, yet without sinning" (Heb 4:15). Jesus, the Son of God, is the authentic, true man. In him we recognize how God willed man to be.

61 *In what does the equality of all men consist?*

All men are equal inasmuch as they have the same origin in the one creative love of God. All men have their Savior in Jesus Christ. All men are destined to find their happiness and their eternal blessedness in God. [360–361]

Hence *all* men are brothers and sisters. Christians should practice solidarity not only with other Christians but with everyone and forcefully oppose racist, sexist, and economic divisions in the one human family.
→ 280, 517

62 *What is the soul?*

The soul is what makes every individual person a man: his spiritual life-principle and inmost being. The soul causes the material body to be a living human body. Through his soul, man is a creature who can say "I" and stand before God as an irreplaceable individual. [362–365, 382]

Men are bodily and spiritual creatures. A man's spirit is more than a function of his body and cannot be explained in terms of man's material composition. Reason tells us that there must be a spiritual principle that is united with the body but not identical to it. We call it the "soul". Although the soul's existence cannot be "proved" scientifically, man cannot be understood as a spiritual or intellectual being without accepting this spiritual principle that transcends matter.
→ 153–154, 163

→ lose their dignity. On the other hand, should he deny the spirit and consider matter, the body, as the only reality, he would likewise lose his greatness.

POPE BENEDICT XVI, *Deus Caritas est*

Open your mouth for the mute, for the rights of all who are left desolate.

Prov 31:8

The soul speaks: I am called to be the companion of the angels, because I am the living breath that God sent forth into dry clay.

ST. HILDEGARD OF BINGEN (1098–1179, Benedictine, mystic)

Man is united with all living creatures by his earthly origin, but only through his soul, which God "breathed into" him, is he man. This confers upon him his irreplaceable dignity but also his unique responsibility.

CHRISTOPH CARDINAL SCHÖNBORN (b. 1945, Archbishop of Vienna)

63   *From where does man get his soul?*

The human soul is created directly by God and is not "produced" by the parents. [366–368, 382]

Man's soul cannot be the product of an evolutionary development out of matter or the result of a generative union of the father and mother. With every man, a unique, spiritual person comes into the world; the Church expresses this mystery by saying that God gives him a soul, which cannot die; even if the person loses his body in death, he will find it again in the resurrection. To say, "I have a soul", means that God created me not only as a creature but as a person and has called me to a never-ending relationship with him.

64   *Why did God create man male and female?*

God, who is love and the archetype of community, created man male and female so that together they might be an image of his nature. [369–373, 383]

God made man in such a way that he is male or female and longs for fulfillment and completion in

So God created man in his own image, in the image of God he created him; male and female he created them.

Gen 1:27

 It is not good that the man should be alone; I will make him a helper fit for him.

Gen 2:18

 Moreover, we read that man cannot exist "alone" (cf. Gen 2:18); he can exist only as a "unity of the two", and therefore *in relation to another human person*. It is a question here of a mutual relationship: man to woman and woman to man. Being a person in the image and likeness of God thus also involves existing in a relationship, in relation to the other "I". This is a prelude to the definitive self-revelation of the Triune God: a living unity in the communion of the Father, Son and Holy Spirit.

POPE JOHN PAUL II (1920–2005) first pope from the East, founder of the World Youth Days, Apostolic Letter *Mulieris dignitatem* (1988)

an encounter with the opposite sex. Men and women have absolutely the same dignity, but in the creative development of their masculinity and femininity they give expression to different aspects of God's perfection. God is not male or female, but he has shown himself to be both fatherly (Lk 6:36) and motherly (Is 66:13). In the love of man and woman, especially in the community of marriage, in which man and woman become "one flesh" (Gen 2:24), people are privileged to sense something of the happiness of the union with God in which every man finds his ultimate wholeness. Just as God's love is faithful, so also their love seeks to be faithful; and it is creative, as God is, because from marriage new life comes forth.

→ 260, 400–401, 416–417

65 *What about people who feel they are homosexual?*

The Church believes that, in the order of creation, man and woman are designed to need each other's complementary traits and to enter into a mutual relationship so as to give life to children. That is why homosexual practices cannot be approved by the Church. Christians owe all persons respect and love, however, regardless of their sexual orientation, because all people are respected and loved by God. [2358–2359]

There is no man on earth who is not descended from a union of a mother and a father. Therefore it is a painful experience for many homosexually oriented people that they do not feel erotically attracted to the opposite sex and necessarily miss out on the physical fruitfulness of the union between man and woman according to human nature and the divine order of creation. Nevertheless, God often leads souls to himself along unusual paths: a lack, a loss, or a wound—if accepted and affirmed—can become a springboard for throwing oneself into the arms of God: the God who brings good out of everything and whose greatness can be discovered in redemption even more than in creation. → 415

66 *Was it part of God's plan for men to suffer and die?*

God does not want men to suffer and die. God's original idea for man was paradise: life forever and peace between God and man and their environment, between man and woman. [374–379, 384, 400]

Often we sense how life ought to be, how *we* ought to be, but in fact we do not live in peace with ourselves, act out of fear and uncontrolled emotions, and have lost the original harmony that man had with the world and ultimately with God. In Sacred Scripture the experience of this alienation is expressed in the story of the Fall. Because sin crept in, Adam and Eve had to leave paradise, in which they were in harmony with each other and with God. The toil of work, suffering, mortality, and the temptation to sin are signs of this loss of paradise.

Fallen Man

67 *What is sin?*

At the core of sin is a rejection of God and the refusal to accept his love. This is manifested in a disregard for his commandments. [385–390]

Sin is more than incorrect behavior; it is not just a psychological weakness. In the deepest sense every rejection or destruction of *something* good is the rejection of *good in itself,* the rejection of God. In its most profound and terrible dimension, sin is separation from God and, thus, separation from the source of life. Only through Jesus do we understand the abysmal dimension of sin: Jesus suffered God's rejection in his own flesh. He took upon himself the deadly power of sin so that it would not strike us. The term that we use for this is redemption. → 224–237, 315–318, 348–468

> We have lost paradise but have received heaven, and therefore the gain is greater than the loss.
>
> ST. JOHN CHRYSOSTOM
> (349/350–407, Doctor of the Church)

> O God, to turn away from you is to fall. To turn to you is to stand up. To remain in you is to have a sure support.
>
> ST. AUGUSTINE
> (354–430)

> Human weakness cannot upset the plans of divine omnipotence. A divine master-builder can work even with falling stones.
>
> MICHAEL CARDINAL VON FAULHABER
> (1869–1952, Archbishop of Munich and Freising)

> Where sin increased, grace abounded all the more.
>
> Rom 5:20b

> When Christ's hands were nailed to the Cross, he also nailed our sins to the Cross.
>
> ST. BERNARD OF CLAIRVAUX
> (1090–1153)

But the serpent said to the woman, "... When you eat of it your eyes will be opened, and you will be like God."

Gen 3:4–5

A moral approach to the world is possible and beneficial only when one takes upon himself the whole awful mess of life, one's share in the responsibility for death and sin, in short, original sin as a whole, and stops seeing guilt always in others.

HERMANN HESSE
(1877–1962, German writer)

The worst thing is not to commit crimes but, rather, not to accomplish the good that one could have done. It is the sin of omission, which is nothing other than to be unloving, and no one accuses himself of it.

LÉON BLOY
(1846–1917, French writer)

68 *Original sin? What does the Fall of Adam and Eve have to do with us?*

Sin in the strict sense implies guilt for which one is personally responsible. Therefore the term "Original Sin" refers, not to a personal sin, but rather to the disastrous, fallen state of mankind into which the individual is born, even before he himself sins by a free decision. [388–389, 402–404]

In talking about Original Sin, Pope Benedict XVI says that we must understand "that we all carry within us a drop of the poison of that way of thinking, illustrated by the images in the Book of → GENESIS ... . The human being does not trust God. Tempted by the serpent, he harbors the suspicion ... that God is a rival who curtails our freedom and that we will be fully human only when we have cast him aside ... . Man does not want to receive his existence and the fullness of his life from God ... . And in doing so, he trusts in deceit rather than in truth and thereby sinks with his life into emptiness, into death" (Pope Benedict XVI, December 8, 2005).

69 *Are we compelled to sin by original sin?*

No. Man, though, is deeply wounded by original sin and is inclined to sin. Nevertheless, with God's help he is capable of doing good. [405]

In no single case are we obliged to sin. In fact, however, we sin again and again, because we are weak, ignorant, and easily misled. A sin committed under compulsion, moreover, would be no sin, because sin always involves a free decision.

70 *How does God draw us out of the whirlpool of evil?*

God does not just look on as man gradually destroys himself and the world around him through the chain reaction of sin. He sends us Jesus Christ, the Savior and Redeemer, who snatches us from the power of sin. [410–412, 420–421]

"No one can help me"—this maxim of human experience is no longer accurate. Wherever man may have strayed by his sins, God the Father has sent his Son there. The consequence of sin is death (cf. Rom 6:23). Another consequence of sin, however, is the marvelous solidarity of God, who sends us Jesus as our friend and Savior. Therefore original sin is also called *felix culpa* (= happy fault): "O happy fault ... which gained for us so great a Redeemer!" (Liturgy of the Easter Vigil).

◇ CHAPTER TWO ◇
I Believe in Jesus Christ, the Only Begotten Son of God

71 *Why are the reports about Jesus called "the Gospel", "the Good News"?*

Without the Gospels we would not know that God sends his Son to us men out of his infinite love, so that despite our sins we might find our way back to eternal fellowship with God. [422–429]

The reports about the life, death, and Resurrection of Jesus are the best news in the world. They testify that the Jew who was born in Bethlehem, Jesus of Nazareth, is "Son of the living God" (Mt 16:16) made man. He was sent by the Father so that "all men might be saved and come to the knowledge of the truth" (cf. 1 Tim 2:4).

72 *What does the name "Jesus" mean?*

**Jesus means in Hebrew "God saves."
[430–435, 452]**

In the Acts of the Apostles Peter says, "There is no other name under heaven given among men by which we must be saved" (Acts 4:12). This is essentially the message that all missionaries brought to people.

And the Word became flesh and dwelt among us, full of grace and truth; we have beheld his glory, glory as of the only-begotten Son from the Father.

Jn 1:14

ΙΧΘΥC ΖΩΝΤΩΝ

In the Roman catacombs we find an ancient Christian secret sign that was a profession of faith in Christ: the word ΙCHTHYS (= fish). If you spell the word out , each letter serves as the beginning of the Greek words Iesous, Christos, THeou (= of God), hYios (= Son), and Soter (= Savior). ΙCHTHYS ΖΟΝΤΟΝ means: Fish of Life.

" That is one of the reasons I believe in Christianity. It is a religion you could not have guessed.

C. S. LEWIS
(1898–1963)

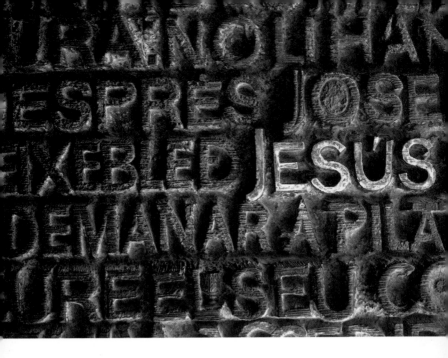

73 *Why is Jesus called "Christ"?*

The brief formula "Jesus is the Christ" expresses the core of the Christian faith: Jesus, the simple carpenter's son from Nazareth, is the long-awaited Messiah and Savior. [436–440, 453]

Both the Greek word "Christos" and the Hebrew word "Messiah" mean "the Anointed One". In Israel kings, priests, and prophets were anointed. The → APOSTLES learned that Jesus was anointed "with the Holy Spirit" (Acts 10:38). We are called *Christians* after *Christ,* as an expression of our exalted vocation.

74 *What does it mean to say that Jesus is "the only-begotten Son of God"?*

When Jesus calls himself "God's only-begotten Son" (or "only Son", Jn 3:16) and Peter and others bear witness to this, the expression means that of all human beings only Jesus is more than a man and has a unique relationship to God, his Father. [441–445, 454]

In many passages of the → NEW TESTAMENT (Jn 1:14, 18; 1 Jn 4:9; Heb 1:2, and so on) Jesus is called "Son". At his baptism and his Transfiguration, the voice from heaven calls Jesus "my beloved Son". Jesus discloses to his disciples his unique relationship to his heavenly Father: "All things have been delivered to me by my Father; and no one knows the Son except the Father, and no one knows the Father except the Son and any one to whom the Son chooses to reveal him" (Mt 11:27). The fact that Jesus Christ really is God's Son comes to light at the Resurrection.

75 Why do Christians address Jesus as "Lord"?

"You call me Teacher and Lord; and you are right, for so I am" (Jn 13:13). [446–451, 455]

The early Christians spoke as a matter of course about Jesus as "Lord", knowing that in the→ OLD TESTAMENT this title was reserved as a form of addressing God. Through many signs Jesus had shown them that he had divine power over nature, demons, sin, and death. The divine origin of Jesus' mission was revealed in his Resurrection from the dead. Thomas confessed, "My Lord and my God!" (Jn 20:28). For us this means that since Jesus is "the Lord", a Christian may not bend his knee to any other power.

76 Why did God become man in Jesus?

"For us men and for our salvation he came down from heaven" (Nicene → CREED). [456–460]

In Jesus Christ, God reconciled the world to himself and redeemed mankind from the imprisonment of sin. "God so loved the world that he gave his only-begotten Son" (Jn 3:16). In Jesus, God took on our mortal human flesh (→ INCARNATION), shared our earthly lot, our sufferings, and our death, and became one like us in all things but sin.

→ Knowledge of Jesus Christ provides the middle ground, because in him we find both God and our misery.

BLAISE PASCAL
(1588–1651)

99 Whereas the life and death of Socrates are the life and death of a wise man, the life and death of Christ are the life and death of a God.

JEAN-JACQUES ROUSSEAU
(1712–1778, French Enlightenment thinker)

99 Wherever God does not have pride of place, ... human dignity is at risk. It is therefore urgent to bring our contemporaries to "rediscover" the authentic face of God, who revealed himself to us in Jesus Christ.

POPE BENEDICT XVI,
August 28, 2005

99 God is so great that he can become small. God is so powerful that he can make himself vulnerable and come to us as a defenseless child, so that we can love him.

POPE BENEDICT XVI,
December 24, 2005

77 *What does it mean to say that Jesus Christ is at the same time true God and true man?*

In Jesus, God really became one of us and thus our brother; nevertheless, he did not cease to be God at the same time and thus our Lord. The Council of Chalcedon in the year 451 taught that the divinity and the humanity in the one person Jesus Christ are united together "without division or confusion". [464–467, 469]

The Church grappled for a long time with the problem of how to express the relation between the divinity and humanity in Jesus Christ. Divinity and humanity are not in competition with each other, which would make Jesus only partially God and only partially man. Nor is it true that the divine and human in Jesus are confused. God took on a human body in Jesus; this was no mere appearance *(Docetism),* but he really became man. Nor are there two different persons in Christ, one human and one divine *(Nestorianism).* Nor is it true, finally, that in Jesus Christ the human nature was absorbed into the divine nature *(Monophysitism).* Contrary to all these heresies, the Church has adhered to the belief that Jesus Christ is at the same time true God and true man in one Person. The famous formula, "without division or confusion" (Council of Chalcedon) does not attempt to explain something that is too sublime for human understanding, but rather draws the boundaries, so to speak, of the faith. It indicates the "line" along which the mystery of the person of Jesus Christ can be investigated.

78 *Why can we grasp Jesus only as a "mystery"?*

Jesus extends into God; therefore we cannot understand him if we exclude the invisible divine reality. [525–530, 536]

The visible side of Jesus points to the invisible. We see in the life of Jesus numerous realities that are powerfully present but that we can understand only as a → MYSTERY. Examples of such mysteries are the divine Sonship, the Incarnation, the Passion, and the Resurrection of Christ.

79 *Did Jesus have a soul, a mind, and a body just as we do?*

Yes. Jesus "worked with human hands, he thought with a human mind. He acted with a human will, and with a human heart he loved" (Second Vatican Council, GS 22, 2). [470–476]

The humanity of Jesus is complete and includes also the fact that Jesus possessed a soul and developed psychologically and spiritually. In this soul dwelled his human identity and his special self-consciousness. Jesus knew about his unity with his heavenly Father in the Holy Spirit, by whom he allowed himself to be guided in every situation of his life.

80 *Why is Mary a Virgin?*

God willed that Jesus Christ should have a true human mother but only God himself as his Father, because he wanted to make a new beginning that could be credited to him alone and not to earthly forces. [484–504, 508–510]

MYSTERY

(Greek *mysterion* = secret): A mystery is a reality (or one aspect of a reality) that in principle eludes rational knowledge.

And Jesus increased in wisdom and in stature.

Lk 2:52

Mary's virginity is not some outdated mythological notion but rather fundamental to the life of Jesus. He was born of a woman but had no human father. Jesus Christ is a new beginning in the world that has been instituted from on high. In the Gospel of Luke, Mary asks the angel, "How can this be, since I have no husband?" (= do not sleep with a man, Lk 1:34); the angel answered, "The Holy Spirit will come upon you" (Lk 1:35). Although the Church from the earliest days was mocked on account of her belief in Mary's virginity, she has always believed that her virginity is real and not merely symbolic. → 117

81 Did Mary have other children besides Jesus?

No. Jesus is the only son of Mary in the physical sense. [500, 510]

Even in the early Church, Mary's perpetual virginity was assumed, which rules out the possibility of Jesus having brothers and sisters from the same mother. In Aramaic, Jesus' mother tongue, there is only one word for sibling and cousins. When the Gospels speak about the "brothers and sisters" of Jesus (for instance, in Mk 3:31–35), they are referring to Jesus' close relatives.

82 Isn't it improper to call Mary the "Mother" of God?

No. Anyone who calls Mary the Mother of God thereby professes that her Son is God. [495, 509]

As early Christianity was debating who Jesus was, the title *Theotokos* ("God-bearer") became the hallmark for the orthodox interpretation of Sacred Scripture: Mary did not give birth merely to a man who then after his birth "became" God; rather, even in her womb her child is the true Son of God. This debate is not about Mary in the first place; rather, it is again the question of whether Jesus is true man and true God at the same time. → 117

83 What does the "Immaculate Conception of Mary" mean?

The Church believes that "the most Blessed Virgin Mary was, from the first moment of her conception, by a singular grace and privilege of almighty God and by virtue of the merits of Jesus Christ, Savior of the human race, preserved immune from all stain of original sin" (Dogma of 1854; → DOGMA) [487–492, 508]

Belief in the Immaculate Conception has existed since the beginning of the Church. The expression is misunderstood today. It is saying that God preserved Mary from original sin from the very beginning. It says nothing about the conception of Jesus in Mary's womb. By no means is it a devaluation of sexuality in Christianity, as though a husband and wife would be "stained" if they conceived a child. → 68–69

84 Was Mary only an instrument of God?

Mary was more than a merely passive instrument of God. The Incarnation of God took place through her active consent as well. [493–494, 508–511]

When the angel told her that she would bear "the Son of God", Mary replied, "Let it be to me according to your word" (Lk 1:38). The redemption of mankind by Jesus Christ thus begins with a request by God and the free consent of a human being—and a pregnancy before Mary was married to Joseph. By such an unusual path Mary became for us the "Gate of Salvation". → 479

85 Why is Mary our mother also?

Mary is our mother because Christ the Lord gave her to us as a mother. [963–966, 973]

"Woman, behold, your son! ... Behold, your mother!" (Jn 19:26b–27a). The second command, which Jesus spoke from the Cross to John, has always been understood by the Church as an act of entrusting the whole Church to Mary. Thus Mary is our mother, too. We may call upon her and ask her to intercede with God. → 147-149

> **"** When faith in the Mother of God declines, faith in the Son of God and God the Father declines also.
>
> LUDWIG FEUERBACH (1804–1872, atheistic philosopher, in *The Essence of Christianity*)

> **"** Mary's response ... is the most momentous word in history.
>
> REINHOLD SCHNEIDER (1903-1958, German writer)

> **"** Mary is the most tender mother of the human race; she is the refuge of sinners.
>
> ST. ALPHONSUS LIGUORI (1696–1787, founder of the Redemptorists, mystic, and Doctor of the Church)

> **"** The more the Church models her life on Mary, the more maternal she becomes and the more a believer can be reborn of God in her and achieve reconciliation.
>
> BROTHER ROGER SCHUTZ (1915–2005, founder and prior of the ecumenical community of Taizé)

86 *Why did Jesus wait thirty years to begin his public life?*

Jesus wanted to share a normal life with us and thus sanctify our everyday routine. [531–534, 564]

Jesus was a child who received love and affection from his parents and was brought up by them. Thus he increased "in wisdom and in stature, and in favor with God and man" (Lk 2:52); he belonged to a Jewish village community and took part in its religious rituals; he learned a trade and had to prove his ability as a craftsman. The fact that God in Jesus willed to be born into a human family and to grow up in it has made the family a place where God is present and a prototype of a helping community.

87 *Why did Jesus allow John to baptize him, although he was without sin?*

To baptize means to immerse. In his baptism, Jesus descended into the sinful history of all mankind. By doing so he established a sign. In order to redeem us from our sins, he would one day be submerged in death but, through his Father's power, reawakened to life. [535–537, 565]

Sinners—soldiers, prostitutes, tax collectors—went out to the prophet John the Baptist because they were looking for the "baptism of repentance for the forgiveness of sins" (Lk 3:3). Strictly speaking, Jesus did not need this baptism, because he was sinless. The fact that he submitted to this baptism shows us two things: Jesus takes *our* sins upon himself. Jesus understands his baptism as an anticipation of his Passion and Resurrection. At this sign of his willingness to die for us, the heavens open: "You are my beloved Son" (Lk 3:22b).

88 *Why was Jesus led into temptation? Could he really be tempted at all?*

Jesus was truly human, and as part of that he was truly susceptible to temptation. In Jesus Christ we do not have the sort of redeemer "who is unable

to sympathize with our weaknesses, but one who in every respect has been tempted as we are, yet without sinning" (Heb 4:15). [538–540, 566]

89 To whom does Jesus promise "the kingdom of God"?

God wills "all men to be saved and to come to the knowledge of the truth" (1 Tim 2:4). The "kingdom of God" begins in those who allow themselves to be transformed by God's love. In Jesus' experience these are above all the poor and the lowly. [541–546, 567]

Even people unaffiliated with the Church find it fascinating that Jesus, with a sort of preferential love, turns first to those who are socially marginalized. In the Sermon on the Mount, it is the poor and the sorrowing, the victims of persecution and violence, all those who seek God with a pure heart, all who seek his mercy, his justice, and his peace, who have prior access to the kingdom of God. Especially invited are sinners also: "Those who are well have no need of a physician, but those who are sick; I came not to call the righteous, but sinners" (Mk 2:17).

90 Did Jesus work miracles, or are they just pious tales?

Jesus really worked miracles, and so did the →APOSTLES. The New Testament authors refer to real incidents. [547–550]

Even the oldest sources tell of numerous miracles, even the raising of the dead, as a confirmation of Jesus' preaching: "But if it is by the Spirit of God that I cast out demons, then the kingdom of God has come upon you" (Mt 12:28). The miracles took place in public; some of the persons involved were known by name, for instance, blind Bartimaeus (Mk 10:46–52) or Peter's mother-in-law (Mt 8:14–15). There were also miracles that in those Jewish circles were considered shocking and outrageous (for example, the cure of a crippled man on the → SABBATH, the cure of lepers). Nevertheless they were not disputed by contemporary Judaism.

Jesus said about his Father: "He has sent me to proclaim release to the captives and recovering of sight to the blind, to set at liberty those who are oppressed, to proclaim the acceptable year of the Lord."

Lk 4:18-19

A miracle does not take place contrary to nature but rather contrary to our knowledge of nature.

ST. AUGUSTINE
(354–430)

Nowhere in the world has so great a miracle occurred as in that little stable in Bethlehem; here God and man became one.

THOMAS À KEMPIS
(1379/1380–1471, German mystic, author of The Imitation of Christ)

And they were astonished beyond measure, saying, "He has done all things well; he even makes the deaf hear and the mute speak."

Mk 7:37

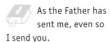 As the Father has sent me, even so I send you.

Jn 20:21b

99 When one has the grace to have a strong experience of God, it is as if one is having an experience similar to that of the disciples during the Transfiguration: →

91 *But why did Jesus work miracles?*

The miracles that Jesus worked were signs that the kingdom of God was beginning. They expressed his love for mankind and reaffirmed his mission. [547–550]

Jesus' miracles were not self-aggrandizing displays of magic. He was filled with the power of God's healing love. Through his miracles he showed that he is the Messiah and that the kingdom of God begins in him. Thus it became possible to experience the dawn of the new world: he freed people from hunger (Jn 6:5–15), injustice (Lk 19:8), sickness, and death (Mt 11:5). By driving out demons, he began his victorious advance against the "ruler of this world" (meaning Satan; see Jn 12:31). Nevertheless, Jesus did not remove all misfortune and evil from the world. He directed his attention principally to freeing man from the slavery of sin. His central concern was faith, which he also elicited through miracles. → 241–242

92 *Why did Jesus call apostles?*

Jesus had a large circle of disciples around him, both men and women. From this circle he selected twelve men whom he called → APOSTLES (Lk 6:12–16). The apostles were specially trained by him and entrusted with various commissions: "He sent them out to preach the kingdom of God and to heal" (Lk 9:2). Jesus took only these twelve apostles with him to the Last Supper, where he gave them the command, "Do this in remembrance of me" (Lk 22:19b). [551–553, 567]

The apostles became witnesses of Jesus' Resurrection and guarantors of the truth about him. They continued Jesus' mission after his death. They chose successors for their ministry: the bishops. To this day, the successors of the apostles exercise the authority conferred by Jesus: They govern and teach and celebrate the liturgy.

The cohesiveness of the apostles became the foundation for the unity of the → CHURCH (→ APOSTOLIC SUCCESSION). Preeminent once again among the Twelve was Peter, on whom Jesus bestowed special authority: "You are Peter, and on this rock I will build my Church" (Mt 16:18). From Peter's special role among the apostles developed the papal ministry. → 137

93 Why was Christ transfigured on the mountain?

The Father wanted to reveal the divine glory of his Son even during Jesus' earthly life. Christ's Transfiguration was meant to help the disciples later to understand his death and Resurrection. [554–556, 568]

Three Gospels relate how Jesus, on the mountaintop, begins to shine (is "transfigured") before the eyes of his disciples. The voice of his heavenly Father calls Jesus his "beloved Son", to whom they are supposed to listen. Peter would like to "make three booths" and capture the moment. Jesus, however, is on the way that leads to suffering. The vision of glory is only to strengthen his disciples.

94 Did Jesus know that he would die when he entered Jerusalem?

Yes. Three times Jesus had predicted his suffering and death before consciously and voluntarily (Lk 9:51) going to the place of his Passion and his resurrection. [557–560, 569–570]

95 Why did Jesus choose the date of the Jewish feast of Passover for his death and Resurrection?

Jesus chose the Passover feast of his people Israel as a symbol for what was to happen through his death and Resurrection. As the people Israel were freed from slavery to Egypt, so Christ frees us from the slavery of sin and the power of death. [571–573]

The Passover was the feast celebrating the liberation of Israel from slavery in Egypt. Jesus went to Jerusalem in order to free us in an even deeper way. He celebrated

→ a momentary foretaste of what will constitute the happiness of Paradise. These are usually brief experiences that are sometimes granted by God, especially prior to difficult trials.

POPE BENEDICT XVI, March 12, 2006

 And he began to teach them that the Son of man must suffer many things, and be rejected by the elders and the chief priests and the scribes.

Mk 8:31

 [He said to them,] "The Son of man will be delivered into the hands of men, and they will kill him; and when he is killed, after three days he will rise."

Mk 9:31b

And the Word became flesh and dwelt among us, full of grace and truth; we have beheld his glory, glory as of the only-begotten son of the father.

Jn 1:14

the Paschal feast with his disciples. During this feast, he made himself the sacrificial Lamb. "For Christ, our Paschal Lamb, has been sacrificed" (1 Cor 5:7), so as to establish once and for all the definitive reconciliation between God and mankind. → 171

96 *Why was a man of peace like Jesus condemned to death on a Cross?*

Jesus posed a decisive question to his contemporaries: Either he was acting with divine authority, or else he was an impostor, a blasphemer, and a violator of the Law and who had to be called to account. [574–576]

In many respects Jesus was a unprecedented challenge to the traditional Judaism of his time. He forgave sins, which God alone can do; he acted as though the Sabbath law were not absolute; he was suspected of blasphemy and brought upon himself the accusation that he was a false prophet. All these were crimes punishable under the Law by death.

97 *Are the Jews guilty of Jesus' death?*

No one can assign collective guilt for the death of Jesus to the Jews. Instead, the Church professes with certainty that all sinners share in the guilt for Jesus' death. [597–598]

The aged prophet Simeon foresaw that Jesus would become "a sign that is spoken against" (Lk 2:34b). And in fact Jesus was resolutely rejected by the Jewish authorities, but among the Pharisees, for example, there were also secret followers of Jesus, like Nicodemus and Joseph of Arimathea. Various Roman and Jewish persons and institutions (Caiaphas, Judas, the Sanhedrin, Herod, Pontius Pilate) took part in Jesus' trial, and only God knows their guilt as individuals. The idea that all Jews of that time or living today are guilty of Jesus' death is irrational and biblically untenable. → 135

98 Did God will the death of his only Son?

The violent death of Jesus did not come about through tragic external circumstances. Jesus was "delivered up according to the definite plan and foreknowledge of God" (Acts 2:23). So that we children of sin and death might have life, the Father in heaven "made him to be sin who knew no sin" (2 Cor 5:21). The magnitude of the sacrifice that God the Father asked of his Son, corresponded to the magnitude of Christ's obedience: "And what shall I say? 'Father, save me from this hour'? No, for this purpose I have come to this hour" (Jn 12:27). On both sides, God's love for men proved itself to the very end on the Cross. [599–609, 620]

In order to save us from death, God embarked on a dangerous mission: He introduced a "medicine of immortality" (St. Ignatius of Antioch) into our world of death—his Son Jesus Christ. The Father and the Son were inseparable in this mission, willing and yearning to take the utmost upon themselves out of love for man. God willed to make an exchange so as to save us forever. He wanted to give us his eternal life, so that we might experience his joy, and wanted to suffer our death, our despair, our abandonment, our death, so as to share with us in everything. So as to love us to the end and beyond. Christ's death is the will of the Father but not his final word. Since Christ died for us, we can exchange our death for his life.

99 What happened at the Last Supper?

Jesus washed the feet of his apostles on the evening before his death; he instituted the →EUCHARIST and founded the priesthood of the New Covenant. [610–611]

Jesus showed his consummate love in three ways: He washed his disciples' feet and showed that he is among us as one who serves (cf. Lk 22:27). He symbolically anticipated his redeeming Passion by speaking these words over the gifts of bread and wine: "This is my body which is given for you. Do this in remembrance of me." And likewise the chalice after supper, saying, "This

> Apart from the Cross there is no other ladder by which we may get to heaven.
>
> ST. ROSE OF LIMA
> (1586–1617, patron saint of Peru, first saint of the Americas)

> It was not the death that pleased him [God the Father], but rather the will of him who freely died, who through that death abolished death, made salvation possible, and restored innocence, who triumphed over principalities and powers, robbed death and enriched heaven, who restored peace to what is in heaven and on earth and united everything.
>
> ST. BERNARD OF CLAIRVAUX
> (1090–1153)

> In a certain sense we can say that the Last Supper itself is the act of foundation of the Church, because he gives himself and thus creates a new community, a community united in communion with himself.
>
> POPE BENEDICT XVI,
> March 15, 2006

? **PASSION**
(Latin *passio* = sickness, suffering): term designating Christ's suffering.

chalice which is poured out for you is the new covenant in my blood." (Lk 22:19f). In this way he instituted the Holy → EUCHARIST. When Jesus commanded the → APOSTLES, "Do this in remembrance of me" (1 Cor 11:24b), he made them priests of the New Covenant. → 208–223

100 *On the Mount of Olives on the night before his death, did Jesus really experience fear of death?*

Since Jesus was true man, he truly experienced fear of death on the Mount of Olives. [612]

With the same human strength that we all possess, Jesus had to fight in order to consent interiorly to

99 God stretched out his hands on the Cross so as to embrace the farthest corners of the universe.

ST. CYRIL OF JERUSALEM (ca. 313–386/387, Father of the Church)

99 When we look at the Cross, we understand the greatness of his love. When we look at the crib, we understand the tenderness of his love for you and for me, for your family and every family.

BL. TERESA OF CALCUTTA (1910–1997)

99 His death on the Cross is the culmination of that turning of God against himself in which he gives himself in order to raise man up and save him. This is love in its most radical form.

POPE BENEDICT XVI, Encyclical *Deus Caritas est*

the Father's will that he give his life for the life of the world. Abandoned in his darkest hour by everyone, even his friends, Jesus managed after a struggle to say Yes. "My Father, if this [cup] cannot pass unless I drink it, your will be done" (Mt 26:42). → 476

101 *Why did Jesus have to redeem us on the Cross, of all places?*

The Cross on which Jesus, although innocent, was cruelly executed is the place of utmost degradation and abandonment. Christ, our Redeemer, chose the Cross so as to bear the guilt of the world and to suffer

the pain of the world. So he brought the world back home to God by his perfect love.
[613–617, 622–623]

God could not show his love more forcibly than by allowing himself in the person of the Son to be nailed to the Cross for us. Crucifixion was the most shameful and most horrible method of execution in antiquity. It was forbidden to crucify Roman citizens, whatever crimes they were guilty of. Thereby God entered into the most abysmal sufferings of mankind. Since then, no one can say "God does not know what I'm suffering."

102 Why are we too supposed to accept suffering in our lives and thus "take up our cross" and thereby follow Jesus?

Christians should not seek suffering, but when they are confronted with unavoidable suffering, it can become meaningful for them if they unite their sufferings with the sufferings of Christ: "Christ ... suffered for you, leaving you an example, that you should follow in his steps" (1 Pet 2:21). [618]

Jesus said, "If any man would come after me, let him deny himself and take up his cross and follow me" (Mk 8:34). Christians have the task of alleviating suffering in the world. Nevertheless, there will still be suffering. In faith we can accept our own suffering and share the suffering of others. In this way human suffering becomes united with the redeeming love of Christ and thus part of the divine power that changes the world for the better.

103 Was Jesus really dead? Maybe he was able to rise again because he only appeared to have suffered death.

Jesus really died on the Cross; his body was buried. All the sources testify to this. [627]

In John 19:33ff., the soldiers even make an explicit determination of death: They open the side of Jesus' dead body with a lance and see blood and water come out. Furthermore, it says that the legs of the men

One of the oldest depictions of the Cross is a caricature from the Palatine Hill in Rome (c. 200), which was intended as a mockery of the Christians' Redeemer. The inscription reads, "Alexamenos worships his God."

> If you carry your cross joyfully, it will carry you.

THOMAS À KEMPIS
(1379/1380–1471)

The Shroud of Turin is a linen cloth apparently from the first century. In 1898 it was photographed for the first time by a photographer in Turin. Upon inspecting the photographic negative, he discovered in the linen fabric the mysterious likeness of a victim of torture from antiquity.

crucified with him were broken—a step that hastened the dying process; this was not required in Jesus' case since his death had already occurred.

104 *Can you be a Christian without believing in the Resurrection of Christ?*

No. "If Christ has not been raised, then our preaching is in vain and your faith is in vain" (1 Cor 15:14). [631, 638, 651]

105 *How did the disciples come to believe that Jesus is risen?*

The disciples, who before had lost all hope, came to believe in Jesus' Resurrection because they saw him in a different way after his death, spoke with him, and experienced him as being alive. [640–644, 656]

The Easter events that took place in Jerusalem in the year 30 are not a made-up story. Following the death of Jesus and the defeat of their whole cause, the disciples fled ("We had hoped that he was the one to redeem Israel", Lk 24:21) or else barricaded themselves behind locked doors. Only their encounter with the risen Christ freed them from their paralysis and filled them with an enthusiastic faith in Jesus Christ, the Lord of life and death.

106 *Are there proofs for the Resurrection of Jesus?*

There are no proofs for the Resurrection of Jesus in the scientific sense. There are, however, very strong individual and collective testimonies by a large number of contemporaries of those events in Jerusalem. [639–644, 647, 656–657]

The oldest written testimony to the Resurrection is a letter that St. Paul wrote to the Corinthians around twenty years after Christ's death: "For I delivered to you as of first importance what I also received, that Christ died for our sins in accordance with the Scriptures, that he was buried, that he was raised on the third day in accordance with the Scriptures, and that he appeared to Cephas, then to the Twelve. Then he appeared to more than five hundred brethren at one time, most of whom are still alive, though some have fallen asleep" (1 Cor 15:3–6). Paul is recording here a living tradition that was present in the original Christian community two or three years after Jesus' death and Resurrection, when he himself became a Christian—on the basis of his own staggering encounter with the risen Lord. The disciples took the fact of the empty tomb (Lk 24:2–3) as the first indication of the reality of the Resurrection. Women, of all people, discovered it—according to the law of that time they were not able to testify. Although we read about the → APOSTLE John that he "saw and believed" (Jn 20:8b) already at the empty tomb, full assurance that Jesus was alive came about only after a series of appearances. The many encounters with the risen Lord ended with Christ's Ascension into heaven. Nevertheless, there were afterward and there are even today encounters with the living Lord: Jesus Christ lives.

Anyone who knows Easter cannot despair.

DIETRICH BONHOEFFER (1906–1945, Lutheran theologian and resistance fighter against Hitler who was put to death in the concentration camp in Flossenbürg)

The love of God passes by radiantly, the Holy Spirit goes through every person in his night like a lightning bolt. In this passing the risen Lord lays hold of you, he burdens himself with everything that is unbearable and takes it all upon himself. Only afterward, often much, much later, do you realize: Christ passed by and bestowed grace out of his superabundance.

BROTHER ROGER SCHUTZ (1915–2005)

107 *Through his Resurrection, did Jesus return to the physical, corporeal state that he had during his earthly life?*

The risen Lord allowed his disciples to touch him; he ate with them and showed them the wounds of his Passion. Nevertheless, his body belonged no longer only to this earth, but rather to the heavenly kingdom of his Father. [645–646]

The risen Christ, who bore the wounds of the Crucified, was no longer bound by space and time. He could enter through locked doors and appear to his disciples in various places in a form in which they did not recognize him immediately. Christ's Resurrection was, therefore, not a return to a normal earthly life, but rather his entrance into a new way of being: "For we know that Christ being raised from the dead will never die again; death no longer has dominion over him" (Rom 6:9).

[Jesus appears to Mary Magdalene, who does not recognize him immediately.] Jesus said to her, "Mary." She turned and said to him in Hebrew, "Rabboni!" (which means Teacher).

Jn 20:16

He who believes in me, though he die, yet shall he live.

Jn 11:25

108 *What changed in the world as a result of the Resurrection?*

Because death is now no longer the end of everything, joy and hope came into the world. Now that death "no longer has dominion" (Rom 6:9) over Jesus, it has no more power over us, either, who belong to Jesus. [655, 658]

Anyone who has heard the Easter proclamation can no longer go around with a tragic expression on his face and lead the humorless existence of a man who has no hope.

FRIEDRICH SCHILLER
(1759–1805, German poet and dramatist)

109 *What does it mean to say that Jesus ascended into heaven?*

With Jesus, one of us has arrived home with God and remains there forever. In his Son, God is close to us men in a human way. Moreover, Jesus says in the Gospel of John, "And I, when I am lifted up from the earth, will draw all men to myself" (Jn 12:32). [659–667]

In the → NEW TESTAMENT, the Ascension of Christ marks the end of forty days during which the risen Lord was especially close to his disciples. At the end of this time, Christ, together with his whole humanity, enters into the glory of God. Sacred Scripture expresses this through the images of "cloud" and "heaven" or sky. "Man", says Pope Benedict XVI, "finds room in God." Jesus Christ is now with the Father, and from there he will come one day "to judge the living and the dead". Christ's Ascension into heaven means that Jesus is no longer visible on earth yet is still present.

"Men of Galilee, why do you stand looking into heaven? This Jesus, who was taken up from you into heaven, will come in the same way as you saw him go into heaven."

Acts 1:11

110 Why is Jesus Christ the Lord of the whole world?

Jesus Christ is Lord of the world and Lord of history because everything was made for his sake. All men were redeemed by him and will be judged by him. [668–674, 680]

He is *over us,* and the only One to whom we bend the knee in worship; he is *with us* as Head of his Church, in which the kingdom of God begins even now; he is *ahead of us* as Lord of history, in whom the powers of darkness are definitively overcome and the destinies of the world are brought to perfection according to God's plan; he *comes to meet us* in glory, on a day we do not know, to renew and perfect the world. We can experience his nearness especially in God's Word, in the reception of the → SACRAMENTS, in caring for the poor, and wherever "two or three are gathered in my name" (see Mt 18:20).
→ 157, 163

In him all things were created, in heaven and on earth, visible and invisible, whether thrones or dominions or principalities or authorities—all things were created through him and for him.

Col 1:16

111 What will it be like when the world comes to an end?

When the world comes to an end, Christ comes—for all to see. [675–677]

The dramatic upheavals (Lk 18:8; Mt 24:3–14) that are foretold in Sacred Scripture—the wickedness that will

... men fainting with fear and with foreboding of what is coming on the world; for the powers of the heavens will be shaken.... Now when these things begin to take place, look up and raise your heads, because your redemption is drawing near.

Lk 21:26, 28

PAROUSIA
(Greek = personal presence): Christ's second coming at the Last Judgment.

CHARISMS
(from the Greek *charis* = gift, grace, favor, charm): a name for the gratuitous gifts of the Holy Spirit as they are described, for example, in 1 Corinthians 12:6ff.: the gift of healing, miraculous powers, prophecy, speaking in tongues, and the gift of interpreting them, wisdom, knowledge, firmness in faith, and so on. Also included are the seven gifts of the Holy Spirit (see question 310); →

be plainly manifest, the trials and persecutions that will put the faith of many to the test—these are only the dark side of the new reality: God's definitive victory over evil will be visible. God's glory, truth, and justice will stand out brilliantly. With Christ's coming there will be "a new heaven and a new earth". "He will wipe away every tear from their eyes, and death shall be no more, neither shall there be mourning nor crying nor pain any more, for the former things have passed away" (Rev 21:4). → 164

112 *What will it be like when Christ judges us and the whole world?*

Even Christ cannot help someone who does not want to know anything about love; such a person judges himself. [678–679, 681–682]

Because Jesus Christ is "the way, and the truth, and the life" (Jn 14:6), he will show what is of lasting value in God's sight and what is not. Held up to the standard of his life, the full truth about all people, things, thoughts, and events will come to light. → 157, 163

CHAPTER THREE
I Believe in the Holy Spirit

113 *What does it mean to say: I believe in the Holy Spirit?*

To believe in the Holy Spirit means to worship him as God just like the Father and the Son. It means to believe that the Holy Spirit comes into our hearts so that we as children of God might know our Father in heaven. Moved by God's Spirit, we can change the face of the earth. [683–686]

Before his death, Jesus promised his disciples that he would send them "another Counselor" (Jn 14:16) when he was no longer with them. Then when the *Holy Spirit* was poured out upon the disciples of the original Church, they learned what Jesus had meant. They experienced a deep assurance and joy in their faith and received particular → CHARISMS; in other words, they could prophesy, heal, and work miracles. To this day there are people in the Church who possess such gifts and have these experiences. → 35–38, 310–311

→ there are special gifts for governing, administering, performing works of charity, and proclaiming the faith.

114 *What role does the Holy Spirit play in the life of Jesus?*

Without the Holy Spirit, we cannot understand Jesus. In his life the presence of God's Spirit, whom we call the Holy Spirit, was manifest in a unique way. [689–691, 702–731]

It was the Holy Spirit who called Jesus to life in the womb of the Virgin Mary (Mt 1:18), endorsed him as God's beloved Son (Lk 4:16–19), guided him (Mk 1:12) and enlivened him to the end (Jn 19:30). On the Cross, Jesus breathed out his Spirit. After his Resurrection, he bestowed the Holy Spirit on his disciples (Jn 20:22). At that the Spirit of Jesus went over to his Church: "As the Father has sent me, even so I send you" (Jn 20:21).

115 *Under what names and signs does the Holy Spirit appear?*

The Holy Spirit descends upon Jesus in the form of a dove. The first Christians experience the Holy Spirit as a healing ointment, living water, a raging storm, or a flaming fire. Jesus Christ himself speaks about the Counselor, Comforter, Teacher, and Spirit of Truth. In the sacraments of the Church, the Holy Spirit is bestowed through the imposition of hands and anointing with oil. [691–693]

The peace that God established in his covenant with mankind after the flood was indicated to Noah through the appearance of a *dove*. Pagan antiquity, too, considered the dove to be a symbol of love. And so the early Christians understood immediately why the Holy Spirit, the love of God in person, came down in the form of a dove when Jesus allowed himself to be baptized in the Jordan. Today the dove is recognized worldwide as the sign of peace and as one of the great symbols for the reconciliation of man with God (cf. Gen 8:10–11).

In Jesus Christ, God himself was made man and allowed us, so to speak, to cast a glance at the intimacy of God himself. And there we see something totally unexpected: ... The mysterious God is not infinite loneliness, he is an event of love.... The Son who speaks to the Father exists, and they are both one in the Spirit, who constitutes, so to speak, the atmosphere of giving and loving which makes them one God.

POPE BENEDICT XVI,
Vigil of Pentecost 2006

And no one can say "Jesus is Lord" except by the Holy Spirit.

1 Cor 12:3b

116 *What does it mean to say that the Holy Spirit has "spoken through the prophets"?*

Already in the Old Covenant God filled men and women with the Spirit, so that they lifted up their voices for God, spoke in his name, and prepared the people for the coming of the Messiah. [683–688, 702–720]

In the Old Covenant God sought out men and women who were willing to let him use them to console, lead, and admonish his people. It was the Spirit of God who spoke through the mouth of Isaiah, Jeremiah, Ezekiel, and other prophets. John the Baptist, the last of these prophets, not only foresaw the coming of the Messiah. He also met him and proclaimed him as the liberator from the power of sin.

117 *How could the Holy Spirit work in, with, and through Mary?*

Mary was totally responsive and open to God (Lk 1:38). Thus she was able to become the "Mother of God" through the working of the Holy Spirit—and as Christ's Mother to become also the Mother of Christians, indeed, the Mother of all mankind. [721–726]

Mary made it possible for the Holy Spirit to work the miracle of all miracles: the Incarnation of God. She gave God her Yes: "Behold, I am the handmaid of the Lord; let it be to me according to your word" (Lk 1:38). Strengthened by the Holy Spirit, she went with Jesus through thick and thin, even to the foot of the Cross. There Jesus gave her to us all as our Mother (Jn 19:25–27). → 80–85, 479

118 What happened on Pentecost?

Fifty days after his Resurrection, the Lord sent the Holy Spirit down from heaven upon his disciples. The age of the → CHURCH began. [731–733]

On Pentecost the Holy Spirit transformed fearful apostles into courageous witnesses to Christ. In a very short time, thousands had themselves baptized: it was the birthday of the Church. The miracle of the languages on → PENTECOST shows that the Church is there for all peoples from the very beginning: She is universal (= the Latin term for the Greek *kat' holon*, catholic) and missionary. She speaks to all men, overcomes ethnic and linguistic barriers, and can be understood by all. To this day the Holy Spirit is the "soul" of the Church, the essential principle of her life.

119 What does the Holy Spirit do in the Church?

The Holy Spirit builds up the → CHURCH and impels her. He reminds her of her → MISSION. He calls people into her service and sends them the necessary gifts. He leads us ever deeper into communion with the Triune God. [733–741, 747]

Even though the Church during her long history has often seemed "abandoned by all good spirits", the Holy Spirit has been at work in her despite all the human failings and inadequacies. The mere fact of her two-

PENTECOST
(from Greek *pentecoste* = "the fiftieth" day after Easter): originally a feast on which Israel celebrated the establishment of the covenant with God on Mount Sinai. Through the Pentecost event in Jerusalem, it became for Christians the feast of the Holy Spirit.

And they were all filled with the Holy Spirit and began to speak in other tongues, as the Spirit gave them utterance. ... Each one heard them speaking in his own language.

Acts 2:4b, 6

"I have yet many things to say to you, but you cannot bear them now. When the Spirit of truth comes, he will guide you into all the truth."

Jn 16:12–13a

FRUITS OF THE HOLY SPIRIT
Love, joy, peace, patience, kindness, goodness, faithfulness, gentleness, self-control (Gal 5:22–23).

THE WORKS OF THE FLESH
According to Gal 5:19ff., these include: immorality, impurity, licentiousness, idolatry, sorcery, enmity, strife, jealousy, anger, selfishness, dissension, division, envy, drunkenness, carousing, and the like.

thousand-year existence and the many saints of all eras and cultures are the visible proof of his presence. The Holy Spirit is the one who maintains the Church as a whole in the truth and leads her ever deeper into the knowledge of God. It is the Holy Spirit who works in the → SACRAMENTS and brings Sacred Scripture to life for us. Even today he gives his gifts of grace (→ CHARISMS) to those who are completely receptive to him.
→ 203–206

120 *What does the Holy Spirit do in my life?*

The Holy Spirit makes me receptive to God; he teaches me to pray and helps me to be there for others. [738–741]

Augustine calls the Holy Spirit "The quiet guest of our soul". Anyone who wants to sense his presence must be quiet. Often this Guest speaks very softly within us and with us, for instance, in the voice of our conscience or through other interior and exterior promptings. Being a "temple of the Holy Spirit" means being there, body and soul, for this Guest, for *God in us.* Our body is therefore God's living room, so to speak. The more receptive we are to the Holy Spirit in us, the more he becomes the master of our life, the sooner he will bestow on us even today his → CHARISMS for the upbuilding of the Church. And so, instead of the → WORKS OF THE FLESH, the → FRUITS OF THE SPIRIT grow in us. → 290–291, 295–297, 310–311

"I Believe in ... the Holy Catholic Church"

121 *What does "Church" mean?*

The Greek word for → CHURCH is *"ekklesia"* **= those who are called forth. All of us who are baptized and believe in God are called forth by the Lord. Together we are the Church. Christ is, as Paul says, the Head of the Church. We are his body. [748–757]**

When we receive the sacraments and hear God's Word, Christ is in us and we are in him—that is the → CHURCH. The intimate communion of life with Jesus that is shared personally by all the baptized is described in Sacred Scripture by a wealth of images: Here it speaks about the People of God and in another passage about the Bride of Christ; now the Church is called Mother, and again she is God's family, or she is compared with a wedding feast. Never is the Church a mere institution,

? CHURCH

(from the Greek *kyriake* = belonging to the Lord): consists of those called together from all nations (from Greek *ex kaleo, ekklesia*) who through Baptism belong to the Body of Christ.

He [Christ] is the head of the body, the Church.

Col 1:18a

99 The Church is an old woman with many wrinkles and furrows. But she is my mother. And no one strikes my mother.

The theologian FR. KARL RAHNER, S.J. (1904–1984), when he heard unseemly criticism of the Church.

never just the "official Church" that we could do without. We will be upset by the mistakes and defects in the → CHURCH, but we can never distance ourselves from her, because God has made an irrevocable decision to love her and does not forsake her despite all the sins of her members. The Church is God's presence among us men. That is why we must love her.

So God created man in his own image, in the image of God he created him.

Gen 1:27

122 *Why does God want there to be a Church?*

God wills the → CHURCH because he wants to redeem us, not individually, but together. He wants to make all mankind his people. [758–781, 802–804]

No one gets to heaven by the asocial route. Someone who thinks only about himself and the salvation of his

own soul is living a-socially. That is impossible both in heaven and on earth. God himself is not a-social; he is not a solitary, self-sufficient being. The Triune God in himself is "social", a communion, an eternal exchange of love. Patterned after God, man also is designed for relationship, exchange, sharing, and love. We are responsible for one another.

123 What is the task of the Church?

The → CHURCH's task is to make the kingdom of God, which has already begun with Jesus, germinate and grow in all nations. [763–769, 774–776, 780]

Wherever Jesus went, heaven touched earth: the kingdom of God was inaugurated, a kingdom of peace and justice. The → CHURCH serves this kingdom of God. She is not an end in herself. She must carry on what Jesus started. She should act as Jesus would act. She continues the sacred signs of Jesus (the → SACRAMENTS). She hands on Jesus' words. That is why the Church, for all her weakness, is a formidable bit of heaven on earth.

Then the Lord said to Cain, "Where is Abel your brother?" He said, "I do not know; am I my brother's keeper?"

Gen 4:9

"As the Father has sent me, even so I send you."

Jn 20:21b

We must be saved together. We must come to God together. Together, we must present ourselves before him. … What would God say to us if some of us were to return without the others?

CHARLES PÉGUY
(1873–1914, French poet)

124 Why is the Church more than an institution?

The Church is more than an institution because she is a →MYSTERY that is simultaneously human and divine. [770–773, 779]

True love does not blind a person but rather makes him see. With regard to the → CHURCH, this is precisely the case: Viewed from outside, the Church is only a historical institution with historical achievements, but also mistakes and even crimes—a Church of sinners. But that is not looking deep enough. After all, Christ became so involved with us sinners that he never abandons his Church, even if we were to betray him daily. This inseparable union of the human and the divine, this intertwining of sin and grace, is part of the mystery of the Church. Seen with the eyes of faith, the Church is therefore indestructibly holy. → 132

125 What is unique about the People of God?

The founder of this people is God the Father. Its leader is Jesus Christ. Its source of strength is the Holy Spirit. The entryway to the People of God is Baptism. Its dignity is the freedom of the children of God. Its law is love. If this people remains faithful to God and seeks first the kingdom of God, it changes the world. [781–786]

In the midst of all the peoples on earth, there is one people that is like no other. It is subject to no one but God alone. It is supposed to be like salt, which adds flavor; like yeast, which permeates everything; like light, which drives away the darkness. Anyone who belongs to the People of God must count on coming into conflict with people who deny God's existence and disregard his commandments. In the freedom of the children of God, however, we have nothing to fear, not even death.

But we have this treasure in earthen vessels, to show that the transcendent power belongs to God and not to us.

2 Cor 4:7

Do all things without grumbling or questioning, that you may be blameless and innocent, children of God without blemish in the midst of a crooked and perverse generation, among whom you shine as lights in the world.

Phil 2:14–15

" The Church cannot behave like a business that changes its product when the demand for it decreases.

KARL CARDINAL LEHMANN (b. 1936)

"But seek first his kingdom and his righteousness, and all these things shall be yours as well."

Mt 6:33

He is the head of the body, the Church.

Col 1:18

" Loving Christ is the same as loving the Church.

BROTHER ROGER SCHUTZ
(1915–2005)

" I would create the whole universe again, just to hear you say that you love me.

Jesus in a vision to
ST. TERESA OF AVILA
(1515–1582)

My beloved speaks and says to me: "Arise, my love, my fair one, and come away."

Song 2:10

The Spirit and the Bride say, "Come." And let him who hears say, "Come." ... Come, Lord Jesus!

Rev 22:17, 20

For we are the temple of the living God; as God said, "I will live in them and move among them, and I will be their God, and they shall be my people."

2 Cor 6:16

126 What does it mean to say that the Church is the "Body of Christ"?

Above all through the → SACRAMENTS of Baptism and Holy → EUCHARIST, an inseparable union comes about between Jesus Christ and Christians. The union is so strong that it joins him and us like the head and members of a human body and makes us one. [787–795] → 146, 175, 179, 200, 208, 217

127 What does it mean to say that the Church is the "Bride of Christ"?

Jesus Christ loves the → CHURCH as a bridegroom loves his bride. He binds himself to her forever and gives his life for her. [796]

Anyone who has ever been in love has some idea of what love is. Jesus knows it and calls himself a bridegroom who lovingly and longingly courts his bride and desires to celebrate the feast of love with her. We are his Bride, the → CHURCH. In the → OLD TESTAMENT God's love for his people is compared to the love between husband and wife. If Jesus seeks the love of each one of us, how often is he then *unhappily in love—* that is to say, with all those who want nothing to do with his love and do not reciprocate it?!

128 What does it mean to say that the Church is the "Temple of the Holy Spirit"?

The → CHURCH is the place in the world where the Holy Spirit is completely present. [797–801, 809]

The people of Israel worshipped God in the Temple of Jerusalem. This temple no longer exists. It has been replaced by the Church, which is not limited to a particular place. "Where two or three are gathered in my name, there am I in the midst of them" (Mt 18:20). What makes her alive is the Spirit of Christ: He lives in the Word of Sacred Scripture and is present in the sacred signs of the → SACRAMENTS. He loves in the hearts of believers and speaks in their prayers. He leads them and bestows charisms on them—simple gifts as well as extraordinary ones. Anyone who enters into a relationship with the Holy Spirit can experience true miracles even today.

→ 113–120, 203–205, 310–311

I Believe in One, Holy, Catholic, and Apostolic Church

129 *Why can there be only <u>one</u> Church?*

Just as there is only one Christ, there can be only one Body of Christ, only one Bride of Christ, and therefore only one → CHURCH of Jesus Christ. He is the Head, the Church is the Body. Together they form the "whole Christ" (St. Augustine). Just as the body has many members yet is one, so too the one Church consists of and is made up of many particular churches (dioceses). [811–816, 866, 870]

Jesus built his Church, which subsists in the Catholic Church, on the foundation of the → APOSTLES. This foundation supports her to this day. The faith of the apostles was handed down from generation to generation under the leadership of the Pope, the Petrine ministry, "which presides in charity" (St. Ignatius of Antioch). The → SACRAMENTS, too, which Jesus entrusted to the apostolic college, still work with their original power.

130 *Are non-Catholic Christians our sisters and brothers also?*

All baptized persons belong to the → CHURCH of Jesus Christ. That is why also those Christians who find themselves separated from the full communion of the Catholic Church, in which the Church of Jesus Christ lives on, are rightly called Christians and are therefore our sisters and brothers. [817–819]

Instances of separation from the one Church of Christ came about through falsifications of Christ's teaching, human failings, and a lack of willingness to be reconciled—usually on the part of representatives on both sides. Christians today are in no way guilty for the

> Most people have no idea what God would make of them if they would only place themselves at his disposal.

ST. IGNATIUS LOYOLA
(1491–1556, founder of the Jesuits)

There is one body and one Spirit, just as you were called to the one hope that belongs to your call, one Lord, one faith, one baptism, one God and Father of us all, who is above all and through all and in all.

Eph 4:4–6

> For with this Church [the Christian community in Rome], by reason of its preeminence, the whole Church, that is the faithful everywhere, must necessarily be in accord, because in it the tradition of the apostles has always been preserved.

ST. IRENAEUS OF LYONS
(ca. 135–202)

CHURCHES AND ECCLESIAL COMMUNITIES
Many Christian communities on earth call themselves churches. According to the Catholic understanding, only those in which the sacraments of Jesus Christ have been preserved in their entirety have remained "Church". This is true especially of the Orthodox and Eastern Churches. In the "ecclesial communities" that resulted from the Protestant Reformation, all the sacraments have not been preserved.

ECUMENISM
(from Greek *oikumene* = the inhabited earth, the globe): efforts to unify divided Christians.

"Say to all the congregation of the sons of Israel, You shall be holy, for I the Lord your God am holy."

Lev 19:2

There is only one tragedy in the end, not to have been a saint.

LÉON BLOY
(1846–1917)

historical divisions of the Church. The Holy Spirit also works for the salvation of mankind in the → CHURCHES AND ECCLESIAL COMMUNITIES that are separated from the Catholic Church. All of the gifts present there, for example, Sacred Scripture, → SACRAMENTS, faith, hope, love, and other charisms, come originally from Christ. Where the Spirit of Christ lives, there is an inner dynamic leading toward "reunion", because what belongs together wants to grow together.

131 *What must we do for the unity of Christians?*

In word and deed we must obey Christ, who expressly wills "that they may all be one" (Jn 17:21). [820–822]

Christian unity is the business of all Christians, regardless of how young or old they are. Unity was one of Jesus' most important concerns. He prayed to the Father, "that they may all be one ... so that the world may believe that you have sent me" (Jn 17:21). Divisions are like wounds on the Body of Christ; they hurt and fester. Divisions lead to enmities and weaken the faith and credibility of Christians. Overcoming the scandal of separation requires the conversion of all concerned but also knowledge of one's own faith convictions, dialogues with others, and especially prayer in common, and collaboration among Christians in serving mankind. Those in authority in the Church must not let the theological dialogue be interrupted.

132 *Why is the Church holy?*

The Church is holy, not because all her members are supposedly holy, but rather because God is holy and is at work in her. All the members of the Church are sanctified by Baptism. [823–829]

Whenever we allow ourselves to be touched by the Triune God, we grow in love and become *holy* and whole. The saints are lovers—not because they are able to love so well, but because God has touched them. They pass on the love they have received from God to other people in their own, often original way. Once God takes

them home, they also sanctify the Church, because they "spend their heaven" supporting us on our path to
→HOLINESS. → 124

133 Why is the Church called catholic?

"Catholic" (Greek *kat' holon*) means related to the whole. The →CHURCH is catholic because Christ called her to profess the *whole* faith, to preserve *all* the →SACRAMENTS, to administer them and proclaim the Good News to *all;* and he sent her to *all* nations. [830–831, 849–856]

134 Who belongs to the Catholic Church?

Anyone who, in union with the →POPE and the bishops, is united to Jesus Christ through profession of the Catholic faith and reception of the →SACRAMENTS is in full communion with the Catholic Church. [836–838]

God willed *one* → CHURCH for *all*. Unfortunately we Christians have been unfaithful to this wish of Christ. Nevertheless, even today we are still deeply united with one another by our faith and common Baptism.

135 What is the relation between the Church and the Jews?

Jews are the "older brethren" of Christians, because God loved them first and spoke to them first. Jesus Christ as man is a Jew, and this fact unites us. The Church recognizes in him the Son of the living God, and this fact separates us. In awaiting the final coming of the Messiah we are one. [839–840]

The Jewish faith is the root of our faith. The Sacred Scripture of the Jews, which we call the Old Testament, is the first part of our Sacred Scripture. The Judeo-Christian concept of man and morality, which is informed by the Ten Commandments, is the foundation of Western democracies. It is shameful that for hundreds of years Christians were unwilling to admit this close relation to Judaism and for pseudo-theological reasons helped foment an anti-Semitism

HOLINESS
The most essential attribute of God. In Latin there is a word, *fanum,* for what is divine, pure, and set apart from profane, everyday things. God is the "totally Other", the Holy One of Israel (Is 30:15); Jesus comes into the world as the "Holy One of God" (Jn 6:69). In him we can see what "holiness" is: to love unconditionally and mercifully, in a helping and healing way, up to perfection in the Cross and Resurrection.

Just as there are also uncatholic things in the Catholic Church, so too we can find something catholic even outside the Catholic Church. Many who seem to be outside are inside; many who seem to be inside are outside.

ST. AUGUSTINE
(354–430)

"Do not think that I have come to abolish the law and the prophets; I have come not to abolish them but to fulfil them."

Mt 5:17

that all too often had lethal effects. During the Holy Year 2000, Pope John Paul II expressly asked forgiveness for this. The Second Vatican Council clearly states that the Jews as a people cannot be charged with any collective guilt for the crucifixion of Christ.

→ 96–97, 335

136 *How does the Church view other religions?*

The → CHURCH respects everything in other religions that is good and true. She respects and promotes freedom of religion as a human right. Yet she knows that Jesus Christ is the sole redeemer of all mankind. He alone is "the way, and the truth, and the life" (Jn 14:6). [841–848]

Whoever seeks God is close to us Christians. There is a special degree of "affinity" to the Muslims. Like Judaism and Christianity, Islam is one of the monotheistic religions (→ MONOTHEISM). The Muslims, too, revere God the Creator and Abraham as their father in faith. Jesus is considered a great prophet in the Qur'an; Mary, his Mother, as the mother of a prophet. The Church teaches that all men who by no fault of their own do not know Christ and his Church but sincerely seek God and follow the voice of their conscience can attain eternal salvation. However, anyone who has

recognized that Jesus Christ is "the way, and the truth, and the life" but is unwilling to follow him cannot find salvation by other paths. This is what is meant by the saying, *Extra ecclesiam nulla salus* (outside of the Church there is no salvation).

→ 199

RELIGIOUS FREEDOM

The right of every man to follow his conscience in choosing and practicing his religion. Acknowledgment of religious freedom is not saying that all religions are equal or equally true.

TWELVE APOSTLES

(Greek *apostolos* = someone sent, messenger): "The names of the twelve apostles are these: first, Simon, who is called Peter, and Andrew his brother; James the son of Zebedee, and John his brother; Philip and Bartholomew; Thomas and Matthew the tax collector; James the son of Alphaeus, and Thaddaeus; Simon the Cananaean, and Judas Iscariot, who betrayed him" (Mt 10:2–4).

137 *Why is the Church called apostolic?*

The → CHURCH is called apostolic because she was founded upon the apostles, holds fast to their Tradition, and is governed by their successors. [857–860, 869, 877]

Jesus called the → APOSTLES to be his closest collaborators. They were his eyewitnesses. After his Resurrection, he appeared to them repeatedly. He bestowed on them the Holy Spirit and sent them as his authoritative messengers to all the world. They assured unity in the early Church. They conferred their mission and authority upon their successors, the bishops, through the laying on of hands. This process is called → APOSTOLIC SUCCESSION. → 92

138 *How is the one, holy, catholic, and apostolic Church structured?*

In the Church there are the → LAITY and clerics (→ CLERGY). As children of God, they are of equal dignity. They have equally important but different

tasks. **The mission of the laity is to direct the whole world toward the kingdom of God. In addition, there are the ordained ministers (clerics), who have the duties of ecclesiastical governance, teaching, and sanctification. In both states of life, there are Christians who place themselves at God's disposal in a special way through celibacy, poverty, and obedience (for example, consecrated religious). [871–876, 934, 935]**

Every Christian has the duty to bear witness to the Gospel by his own life. But God walks a special path with each person. Some he sends as laymen, so that they might build up the kingdom of God by their family and occupation in the midst of the world. For this purpose, he bestows on them in Baptism and → CONFIRMATION all the necessary gifts of the Holy Spirit. Others he entrusts with the pastoral ministry; they are to govern, teach, and sanctify his people. No one can take this duty upon himself; the Lord himself must send him on his way with his divine power through Holy Orders, so that he can act in the place of Christ and administer the → SACRAMENTS. → 259

139 *What is the lay vocation?*

The → LAITY are sent to engage in society so that the kingdom of God can grow among men. [897–913, 940–943]

A lay person is not a second-class Christian, for he shares in the priestly ministry of Christ (the universal priesthood). He sees to it that the people in his walk of life (in school, family and work) come to know the Gospel and learn to love Christ. Through his faith he leaves a mark on society, business, and politics. He supports the life of the Church, for instance, by becoming a lector or an extraordinary minister, by volunteering as a group leader, or by serving on church committees and councils (for example, the parish council or the board of directors of an institution). Young people especially should give serious thought to the question of what place God might want them to have in the Church.

HIERARCHY
(from Greek *hieros* and *arché* = holy origin): the gradated structure of the Church under Christ, from whom all power and authority proceeds.

POPE
(from Greek *pappas* = father): successor of the apostle Peter, Bishop of Rome. Because Peter was the first among the apostles, the Pope, as his successor, presides over the college of bishops. As Christ's Vicar or representative, he is the supreme pastor, priest and teacher of the Church.

BISHOP
(from Greek *episkopein* = to supervise): successor of the apostles; leader of a diocese (local Church); as a member of the college of bishops, under the leadership of the Pope, the bishop has a share in the responsibility for the universal Church.

140 *Why is the Church not a democratic organization?*

Democracy operates on the principle that all power comes from the people. In the → CHURCH, however, all power comes from Christ. That is why the Church has a hierarchical structure. At the same time, however, Christ gave her a collegial structure as well. [874–879]

The *hierarchical* element in the → CHURCH consists in the fact that Christ himself is the one who acts in the Church when ordained ministers, by God's grace, do or give something that they could not do or give by themselves, in other words, when they administer the → SACRAMENTS in Christ's place and teach with his authority. The *collegial* element in the Church consists in the fact that Christ entrusted the entire faith to a group of twelve apostles, whose successors govern the Church, with the Pope, the Petrine ministry presiding. Given this collegial approach, councils are an indispensable part of the Church. Yet even in other administrative bodies of the Church, in synods and councils, the manifold gifts of the Spirit and the universality of the Church throughout the world can be fruitful.

PRIEST

(from Greek *presbyteros* = elder): co-worker with the BISHOP in proclaiming the Gospel and administering the sacraments. He carries out his ministry in communion with the other priests, under the leadership of the bishop.

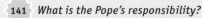

141 *What is the Pope's responsibility?*

As successor of St. Peter and head of the college of bishops, the → POPE is the source and guarantor of the → CHURCH's unity. He has the supreme pastoral authority and the final authority in doctrinal and disciplinary decisions. [880–882, 936–937]

Jesus gave Peter a unique position of preeminence among the apostles. This made him the supreme authority in the early Church. → ROME—the local Church that Peter led and the place of his martyrdom— became after his death the internal reference point of the young Church. Every Christian community had to

DEACON

(Greek *diakonos* = servant, helper): He is ordained for the ministry (diakonía) of the Word, the LITURGY, and charitable works. His ordination includes the authority to baptize, to preach at Mass, and to preside at the sacrament of Matrimony.

agree with Rome; that was the standard for the true, complete, and unadulterated apostolic faith. To this day every → BISHOP of Rome has been, like Peter, the supreme shepherd of the Church, whose real Head is Christ. Only in this capacity is the Pope "Christ's Vicar on earth". As the highest pastoral and doctrinal authority, he watches over the transmission of the true faith. If need be, he must revoke commissions to teach doctrine or relieve ordained ministers of their office in cases of serious failures in matters of faith and morals. Unity in matters of faith and morals, which is guaranteed by the Church's → MAGISTERIUM, or teaching authority, with the Pope at the head, is one reason for the remarkable resilience and influence of the Catholic Church.

142 *Can bishops act and teach against the Pope, or the Pope against the bishops?*

Bishops cannot act and teach against the → POPE, but only with him. In contrast, the Pope can make decisions in clearly defined cases even without the approval of the bishops. [883–885, 880–890]

Of course the → POPE in all his decisions is bound by the Church's faith. There is something like a general sense of the faith in the Church, a fundamental conviction in matters of faith that is brought about by the Holy Spirit and present throughout the Church, the Church's "common sense", so to speak, which recognizes "what has always and everywhere been believed by all" (Vincent of Lerins).

143 *Is the Pope really infallible?*

Yes. But the → POPE speaks infallibly only when he defines a dogma in a solemn ecclesiastical act ("ex cathedra"), in other words, makes an authoritative decision in doctrinal questions of faith and morals. Magisterial decisions of the college of bishops in communion with the Pope also possess an infallible character, for example, decisions of an ecumenical council. [888–892]

The infallibility of the → POPE has nothing to do with his moral integrity or his intelligence. What is infallible is actually the *Church*, for Jesus promised her the Holy Spirit, who keeps her in the truth and leads her ever deeper into it. When a truth of the faith that has been taken for granted is suddenly denied or misinterpreted, the Church must have one final voice that authoritatively says what is true and what is false. This is the voice of the Pope. As the successor of Peter and the first among the bishops, he has the authority to formulate the disputed truth according to the Church's Tradition of faith in such a way that it is presented to the faithful for all times as something "to be believed with certainty". We say then that *the Pope defines a dogma*. Therefore such a dogma can never contain something substantially "new". Very rarely is a dogma defined. The last time was in 1950.

ROME

From the very beginning, the Christian community in Rome was regarded as "the greatest and most ancient Church known to all, founded and organized at Rome by the two most glorious apostles, Peter and Paul. ...
[W]ith this Church, because of her superior origin, all Churches must agree, that is, all the faithful in the whole world; and it is in her that the faithful everywhere have maintained the Tradition of the APOSTLES" (St. Irenaeus of Lyons, 135–202). The fact that both apostles suffered martyrdom in Rome lent additional significance to the Roman community.

"I have yet many things to say to you, but you cannot bear them now. When the Spirit of truth comes, he will guide you into all the truth."

Jn 16:12–13

ECUMENICAL COUNCIL

(Greek *oikumene* = the entire inhabited world): assembly of the Catholic bishops from all over the world; not to be confused with "ecumenism" in the sense of efforts to bring about unity among all Christians.

DOGMA

(Greek *dogma* = opinion, decision, doctrine): an article of faith proclaimed by a Council or the Pope as divine *revelation* contained in Scripture and Tradition.

EX CATHEDRA

(Latin = from the chair, symbol of teaching authority): This technical expression designates the special case of an infallible magisterial decision of the Pope.

"He who hears you hears me, and he who rejects you rejects me, and he who rejects me rejects him who sent me."

Lk 10:16

144 What is the task of the bishops?

Bishops have responsibility for the local Church that is entrusted to them and a share in the responsibility for the whole → CHURCH. They exercise their authority in communion with one another and for the benefit of the whole Church under the leadership of the → POPE. [886–887, 893–896, 938–939]

Bishops must first of all be → APOSTLES—faithful witnesses of Jesus, who personally called them to follow him and then sent them. So they bring Christ to mankind and mankind to Christ. This happens through their preaching, the celebration of the sacraments, and their governance of the → CHURCH. As a successor of the apostles, a bishop exercises his ministry by virtue of his own apostolic authority; he is not an agent or a sort of assistant to the Pope. Yet he acts with and under the Pope.

145 Why does Jesus want there to be Christians who live their whole lives in poverty, unmarried chastity, and obedience?

God is love. He longs for our love also. One form of loving surrender to God is *to live as Jesus did*—poor, chaste, and obedient. Someone who lives in this way has head, heart, and hands free for God and neighbor. [914–933, 944–945]

In every age individual Christians let themselves be completely taken over by Jesus, so that "for the sake of the kingdom of heaven" (Mt 19:12) they give everything away for God—even such wonderful gifts as their own property, self-determination, and married love. This life according to the → EVANGELICAL COUNSELS in poverty, → CHASTITY, and obedience shows all Christians that the world is not everything. Only an encounter with the divine Bridegroom "face to face" will ultimately make a person happy.

? **EVANGELICAL COUNSELS**

Poverty, unmarried chastity, and obedience are the counsels given in the Gospel for imitating Jesus.

And Jesus looking upon him loved him, and said to him, "You lack one thing; go, sell what you have ... and come, follow me."

Mk 10:21

99 After I recognized that there is a God, it was impossible for me not to live for him alone.

BL. CHARLES DE FOUCAULD
(1858–1916, Christian hermit in the Sahara Desert)

"I Believe in ... the Communion of Saints"

146 *What does the "communion of saints" mean?*

The "communion of saints" is made up of all men who have placed their hope in Christ and belong to him through Baptism, whether they have already died or are still alive. Because in Christ we are one Body; we live in a communion that encompasses heaven and earth. [946–962]

The Church is larger and more alive than we think. Among her members are the living and the deceased (whether they are still undergoing a process of purification or are already in the glory of God), individuals known and unknown, great saints and inconspicuous persons. We can help one another even beyond the grave. We can call on our patrons and favorite saints, but also our departed relatives and friends whom we believe are already with God. Conversely, by our

If one member suffers, all suffer together; if one member is honored, all rejoice together.

1 Cor 12:26

intercessory prayer, we can come to the aid of our dear departed who are still undergoing purification. Whatever the individual does or suffers in and for Christ benefits all. Conversely, this unfortunately means also that every sin harms the communion. → 126

147 *Why does Mary have such a preeminent place in the communion of saints?*

Mary is the Mother of God. She was united with Jesus on earth as no other human being was or could be—in an intimacy that does not cease in heaven. Mary is the Queen of Heaven, and in her motherhood she is quite close to us. [972]

Because she committed herself, body and soul, to a divine yet dangerous undertaking, Mary was taken up body and soul into heaven. Anyone who lives and believes as Mary did will get to heaven. → 80–85

148 *Can Mary really help us?*

Yes. Since the beginning of the Church, experience has taught that Mary helps. Millions of Christians testify to it. [967–970]

Being the Mother of Jesus, Mary is also our Mother. Good mothers always stand up for their children. Certainly this Mother does. While still on earth she interceded with Jesus for others; for example, she protected a bride and groom in Cana from embarrassment. In the Upper Room on Pentecost she prayed in the midst of the disciples. Because her love for us never ceases, we can be sure that she will plead for us in the two most important moments of our life: "*now* and at the hour of our death". → 85

149 *May we worship Mary?*

No. Only God can be worshipped. But we can revere Mary as the Mother of our Lord. [971]

By worship we mean the humble, unconditional acknowledgment of the absolute superiority of God over all creatures. Mary is a creature like us. In faith she is our Mother. And we should honor our parents. There is a biblical basis for this, since Mary herself says, "For behold, henceforth all generations will call me blessed" (Lk 1:48b). So the Church has Marian shrines and places of pilgrimage, feast days, hymns, and prayers, for instance, the → ROSARY. It is a compendium of the Gospels. → 353, 484

"I Believe in ... the Forgiveness of Sins"

150 *Can the Church really forgive sins?*

Yes. Jesus not only forgave sins himself, he also conferred on the → CHURCH the mission and the power to free men from their sins. [981–983, 986–987]

Through the ministry of the → PRIEST, the penitent receives God's forgiveness, and his guilt is wiped away as completely as if it had never existed. A priest can do this only because Jesus allows him to participate in his own divine power to forgive sins. → 225–239

151 *What possibilities are there for the forgiveness of sins in the Church?*

Fundamentally the forgiveness of sins occurs in the → SACRAMENT of Baptism. After that the sacrament of Reconciliation (Penance, confession) is necessary for the forgiveness of serious sins. For less serious sins, confession is recommended. But reading Sacred Scripture, prayer, fasting, and the performance of good works also have the effect of forgiving sins. [976–980, 984–987] → 226–239

"I Believe in ... the Resurrection of the Dead"

152 *Why do we believe in the resurrection of the dead?*

We believe in the resurrection of the dead because Christ rose from the dead, lives forever, and causes us to share in this eternal life. [988–991]

→ if Christ has not been raised, then our preaching is in vain and your faith is in vain. ... If for this life only we have hoped in Christ, we are of all men most to be pitied. But in fact Christ has been raised from the dead, the first fruits of those who have fallen asleep.

1 Cor 15:13–14, 19–20

And the Word [of God] became flesh and dwelt among us.

Jn 1:14a

Creation itself will be set free from its bondage to decay and obtain the glorious liberty of the children of God.

Rom 8:21

But some one will ask, "How are the dead raised? With what kind of body do they come?" You foolish man! What you sow does not come to life unless it dies. And what you sow is not the body which is to be, but a bare kernel, perhaps of wheat or of some other grain.

1 Cor 15:35–37

When someone dies, his body is buried or cremated. Nevertheless, we believe that there is a life after death for that person. In his Resurrection, Jesus showed that he is Lord over death; his word is trustworthy: "I am the resurrection and the life; he who believes in me, though he die, yet shall he live" (Jn 11:25b).

→ 103–108

153 *Why do we believe in the resurrection of the "body"?*

In Jesus Christ, God himself took on "flesh" (→INCARNATION) in order to redeem mankind. The biblical word "flesh" characterizes man in his weakness and mortality. Nevertheless, God does not regard human flesh as something inferior. God does not redeem man's spirit only; he redeems him entirely, body and soul. [988–991, 997–1001, 1015]

God created us with a body (flesh) and a soul. At the end of the world he does not drop the "flesh" like an old toy. On the "Last Day" he will remake all creation and raise us up in the flesh—this means that we will be transformed but still experience ourselves in *our element.* For Jesus, too, being in the flesh was not just a phase. When the risen Lord showed himself, the disciples saw the wounds on his body.

154 *What happens to us when we die?*

In death body and soul are separated. The body decays, while the soul goes to meet God and waits to be reunited with its risen body on the Last Day. [992–1004, 1016–1018]

How the resurrection will take place is a mystery. An image can help us to accept it: When we look at a tulip bulb we cannot tell into what a marvelously beautiful flower it will develop in the dark earth. Similarly, we know nothing about the future appearance of our new body. Paul is nevertheless certain: "It is sown in dishonor, it is raised in glory" (1 Cor 15:43a).

155 How does Christ help us at our death, if we trust in him?

Christ comes to meet us and leads us into eternal life. "Not death, but God will take me" (St. Thérèse of Lisieux). [1005–1014, 1016, 1019]

In view of Jesus' suffering and death, death itself can become easier. In an act of trust and love for the Father, we can say Yes, as Jesus did in the Garden of Gethsemane. Such an attitude is called "spiritual sacrifice": the dying person unites himself with Christ's sacrifice on the Cross. Someone who dies this way, trusting in God and at peace with men, and thus without serious sin, is on the way to communion with the risen Christ. Our dying makes us fall no farther than into his hands. A person who dies does not travel to nowhere but rather goes home into the love of God, who created him. → 102

"I Believe ... in Life Everlasting"

156 What is eternal life?

Eternal life begins with Baptism. It continues through death and will have no end. [1020]

Even when we are simply in love, we want this state of affairs to last forever. "God is love", says the First Letter of John (1 Jn 4:16). "Love", says the First Letter to the Corinthians, "never ends" (1 Cor 13:8). God is eternal because he is love; and love is everlasting because it is divine. If we are in love, we enter into God's endless presence. → 285

157 Will we be brought to judgment after death?

The so-called particular or personal judgment occurs at the moment of death of the individual. The general judgment, which is also called the Last Judgment, occurs on the Last Day, at the end of the world, when the Lord comes again. [1021–1022]

In dying every man arrives at the moment of truth. Now it is no longer possible to repress or conceal anything;

If we live, we live to the Lord, and if we die, we die to the Lord; so then, whether we live or whether we die, we are the Lord's.

Rom 14:8

I want to see God and, in order to see him, I must die.

ST. TERESA OF AVILA (1515–1582)

I am not dying; I am entering life.

ST. THÉRÈSE OF LISIEUX (1873–1897)

But do not ignore this one fact, beloved, that with the Lord one day is as a thousand years, and a thousand years as one day.

2 Pet 3:8

Nature is mortal; we shall outlive her. When all the suns and nebulae have passed away, each one of us will still be alive.

C. S. LEWIS (1898–1963)

> Your place in heaven will seem to be made for you and you alone, because you were made for It—made for it stitch by stitch as a glove is made for a hand.

C. S. LEWIS
(1898–1963)

? JUDGMENT
The so-called particular or personal judgment occurs at the death of the individual. The Last or General Judgment occurs on the Last Day, at the end of the world, when the Lord comes again.

For now we see as in a mirror dimly, but then face to face. Now I know in part; then I shall understand fully, even as I have been fully understood.

1 Cor 13:12

The fire will test what sort of work each one has done. If the work which any man has built on the foundation survives, he will receive a reward. If any man's work is burned up, he will suffer loss, though he himself will be saved, but only as through fire.

1 Cor 3:13–15

nothing more can be changed. God sees us as we are. We come before his tribunal, where he proclaims and brings about what is just. Perhaps we will still have to undergo a process of purification, or maybe we will be able to fall into God's arms immediately. But perhaps we will be so full of wickedness, hatred, and denial of everything that we will turn our face away from love forever, away from God. A life without love, however, is nothing but hell. → 163

158 *What is heaven?*

Heaven is the endless moment of love. Nothing more separates us from God, whom our soul loves and has sought our whole life long. Together with all the angels and saints we will be able to rejoice forever in and with God. [1023–1026, 1053]

If you have ever observed a couple looking at each other lovingly or seen a baby nursing who looks for his mother's eyes as though it wanted to store up every smile forever, then you have some inkling of heaven. To be able to see God face to face—that is like one, single, never-ending moment of love. → 52

159 *What is purgatory?*

Purgatory, often imagined as a place, is actually a condition. Someone who dies in God's grace (and therefore at peace with God and men) but who still needs purification before he can see God face to face is in purgatory. [1030–1031]

When Peter had betrayed Jesus, the Lord turned around and looked at Peter: "And Peter went out and wept bitterly"—a feeling *like being in purgatory*. Just such a purgatory probably awaits most of us at the moment of our death: the Lord looks at us full of love—and we experience burning shame and painful remorse over our wicked or "merely" unloving behavior. Only after this purifying pain will we be capable of meeting his loving gaze in untroubled heavenly joy.

160 *Can we help the departed who are in the condition of purgatory?*

Yes, since all those who are baptized into Christ form one communion and are united with one another, the living can also help the souls of the faithful departed in purgatory. [1032, 1414]

When a man is dead, he can do nothing more for himself. The time of active probation is past. But we can do something for the faithful departed in purgatory. Our love extends into the afterlife. Through our fasting, prayers, and good works, but especially through the celebration of Holy → EUCHARIST, we can obtain grace for the departed. → 146

161 *What is hell?*

Hell is the condition of everlasting separation from God, the absolute absence of love. [1033–1037]

Someone who consciously and with full consent dies in serious sin, without repenting, and refuses God's merciful, forgiving love forever, excludes himself from communion with God and the saints. Our freedom makes that decision possible. Jesus warns us again and again not to separate ourselves definitively from him by shutting our hearts against the need of *his* brothers and sisters: "Depart from me, you cursed .... As you did it not to one of the least of these, you did it not to me" (Mt 25:41, 45). → 53

162 *But if God is love, how can there be a hell?*

God does not damn men. Man himself is the one who refuses God's merciful love and voluntarily deprives himself of (eternal) life by excluding himself from communion with God. [1036–1037]

Therefore he [Judas Maccabeus] made atonement for the dead, that they might be delivered from their sin.

2 Mac 12:45

Let us not hesitate to help those who have died and to offer our prayers for them.

ST. JOHN CHRYSOSTOM (349/350–407)

At the evening of life, we shall be judged on love.

ST. JOHN OF THE CROSS (1542–1591, Spanish mystic, Doctor of the Church and poet)

"And if your hand causes you to sin, cut it off; it is better for you to enter life maimed than with two hands to go to hell, to the unquenchable fire."

Mk 9:43

I ask myself: What does hell mean? I maintain that it is the inability to love.

FYODOR M. DOSTOYEVSKY (1821–1881, Russian writer)

The Lord is not slow about his promise as some count slowness, but is forbearing toward you, not wishing that any should perish, but that all should reach repentance.

2 Pet 3:9

[He] desires all men to be saved and to come to the knowledge of the truth.

1 Tim 2:4

"When the Son of man comes in his glory, and all the angels with him, then he will sit on his glorious throne. Before him will be gathered all the nations, and he will separate them one from another as a shepherd separates the sheep from the goats, and he will place the sheep at his right hand, but the goats at the left. ... And they will go away into eternal punishment, but the righteous into eternal life."

Mt 25:31–33, 46

God yearns for communion even with the worst sinner; he wants everyone to convert and be saved. Yet God created man to be *free* and respects his decisions. Even God cannot compel love. As a lover he is "powerless" when someone chooses hell instead of heaven.
→ 51, 53

163 *What is the Last Judgment?*

The Last Judgment will take place at the end of the world, at the second coming of Christ. "All who are in the tombs will hear his voice and come forth, those who have done good, to the resurrection of life, and those who have done evil, to the resurrection of judgment" (Jn 5:29). [1038–1041, 1058–1059]

When Christ comes again in glory, his full splendor will shine upon us. The truth will come plainly to light: our thoughts, our deeds, our relationship to God and to other men—nothing will remain hidden. We will recognize the ultimate meaning of creation,

comprehend God's marvelous ways for the sake of our salvation, and finally receive also an answer to the question of why evil can be so powerful if God is in fact the Almighty. The Last Judgment is also our day in court. Here it is decided whether we will rise to eternal life or be separated from God forever. Toward those who have chosen life, God will act creatively once again. In a "new body" (see 2 Cor 5) they will live forever in God's glory and praise him with body and soul.
→ 110–112, 157

164 *How will the world come to an end?*

At the end of time, God will create a new heaven and a new earth. Evil will no longer have any power or attractiveness. The redeemed will stand face to face with God—as his friends. Their yearning for peace and justice will be fulfilled. To behold God will be their blessedness. The Triune God will dwell among them and wipe away every tear from their eyes; there will be no more death, sorrow, lamentation, or trouble. [1042–1050, 1060] → 110–112

165 *Why do we say "Amen" to the profession of our faith?*

We say Amen—"Yes"—to the profession of our faith because God appoints us witnesses to the faith. Anyone who says Amen assents freely and gladly to God's work in creation and redemption. [1061–1065]

The Hebrew word *amen* comes from a family of words that mean both "faith" and "steadfastness, reliability, fidelity". "He who says *amen* writes his signature" (St. Augustine). We can pronounce this unconditional Yes only because Jesus in his death and Resurrection has proved to be faithful and trustworthy for us. He himself is the human Yes to all God's promises, just as he is also God's definitive Yes to us. → 527

According to his promise we wait for new heavens and a new earth in which righteousness dwells.

2 Pet 3:13.

AMEN
The word *amen* (from Hebrew *aman* = to be steadfast, trustworthy) is used in the Old Testament most often in the sense of "so be it", to reaffirm one's desire for God to act or to join in the praise of God. In the New Testament it is commonly the affirmative concluding word of a prayer. Most often, however, Jesus himself uses it as an otherwise unusual introduction to a speech. It underscores the authority of his words.

For all the promises of God find their Yes in him. That is why we utter the Amen through him, to the glory of God.

2 Cor 1:20

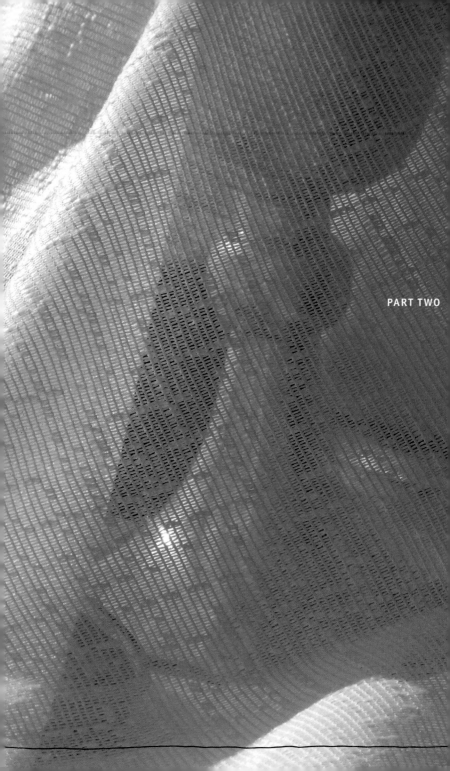

PART TWO

How We Celebrate
the Christian Mysteries

? **LITURGY**
(from Greek
leiturgia = public work,
service, achievement by
and for the people): In
the Christian Tradition,
liturgy means that the
People of God participate
in the "work of God".
The centerpiece of
liturgical celebrations
is the Holy Eucharist;
the other liturgies—for
example, the celebration
of other sacraments,
devotions, blessings,
processions, and the
Liturgy of the Hours—are
ordered to it.

Celebrating the Christian mysteries (→ SACRAMENTS)
is about encountering Jesus Christ in time. Until the
end of time he is present in his → CHURCH. The most
profound encounter with him on earth is the → LITURGY
(divine worship). Therefore the *Rule of St. Benedict*
says:

> "Nothing may have priority over the liturgy."
>
> ST. BENEDICT OF NURSIA (ca. 480-547, founder of Western monasticism).

◇ SECTION ONE ◇
God Acts in Our Regard
by Means of Sacred Signs

166 *Why does the Church celebrate the liturgy
so often?*

**The people of Israel interrupted their work "seven
times a day" (Ps 119:164) in order to praise God.
Jesus participated in the liturgy and prayer of his
people; he taught his disciples to pray and gathered
them in the Upper Room so as to celebrate with them
the → LITURGY of all liturgies: the gift of himself in
the Last Supper. The → CHURCH, which calls us to the
liturgy, obeys his command, "Do this in remembrance
of me" (1 Cor 11:24b). [1066–1070]**

Just as a man breathes air in order to stay alive, so too
the → CHURCH lives and breathes by celebrating the
liturgy. God himself is the one who breathes new life
into her day by day and enriches her with gifts through
his Word and his → SACRAMENTS. We can use another
image, too: every → LITURGY is like a rendezvous of
love that God writes on our calendar. Anyone who has
already experienced God's love is glad to go to church.
Someone who from time to time feels nothing and goes
nevertheless shows God his faithfulness.

99 The liturgy is
never a mere meeting of
a group of people, who
make up their own form
of celebration. ...
[T]hrough our sharing in
Jesus' appearing before
the Father, we stand
both as members of the
worldwide community
of the whole Church and
also of the communion of
saints. Yes, in a certain
sense this is the liturgy
of heaven.

JOSEPH CARDINAL
RATZINGER / POPE
BENEDICT XVI, in *God and
the World*

167 *What is liturgy?*

**→ LITURGY is the official divine worship of
the → CHURCH. [1077–1112]**

A → LITURGY is not an event that depends on good ideas and great songs. No one makes or invents a liturgy. It is something living that grew over millennia of faith. A Mass is a holy, venerable action. Liturgy becomes exciting when one senses that God himself is present under its sacred signs and its precious, often ancient prayers.

168 *Why does the liturgy have priority in the life of the Church and of the individual?*

"The → LITURGY is the summit toward which the activity of the Church is directed; it is also the font from which all her power flows" (Second Vatican Council, *Sacrosanctum concilium* 10). [1074]

During Jesus' lifetime, multitudes of people flocked to him, because they were seeking his healing presence. Even today we can find him, for he lives in his Church. He assures us of his presence in two places: in service to the poor (Mt 25:40) and in the → EUCHARIST. There we run directly into his arms. And when we let him get close to us, he teaches us, feeds us, transforms us, heals us, and becomes one with us in the Holy Sacrifice of the Mass.

169 *What happens to us when we celebrate the liturgy?*

When we celebrate the liturgy, we are drawn into the love of God, healed, and transformed. [1076]

The sole purpose of all liturgies of the → CHURCH and all her → SACRAMENTS is that we might have life and have it abundantly. When we celebrate the liturgy, we encounter the One who said about himself, "I am the way, and the truth, and the life" (Jn 14:6). Someone who is forsaken and goes to Mass receives protection and consolation from God. Someone who feels lost and goes to Mass finds a God who is waiting for him.

Power came forth from him and healed them all.

Lk 6:19b

> Without the Sunday Eucharist, we cannot live. Do you not know that the Christian exists for the Eucharist and the Eucharist for Christians?

Answer of the martyr SATURNINUS (305) during cross-examination to the accusation that he had taken part in the forbidden assembly on Sunday.

"I came that they may have life, and have it abundantly."

Jn 10:10b

While he was yet at a distance, his father saw him and had compassion, and ran and embraced him and kissed him.

Lk 15:20

? BLESSING

A blessing is something good that comes from God (Latin *bene-dicere;* Greek *eu-logein* = to call good); to bless is a divine, life-giving, and life-preserving action. God, the Father and Creator of all being, says: It is good that you exist. The fact that you are is something beautiful.

Then I will go to the altar of God, the God my exceeding joy; and I will praise you with the lyre, O God, my God.

Ps 43:4

<> **CHAPTER ONE** <>
God and the Sacred Liturgy

170 *What is the most profound origin of the liturgy?*

The most profound origin of the → LITURGY is God, in whom there is an eternal, heavenly banquet of love—the joy of the Father, the Son, and the Holy Spirit. Because God is love, he would like to let us participate in the feast of his joy and to grant us his → BLESSINGS. [1077–1109]

Our earthly liturgies must be celebrations full of beauty and power: Feasts *of the Father who created us*—that is why the gifts of the earth play such a great part: the bread, the wine, oil and light, incense, sacred music, and splendid colors. Feasts *of the Son who redeemed us*—that is why we rejoice in our liberation, breathe deeply in listening to the Word, and are strengthened in eating the Eucharistic Gifts. Feasts *of the Holy Spirit* who lives in us—that is why there is a wealth of consolation, knowledge, courage, strength, and blessing that flows from these sacred assemblies.
→ 179

171 What is the essence of every liturgy?

→ **LITURGY is always in the first place communion or fellowship with Jesus Christ. Every liturgy, not just the celebration of the Eucharist, is an Easter in miniature. Jesus reveals his passage from death to life and celebrates it with us. [1085]**

The most important → LITURGY in the world was the Paschal liturgy that Jesus celebrated with his disciples in the Upper Room on the night before his death. The disciples thought that Jesus would be commemorating the liberation of Israel from Egypt. Instead, Jesus celebrated the liberation of all mankind from the power of death. Back in Egypt it was the "blood of the lamb" that preserved the Israelites from the angel of death. Now he himself would be the Lamb whose blood saves mankind from death. For Jesus' death and Resurrection is the proof that someone can die and nevertheless gain life. This is the genuine substance of every Christian liturgy. Jesus himself compared his death and Resurrection with Israel's liberation from slavery in Egypt. Therefore, the redemptive effect of Jesus' death and Resurrection is called the *Paschal mystery*. There is an analogy between the life-saving blood of the lamb at the Exodus of the Israelites from Egypt (Ex 12) and Jesus, the true Paschal Lamb that has redeemed mankind from the bondage of death and sin.

172 How many sacraments are there, and what are their names?

The → CHURCH has seven → SACRAMENTS: Baptism, → CONFIRMATION, → EUCHARIST, Penance, Anointing of the Sick, Holy Orders, and Matrimony. [1210]

173 Why do we need sacraments in the first place?

We need → SACRAMENTS in order to outgrow our petty human life and to become like Jesus through Jesus: children of God in freedom and glory. [1129]

In Baptism the fallen children of men become cherished children of God; through → CONFIRMATION the weak become strong, committed Christians; through Penance

"The blood [of the lamb] shall be a sign for you, upon the houses where you are; and when I see the blood, I will pass over you, and no plague shall fall upon you to destroy you, when I strike the land of Egypt."

Ex 12:12–13f

SACRAMENT
(Latin *sacramentum* = military oath of allegiance; the usual translation for the Greek *mysterion* = mystery): Sacraments are holy, visible signs instituted by Christ of an invisible reality, in which Christians can experience the healing, forgiving, nourishing, strengthening presence of God that enables them to love in turn; this is possible because God's grace works in the sacraments.

the guilty are reconciled; through the → EUCHARIST the
hungry become bread for others; through Matrimony
and Holy Orders individualists become servants of
love; through the Anointing of the Sick the despairing
become people of confidence. The sacrament in all the
sacraments is Christ himself. In him we men, lost in
selfishness, grow and mature into the true life that has
no end.

174 *Why is faith in Jesus Christ not enough?*
Why does God give us the sacraments, too?

**We can and should come to God with all our senses,
not just with the intellect. That is why God gives
himself to us in earthly signs—especially in bread
and wine, the Body and Blood of Christ.
[1084, 1146–1152]**

People saw Jesus, heard him, could touch him and
thereby experience salvation and healing in body and
soul. The sensible signs of the → SACRAMENTS show
this same signature of God, who desires to address the
whole man—not just his head.

175 *Why do the sacraments belong to the Church?*
Why cannot anyone use them however he wants?

**→ SACRAMENTS are Christ's gift to his Church. It is her
duty to administer them and to protect them from
misuse. [1117–1119, 1131]**

Jesus entrusted his words and signs to specific men,
namely, the apostles, who were to hand them on; he
did not hand them over to an anonymous crowd. Today
we would say: He did not post his inheritance on the
Internet for free access but rather registered it under
a domain name. Sacraments exist *for* the Church and
through the Church. They are *for* her, because the
Body of Christ, which is the Church, is established,
nourished, and perfected through the sacraments.
They exist *through her,* because the sacraments are
the power of Christ's Body, for example in confession,
where Christ forgives our sins through the → PRIEST.

176 *Which sacraments can be received only once in a lifetime?*

Baptism, → CONFIRMATION, and Holy Orders. These → SACRAMENTS imprint an indelible mark on the soul of the Christian. Baptism and Confirmation make him once and for all a child of God and Christlike. Holy Orders similarly leaves an imprint on a Christian man. [1121]

Just as someone always is and remains a child of his parents (and not just "sometimes" or "a little bit"), so also through Baptism and Confirmation one becomes forever a child of God, Christlike, and a member of his Church. Similarly, Holy Orders is not a "job" that a man does until retirement; rather, it is an irrevocable charism (gift of grace). Because God is faithful, the effect of these sacraments is maintained forever for the Christian—as receptivity to God's call, as a vocation, and as protection. Consequently these sacraments cannot be repeated.

177 *Why is faith a prerequisite for the sacraments?*

→ SACRAMENTS are not magic. A Sacrament is effective of itself, however, to be fruitful it must be accepted in faith. Sacraments not only presuppose faith, they also strengthen it and give expression to it. [1122–1126]

Jesus commissioned the → APOSTLES first to make people disciples through their preaching, in other words, to awaken their faith and only *then* to baptize them. There are two things, therefore, that we receive from the → CHURCH: faith and the sacraments. Even today someone becomes a Christian, not through a mere ritual or by being listed in a register, but rather through acceptance of the true faith. We receive the true faith from the Church. She vouches for it. Because the Church's faith is expressed in the → LITURGY, no sacramental ritual can be changed or manipulated at the discretion of an individual minister or a congregation.

When the goodness and loving kindness of our Saviour appeared, he saved us ... by the washing of regeneration and renewal in the Holy Spirit.

Tit 3:4–5

This is how one should regard us, as servants of Christ and stewards of the mysteries of God.

1 Cor 4:1

What was visible in our Savior has passed over into his mysteries.

ST. LEO THE GREAT
(ca. 400–461, Pope and
Father of the Church)

For I delivered to you as of first importance what I also received.

1 Cor 15:3

As one candle is lit from the flame of another, so is faith kindled by faith.

ROMANO GUARDINI
(1885–1968)

178 *If a sacrament is administered by someone who is unworthy, does it fail to have its effect?*

No. The → SACRAMENTS are effective on the basis of the sacramental action that is carried out *(ex opere operato),* in other words, independently of the moral conduct or spiritual outlook of the minister. It is enough for him to intend to do what the → CHURCH does. [1127–1128, 1131]

By all means, ministers of the sacraments ought to live an exemplary life. But the sacraments take effect, not because of the → HOLINESS of their ministers, but rather because Christ himself is at work in them. In any case, he respects our freedom when we receive the sacraments. That is why they have a positive effect only if we rely on Christ.

And so, with the Angels and all the Saints we proclaim your glory, as with one voice we sing: Holy, Holy, Holy Lord God of hosts. ...

Eucharistic Prayer II of the Church

It (the liturgy) is entering into the liturgy of the heavens that has always been taking place. ... It is not the case that you think something up and then sing it; instead, the song comes to you from the angels.

JOSEPH RATZINGER / POPE BENEDICT XVI, "In the Presence of the Angels I Will Sing Your Praise" in *A New Song for the Lord*

<>CHAPTER TWO<>
How We Celebrate the Mysteries of Christ

179 *Who celebrates the liturgy?*

In all earthly liturgies, Christ the Lord himself is the one who celebrates the cosmic → LITURGY, which encompasses angels and men, the living and the dead, the past, present, and future, heaven and earth. → PRIESTS and believers participate in different ways in Christ's divine worship. [1136–1139]

When we celebrate the → LITURGY, we must prepare ourselves interiorly for the great thing that takes place in it: here and now Christ is present and, with him, all of heaven. There everyone is filled with unspeakable joy and at the same time with loving care for us. The last book of Sacred Scripture, Revelation, portrays in mysterious images this liturgy to which we here on earth join our voices. → 170

180 *Why is the Mass sometimes referred to as a "worship service"?*

A worship service is in the first place a service that God performs for us—and only then is it our service offered to God. God gives himself to us under the form of holy signs—so that we might do the same: give ourselves unreservedly to him. [1145–1192]

Jesus is there in Word and → SACRAMENT—God is present. That is the first and most important thing about every liturgy. Only then do we enter the picture. Jesus sacrifices his life for us so that we might offer to him the spiritual sacrifice of our life. In the → EUCHARIST, Christ gives himself to us, so that we might give ourselves to him. Thus we take part in the redeeming and transforming sacrifice of Christ. Our little life is burst open and led into the kingdom of God. God can live his life in our lives.

181 *Why are there so many signs and symbols in the liturgies?*

God knows that we men are not only spiritual but also bodily creatures; we need signs and symbols in order to perceive and describe spiritual or interior realities. [1145–1152]

Whether it is red roses, a wedding ring, black clothing, graffiti, or AIDS armbands—we always express our interior realities through signs and are understood immediately. The incarnate Son of God gives us human signs in which he is living and active among us: bread and wine, the water of Baptism, the anointing with the Holy Spirit. Our response to God's sacred signs instituted by Christ consists in signs of reverence: genuflecting, standing while listening to the Gospel, bowing, folding our hands. And as though for a wedding we decorate the place of God's presence with the most beautiful things we have: flowers, candles, and music. In any case, signs also require words to interpret them.

182 *Why do the sacred signs of the liturgy need words, too?*

Celebrating the → LITURGY means encountering God; allowing him to act, listening to him, responding to him. Such dialogues are always expressed in gestures and words. [1153–1155, 1190]

> Symbols are the language of something invisible spoken in the visible world.
>
> GERTRUD VON LE FORT
> (1876-1971)

> I consider the language of symbols to be the only foreign language that every one of us ought to learn.
>
> ERICH FROMM
> (1900-1980, psychoanalyst)

> And whoever would be the first among you must be the slave of all. For the Son of man also came not to be served but to serve, and to give his life as a ransom for many.
>
> Mk 10:44–45

> And one [of the angels] called to another and said: "Holy, holy, holy is the Lord of hosts; the whole earth is full of his glory."
>
> Is 6:3

Jesus spoke to men through signs and words. So it is in the → CHURCH, also, when the priests offers the gifts and says, "This is my Body ... this is my Blood ... ." Only these interpreting words of Jesus cause the signs to become sacraments: signs that bring about what they signify.

183 *Why is there music at liturgies, and what kind of music must it be to be suitable for liturgy?*

Where words are not enough to praise God, music comes to our aid. [1156–1158, 1191]

When we turn to God, there is always something ineffable and unsaid left over. Then music can help out. In rejoicing, language becomes song—that is why the angels *sing*. Music in a worship service should make prayer more beautiful and more fervent, move more deeply the hearts of all in attendance and bring them closer to God, and prepare for God a feast of melody.

Be filled with the Spirit, addressing one another in psalms and hymns and spiritual songs, singing and making melody to the Lord with all your heart.

Eph 5:19

184 *How does the liturgy affect time?*

In the liturgy time becomes *time for God*.

Often we do not know what to do with our time—we look for a *pastime*. In the liturgy, time becomes quite dense, because every second is filled with meaning. When we celebrate the liturgy, we experience the fact that God has sanctified time and made every second a gateway into eternity.

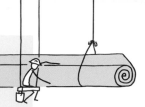

185 *Why does the liturgy repeat itself every year?*

Just as we celebrate a birthday or a wedding anniversary each year, so too the → LITURGY celebrates over the course of the year the most important events in Christian salvation history. With one important difference, however: All time is God's time. "Memories" of Jesus' life and teaching are simultaneously encounters with the living God. [1163–1165, 1194–1195]

The Danish philosopher Søren Kierkegaard once said, "Either we are contemporaries of Jesus, or we can have nothing at all to do with it." Following the Church year in faith makes us indeed contemporaries of Jesus. Not because we can imagine ourselves so precisely as part of *his* time and *his* life, but rather because he comes into *my* time and *my* life, if I make room for him in this way, with his healing and forgiving presence, with the explosive force of his Resurrection.

186 *What is the liturgical year (the Church year)?*

The liturgical year, or the Church year, superimposes the mysteries of the life of Christ—from his Incarnation to his second coming in glory—on the normal course of the year. The liturgical year begins with Advent, the time of waiting for the Lord, and has its first high point in the Christmas season and its second, even greater climax in the celebration of the redemptive suffering, death, and Resurrection of Christ at Easter. The Easter season ends with the feast of Pentecost, the descent of the Holy Spirit on the → CHURCH. The liturgical year is repeatedly interrupted by feasts of the Lord, Mary, and the saints, in which the Church praises God's grace, which has led mankind to salvation. [1168–1173, 1194–1195]

 [Make] the most of the time.

Eph 5:16

" God's eternity is not mere time-lessness, the negation of time, but a power over time that is really present with time and in time.

JOSEPH RATZINGER / POPE BENEDICT XVI, in *The Spirit of the Liturgy*

" The Church year, which makes present and portrays anew the life of Christ, is mankind's greatest work of art; and God has acknowledged it and allows it year after year, always granting it new light, as though one were encountering it for the first time.

JOCHEN KLEPPER (1903–1942, German writer)

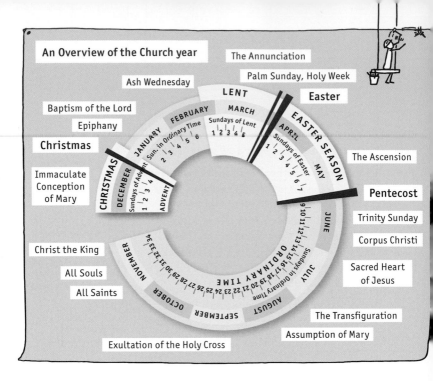

An Overview of the Church year

The Annunciation

Palm Sunday, Holy Week

Ash Wednesday

LENT

Easter

MARCH

Baptism of the Lord

Epiphany

FEBRUARY

Sundays of Lent
1 2 3 4 5

EASTER SEASON

APRIL

Christmas

JANUARY

2 3 4 5 Advent Sun. in Ordinary Time

Sundays of Easter
1 2 3 4 5 6 7

MAY

The Ascension

Immaculate
Conception
of Mary

CHRISTMAS

DECEMBER

Sundays of Advent
1 2 3 4

ADVENT

Pentecost

9 10 11 12 13

JUNE

Trinity Sunday

Corpus Christi

Christ the King

34 33

NOVEMBER

14 15 16 17 18 Sundays in Ordinary Time 19 20 21 22 23 24 25 26 27 28 29 30 31 32

ORDINARY TIME

JULY

Sacred Heart
of Jesus

All Souls

All Saints

OCTOBER

SEPTEMBER

AUGUST

The Transfiguration

Assumption of Mary

Exultation of the Holy Cross

The Church's New Year
begins on the first
Sunday of Advent and
reaches its highpoint at
Easter.

187 *How important is Sunday?*

**Sunday is the center of Christian time, for on
Sunday we celebrate Christ's Resurrection,
and every Sunday is a miniature Easter.
[1163–1167, 1193]**

If Sunday is disregarded or abolished, only work-
days are left in the week. Man, who was created for
joy, degenerates into a workhorse and a mindless
consumer. We must learn on earth how to celebrate
properly, or else we will not know what to do in
heaven. Heaven is an endless Sunday.

→ 104–107

188 *What is the Liturgy of the Hours?*

**The Liturgy of the Hours is the universal, pub-
lic prayer of the → CHURCH. Biblical readings
lead the person who prays it ever deeper
into the mystery of the life of Jesus Christ.**

Throughout the world this gives the Triune God the opportunity at every hour of the day to transform gradually those who pray and also the world. The Liturgy of the Hours is prayed not only by → PRIESTS and religious. Many Christians who take their faith seriously join their voices with the many thousands of praises and petitions that ascend to God from all over the world. [1174–1178, 1196]

The seven "hours of prayer" are like a treasury of the → CHURCH's prayers. It also loosens our tongues when we have become speechless because of joy, sorrow, or fear. Again and again one is astonished in reciting the Liturgy of the Hours: an entire reading "coincidentally" applies precisely to my situation. God hears us when we call to him. He answers us in these texts—often in a way that is so specific as to be almost disconcerting. In any case he also allows us to have long periods of silence and dryness so that we can demonstrate our fidelity.
→ 473, 492

189 *How does the liturgy affect the spaces in which we live?*

By his victory, Christ has penetrated all places in the world. He himself is the true Temple, and the worship of God "in spirit and truth" (Jn 4:24) is no longer bound up with a particular place. Nevertheless, the Christian world is filled with churches and sacred signs, because men need specific places in which to meet and signs to remind them of this new reality. Every house of God is a symbol for our heavenly Father's house, to which we are journeying. [1179–1181, 1197–1198]

Certainly one can pray anywhere—in the forest, on the beach, in bed. But since we men are not merely spiritual but also have a body, we need to see, hear, and feel one another; we need a specific place if we want to meet so as to be the Body of Christ; we must kneel down if we want to worship God; we must eat the transformed bread when it is offered; we must set our bodies in motion when *he* calls us. And a cross on the roadside will remind us of who owns the world and where our journey is taking us.

The seven times for prayer in the Liturgy of the Hours are:
- Matins (Office of Readings or Vigils, in the early morning hours)
- Lauds (Morning Prayer)
- Terce (9:00 a.m., Midmorning Prayer)
- Sext (12:00 noon, Midday Prayer)
- None (3:00 p.m., Midafternoon Prayer)
- Vespers (Evening Prayer)
- Compline (Night Prayer)

190 What is a Christian house of prayer?

A Christian house of prayer is both a sign of the ecclesial communion of people at a specific place and also a symbol of the heavenly dwellings that God has prepared for us all. In God's house we gather together to pray in common or alone and to celebrate the →SACRAMENTS, especially the →EUCHARIST. [1179–1186, 1197–1199]

"It smells like heaven here." "Here you can be very quiet and reverent." Many churches surround us perceptibly in a thick atmosphere of prayer. We sense that God is present here. The beauty of church buildings directs our attention to the beauty, greatness, and love of God. Churches are not just stone messengers of the faith, but dwelling places of God, who is really and truly and substantially present in the sacrament of the altar.

191 What liturgical spaces define a house of God?

The central places of a house of God are the altar with the crucifix, the →TABERNACLE, the celebrant's chair, the ambo, the baptismal font, and the confessional. [1182–1188]

The *altar* is the central point of the church. On it Jesus Christ's sacrifice on the Cross is made present in the celebration of the Eucharist and the Easter meal is prepared. It is also the table to which the People of God are invited. The *tabernacle,* a kind of sacred safe, houses with the greatest honor in a most worthy place in the church the Eucharistic species in which the Lord himself is present. The so-called *perpetual lamp* indicates that the tabernacle is "occupied". If the lamp is not burning, the tabernacle is empty. The raised *chair* (Latin *cathedra*) of the → BISHOP or the priest means that ultimately Christ is the one who leads the congregation. The *ambo* (from Greek *anabainein* = to climb up), the lectern for the Word of God, should manifest the value and dignity of the biblical readings as the Word of the living God. Baptisms are performed at the *baptismal font,* and the *holy water font* should be a vivid reminder of our baptismal promises. A *confessional* or *confession room* is there so that we can acknowledge our guilt and receive forgiveness.

192 *Can the Church also change and renew the liturgy?*

There are changeable and unchangeable components of the → LITURGY. Unchangeable is everything that is of divine origin, for instance, the words of Jesus at the Last Supper. Then there are changeable parts, which the Church occasionally must change. After all, the mystery of Christ must be proclaimed, celebrated, and lived out at all times and in all places. [1200–1209]

Jesus effectively addressed the entire person: mind and understanding, heart and will. That is precisely what he wants to do today also in the → LITURGY. That is why it has different characteristics in Africa and in Europe, in nursing homes and at World Youth Days, and differs in appearance in parishes and monasteries. But it must still be recognizable that it is the one liturgy of the whole worldwide Church.

There is … one Lord, one faith, one baptism, one God and Father of us all.

Eph 4:5–6

INITIATION
(from Latin *initium* = beginning): the term for the introduction and integration of an outsider into an already existing community or fellowship.

We were buried therefore with him by baptism into death, so that as Christ was raised from the dead by the glory of the Father, we too might walk in newness of life.

Rom 6:4

Through Baptism each child is inserted into a gathering of friends who never abandon him in life or in death. ... This group of friends, this family of God, into which the child is now admitted, will always accompany him, even on days of suffering and in life's dark nights; it will give him consolation, comfort, and light.

POPE BENEDICT XVI,
January 8, 2006

Therefore if any one is in Christ, he is a new creation; the old has passed away, behold, the new has come.

2 Cor 5:17

◇ SECTION TWO ◇
The Seven Sacraments of the Church

193 *Is there some inner logic that unites the sacraments with each other?*

All → SACRAMENTS are an encounter with Christ, who is himself the original sacrament. There are sacraments of → INITIATION, which introduce the recipient into the faith: Baptism, → CONFIRMATION, and → EUCHARIST. There are sacraments of healing: Reconciliation and the Anointing of the Sick. And there are sacraments of communion and mission: Matrimony and Holy Orders. [1210–1211]

Baptism joins us with Christ. Confirmation gives us his Spirit. The Eucharist unites us with him. Confession reconciles us with Christ. Through the Anointing of the Sick, Christ heals, strengthens, and consoles. In the sacrament of Matrimony, Christ promises his love in our love and his fidelity in our fidelity. Through the sacrament of Holy Orders, → PRIESTS have the privilege of forgiving sins and celebrating the Holy Sacrifice of the Mass.

◇ CHAPTER ONE ◇
The Sacraments of Initiation

The Sacrament of Baptism

194 *What is Baptism?*

Baptism is the way out of the kingdom of death into life, the gateway to the → CHURCH, and the beginning of a lasting communion with God. [1213–1216, 1276–1278]

Baptism is the foundational → SACRAMENT and the prerequisite for all other sacraments. It unites us with Jesus Christ, incorporates us into his redemptive death on the Cross, thereby freeing us from the power of Original Sin and all personal sins, and causes us to rise with him to a life without end. Since Baptism is a covenant with God, the individual must say Yes to it.

In the baptism of children, the parents confess the Faith on behalf of the children. → 197

→ 197

195 How is Baptism administered?

The classical form of administering Baptism is the threefold immersion of the candidate in the water. Usually, however, water is poured three times over the head of the candidate, while the minister of the sacrament speaks the words, "N., I baptize you in the name of the Father, and of the Son, and of the Holy Spirit." [1229–1245, 1278]

Water symbolizes cleansing and new life, which was already expressed in the baptism of repentance performed by John the Baptist. The Baptism that is administered with water "in the name of the Father, and of the Son, and of the Holy Spirit" is more than a sign of conversion and repentance; it is *new life in Christ*. That is why the ceremony also includes the signs of anointing, the white garment, and the baptismal candle.

196 Who can be baptized, and what is required of a candidate?

Any person who is not yet baptized can be baptized. The only prerequisite for Baptism is faith, which must be professed publicly at the Baptism. [1246–1254]

A person who turns to Christianity is not just changing a world view. He travels a path of learning (the → CATECHUMENATE), in which he becomes a new man through personal conversion, but especially through the gift of Baptism. He is now a living member of the Body of Christ.

197 Why does the Church adhere to the practice of infant Baptism?

From antiquity the → CHURCH has practiced infant Baptism. There is one reason for this: before we decide on God, God has decided on us. Baptism is therefore a grace, an undeserved gift of God, who

Go therefore and make disciples of all nations, baptizing them in the name of the Father and of the Son and of the Holy Spirit.

Mt 28:19

The night is far gone, the day is at hand. Let us then cast off the works of darkness and put on the armor of light … Put on the Lord Jesus Christ [like a new garment].

Rom 13:12, 14

CATECHUMENATE (from Greek *kat' echein* = to instruct, to teach by word of mouth): Especially in the early Church candidates for adult Baptism (catechumens) went through a three-stage preparation, the catechumenate, in which they were instructed in the faith and were gradually allowed to participate in the Liturgy of the Word.

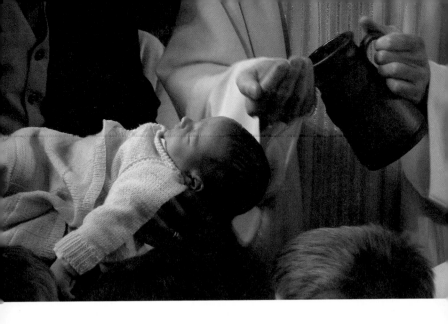

> The gift received by newborn infants needs to be accepted by them freely and responsibly once they have reached adulthood: the process of growing up will then bring them to receive the sacrament of Confirmation, which precisely strengthens the baptized and confers upon each one the "seal" of the Holy Spirit.
>
> POPE BENEDICT XVI, January 8, 2006

accepts us unconditionally. Believing parents who want what is best for their child want Baptism also, in which the child is freed from the influence of original sin and the power of death. [1250, 1282]

Infant Baptism presupposes that Christian parents will raise the baptized child in the faith. It is an injustice to deprive the child of Baptism out of a mistaken liberality. One cannot deprive a child of love so that he can later decide on love for himself; so too it would be an injustice if believing parents were to deprive their child of God's grace in Baptism. Just as every person is born with the ability to speak yet must learn a language, so too every person is born with the capacity to believe but must become acquainted with the faith. At any rate, Baptism can never be imposed on anyone. If someone has received Baptism as a little child, he must "ratify" it later in life – this means he must say Yes to it, so that it becomes fruitful.

198 *Who can administer Baptism?*

Normally a → BISHOP, a → PRIEST, or a → DEACON administers the sacrament of Baptism. In an emergency, any Christian, indeed anyone, can baptize

by pouring water over the head of the recipient and pronouncing the baptismal formula, "I baptize you in the name of the Father and of the Son and of the Holy Spirit." [1256, 1284]

Baptism is so important that even a non-Christian can administer it. In doing so, however, he must have the intention of doing what the → CHURCH does when she baptizes.

199 Is Baptism in fact the only way to salvation?

For all those who have received the Gospel and have heard that Christ is "the way, and the truth, and the life" (Jn 14:6), Baptism is the only way to God and salvation. At the same time, however, it is true that Christ died for all mankind. Therefore all men who have had no opportunity to learn about Christ and the faith but seek God sincerely and live according to their conscience also find salvation (the so-called *Baptism of desire*)**. [1257–1261, 1281, 1283]**

God has made salvation dependent on the → SACRAMENTS. Therefore the Church must tirelessly offer them to mankind. To give up her missionary work would be a betrayal of God's commission. God himself, however, is not dependent on his sacraments. In places where the Church does not exist or has had no success—whether by her own fault or for other reasons—God himself paves for the people other ways to salvation in Christ. → 136

200 What happens in Baptism?

In Baptism we become members of the Body of Christ, sisters and brothers of our Redeemer, and children of God. We are freed from sin, snatched from death, and destined from then on for a life in the joy of the redeemed. [1262–1274, 1279–1280]

Being baptized means that my personal life story is submerged in the stream of God's love. "Our life", says Pope Benedict XVI, "now belongs to Christ, and no longer to ourselves … . At his side and, indeed, drawn up in his love, we are freed from fear. He enfolds us and

[He] desires all men to be saved and to come to the knowledge of the truth.

1 Tim 2:4

"Unless one is born of water and the Spirit, he cannot enter the kingdom of God."

Jn 3:5

If we live, we live to the Lord, and if we die, we die to the Lord; so then, whether we live or whether we die, we are the Lord's.

Rom 14:8

For by one Spirit we were all baptized into one body—Jews or Greeks, slaves or free—and all were made to drink of one Spirit.

1 Cor 12:13

And if [we are] children, then heirs, heirs of God and fellow heirs with Christ.

Rom 8:17

? CONFIRMATION
(from Latin *confirmatio* = strengthening, consolidation): Confirmation, like Baptism and the Eucharist, is one of the three sacraments of initiation of the Catholic Church. As the Holy Spirit descended upon the disciples who were gathered on Pentecost, so the Holy Spirit comes to every baptized person for whom the Church requests the gift of the Holy Spirit. It secures and strengthens him to be a living witness to Christ.

? CHRISM
(from Greek *chrisma* = oil of anointing; and *christos* = anointed one): Chrism is an ointment made out of a mixture of olive oil and balsam. On the morning of Holy Thursday, the bishop consecrates it, so that it can be used in Baptism, Confirmation, priestly and episcopal ordination, and also the consecration of altars and bells. Oil is a symbol of joy, strength, and health. People anointed with chrism are supposed to spread "the aroma of Christ" (2 Cor 2:15).

carries us wherever we may go—he who is Life itself" (April 7, 2007). → 126

201 What is the significance of receiving a name in Baptism?

Through the name that we receive in Baptism God tells us: "I have called you by name, you are mine" (Is 43:1). [2156–2159, 2165]

In Baptism a person is not dissolved into an anonymous divinity, but rather is affirmed precisely in his individuality. To be baptized by a name signifies that God knows me, he says Yes to me and accepts me forever in my unrepeatable uniqueness. → 361

202 Why should Christians choose the names of saints at Baptism?

There are no better examples than the saints and no better helpers. If my namesake is a saint, I have a friend with God. [2156–2159, 2165–2167]

The Sacrament of Confirmation

203 What is Confirmation?

→CONFIRMATION is the →SACRAMENT that completes Baptism; in it the gift of the Holy Spirit is bestowed upon us. Anyone who freely decides to live a life as God's child and asks for God's Spirit under the signs of the imposition of hands and anointing with →CHRISM receives the strength to witness to God's love and might in word and deed. He is now a full-fledged, responsible member of the Catholic →CHURCH. [1285–1314]

When a coach sends a soccer player onto the playing field, he puts his hand on his shoulder and gives him final instructions. We can understand Confirmation in a similar way. A hand is placed upon us. We step out onto the field of life. Through the Holy Spirit we know what we have to do and we have been given the power to do it. He has motivated us. His mission resounds in our ears. We sense his help. We will not betray his trust or

disappoint him; we will win the game for him. We just have to want to do it and listen to him. → 119, 120

204 *What does Sacred Scripture say about the sacrament of Confirmation?*

In the → OLD TESTAMENT, the People of God expected the outpouring of the Holy Spirit upon the Messiah. Jesus lived his life in a special Spirit of love and of perfect unity with his Father in heaven. This Spirit of Jesus was the "Holy Spirit" for whom the people of Israel longed; this was the same Spirit whom Jesus promised to his disciples, the same Spirit who descended upon the disciples fifty days after Easter, on the feast of Pentecost. And it is again this same Holy Spirit of Jesus who descends upon everyone who receives the → SACRAMENT of → CONFIRMATION. [1285–1288, 1315]

In the Acts of the Apostles, which were written a few decades after the death of Jesus, we see Peter and John traveling about to confirm new Christians by imposing hands on those who previously "had only been baptized

Now when the apostles at Jerusalem heard that Samaria had received the word of God, they sent to them Peter and John, who came down and prayed for them that they might receive the Holy Spirit; for the Spirit had not yet fallen on any of them, but they had only been baptized in the name of the Lord Jesus.

Acts 8:14–16

in the name of the Lord Jesus", so that their hearts might be filled with the Holy Spirit.
→ 113–120, 310–311

205 *What happens in Confirmation?*

In →Confirmation the soul of a baptized Christian is imprinted with a permanent seal that can be received only once and marks this individual forever as a Christian. The gift of the Holy Spirit is the strength from above in which this individual puts the grace of his Baptism into practice through his life and acts as a "witness" for Christ. [1302–1305, 1317]

To be confirmed means to make a "covenant" with God. The confirmand says, "Yes, I believe in you, my God; give me your Holy Spirit, so that I might belong entirely to you and never be separated from you and may witness to you throughout my whole life, body and soul, in my words and deeds, on good days and bad." And God says, "Yes, I believe in you, too, my child—and I will give you my Spirit, my very self. I will belong entirely to you. I will never separate myself from you, in this life or eternally in the next. I will be in your body and your soul, in your words and deeds. Even if you forget me, I will still be there—on good days and bad". → 120

206 *Who can be confirmed, and what is required of a candidate for Confirmation?*

Any Catholic Christian who has received the →sacrament of Baptism and is in the "state of grace" can be admitted to →Confirmation. [1306–1311, 1319]

To be "in the state of grace" means not to have committed any serious sin (mortal sin). By a serious sin a person separates himself from God and can be reconciled with God only by making a good confession. A (young) Christian who is preparing for Confirmation finds himself in one of the most important phases of his life. He will do everything possible to grasp the faith with his heart and his understanding; he will pray alone and with others for the Holy Spirit; he will reconcile himself in every way with himself, with the people around him, and with God. Confession is part of this, since it brings one closer to God even if one has not committed a mortal sin. → 316–317

207 Who may confirm?

The → SACRAMENT of → CONFIRMATION is normally administered by the → BISHOP. For weighty reasons when necessary, the bishop can also delegate a priest to do it. In danger of death, any priest can administer Confirmation. [1312–1314]

The Sacrament of the Eucharist

208 What is Holy Eucharist?

Holy Eucharist is the → SACRAMENT in which Jesus Christ gives his Body and Blood—himself—for us, so that we too might give ourselves to him in love and be united with him in Holy → COMMUNION. In this way we are joined with the one Body of Christ, the → CHURCH. [1322, 1324, 1409, 1413]

After Baptism and → CONFIRMATION, the Eucharist is the third sacrament of initiation of the Catholic Church. The Eucharist is the mysterious center of all these sacraments, because the historic sacrifice of Jesus on the Cross is made present during the words of consecration in a hidden, unbloody manner. Thus the celebration of the Eucharist is "the source and summit of the Christian life" (Second Vatican Council, *Lumen gentium* [LG], 11). Everything aims at this; besides this there is nothing greater that one could attain. When we eat the broken Bread, we unite ourselves with the love of Jesus, who gave his body for us on the wood of the Cross; when we drink from the chalice, we unite ourselves with him who even poured out his blood out of love for us. We did not invent this ritual. Jesus himself celebrated the Last Supper with his disciples and therein anticipated his death; he gave himself to his disciples under the signs of bread and wine and commanded them from then on, even after his death, to celebrate the → EUCHARIST. "Do this in remembrance of me" (1 Cor 11:24).
→ 126, 193, 217

> God would have given us something greater if he had had something greater than himself.

ST. JOHN VIANNEY (1786–1859, the "Curé of Ars")

> The actual effect of the Eucharist is the transformation of man into God.

ST. THOMAS AQUINAS (1225–1274)

? EUCHARIST (Greek *eucharistia* = thanksgiving): Eucharist was at first the name for the prayer of thanksgiving that preceded the transformation of the bread and wine into Christ's Body and Blood in the liturgy of the early Church. Later the term was applied to the whole celebration of the Mass.

Draw near to God and he will draw near to you.

Jas 4:8

209 When did Christ institute the Eucharist?

Christ instituted the Holy → EUCHARIST on the evening before his death, "on the night when he was betrayed" (1 Cor 11:23), when he gathered the → APOSTLES around him in the Upper Room in Jerusalem and celebrated the Last Supper with them. [1323, 1337–1340]

210 How did Christ institute the Eucharist?

"For I received from the Lord what I also delivered to you, that the Lord Jesus on the night when he was betrayed took bread, and when he had given thanks, he broke it, and said, 'This is my body, which is for you. Do this in remembrance of me.' In the same way also the chalice, after supper, saying, 'This chalice is the new covenant in my blood. Do this, as often as you drink it, in remembrance of me'" (1 Cor 11:23–25).

This, the oldest account of the events in the Upper Room at the Last Supper, is by the → APOSTLE Paul, who was not an eyewitness himself, but rather wrote down what was being preserved as a holy mystery by the young Christian community and was being celebrated in the liturgy. → 99

211 How important is the Eucharist for the Church?

The celebration of the → Eucharist is the heart of the Christian communion. In it the → CHURCH becomes Church. [1325]

We are not Church because we get along well, or because we happen to end up in the same parish community, but rather because in the Eucharist we receive the Body of Christ and are increasingly being transformed into the Body of Christ. → 126, 217

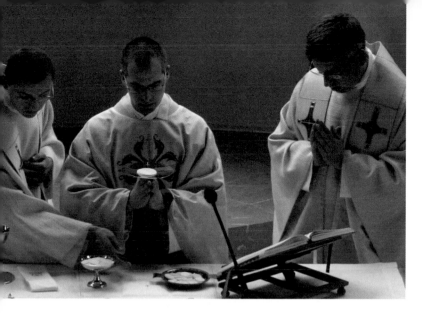

212 *What names are there for Jesus' meal with us, and what do they mean?*

The different names indicate the unfathomable richness of this mystery: the Holy Sacrifice, Holy Mass, the Sacrifice of the Mass—the Lord's Supper—the Breaking of Bread—the Eucharistic assembly—the memorial of the Lord's Passion, death, and Resurrection—the Holy and Divine Liturgy, the Sacred Mysteries—Holy → COMMUNION. [1328–1332]

Holy Sacrifice, Holy Mass, the Sacrifice of the Mass: The one sacrifice of Christ, which completes and surpasses all sacrifices, is made present in the celebration of the Eucharist. The → CHURCH and the faithful, through their self-offering, unite themselves with Christ's sacrifice. The word Mass comes from the Latin dismissal, *Ite, missa est,* "Go now, you are sent."

The Lord's Supper: Every celebration of the Eucharist is still the one supper that Christ celebrated with his disciples and, at the same time, the anticipation of the banquet that the Lord will celebrate with the redeemed at the end of time. We men do not make the worship service; the Lord is the one who calls us to worship God and is mysteriously present in the liturgy.

In the Holy Eucharist we become one with God like food with the body.

ST. FRANCIS DE SALES (1567–1622)

124
125

Your life must be woven around the Eucharist. Direct your eyes to Him, who is the Light; bring your hearts very close to His Divine Heart; ask Him for the grace to know Him, for the charity to love Him, for the courage to serve Him. Seek him longingly.

BL. TERESA OF CALCUTTA (1910–1997)

CONSECRATION
(from Latin
consecratio = hallow-
ing, sanctification): A
consecration is a solemn
act of making something
holy. Thus during Holy
Mass at the consecra-
tion, bread and wine
are "consecrated" and
thereby transformed into
the Body and Blood of
Christ. Bishops, priests,
and deacons are conse-
crated too, as are certain
things for the service
of God, such as church
buildings and altars.

The breaking of bread: "The breaking of bread" was
an old Jewish ritual at meals, which Jesus employed
at the Last Supper to express his gift of self "for us"
(Rom 8:32). In the "breaking of bread" the disciples
recognized him again after the Resurrection. The early
Church called their liturgical feasts "the breaking of
bread".

Eucharistic assembly: The celebration of the Lord's Supper is also an assembly of "thanksgiving", in which the
→ CHURCH finds her visible expression.

Memorial of the Lord's Passion, death, and Resurrection:
In the celebration of the Eucharist, the congregation
does not celebrate itself; rather it discovers and celebrates again and again the presence of Christ's saving
passage through suffering and death to life.

Holy and Divine Liturgy, Sacred Mysteries: In the celebration of the Eucharist, the Church in heaven and on
earth unite in one feast. Because the Eucharistic Gifts
in which Christ is present are, so to speak, the holi-
est thing in the world, we also speak about the Most
Blessed Sacrament.

Holy Communion: Because we unite ourselves with
Christ at Holy Mass, and through him are united with
one another, we speak about Holy Communion (*communio* = fellowship).

213 *What elements are essential to a Holy Mass?*

**Every Holy Mass (celebration of the Eucharist)
unfolds in two main parts, the Liturgy of the Word
and the Liturgy of the Eucharist. [1346–1347]**

In the Liturgy of the Word, we hear readings from the
Old and → NEW TESTAMENT and also the Gospel. Besides
that there is an opportunity for preaching and general
intercessory prayers. In the subsequent Liturgy of the
Eucharist, bread and wine are offered, consecrated, and
distributed to the faithful at → COMMUNION.

Holy Mass begins with the gathering of the faithful and the entrance of the priest and the others who serve in the sanctuary (altar servers, lectors, cantors, and so on). After the greeting comes the Penitential Rite, which concludes with the →KYRIE. On Sundays (outside of Advent and Lent) and feast days, the →GLORIA is then sung or recited. The prayer of the day introduces one or two readings from the →OLD and →NEW TESTAMENT, followed by the responsorial psalm. Before the Gospel is read, there is an →ALLELUIA, or acclamation. After the proclamation of the Gospel on Sundays and feast days, the →PRIEST or →DEACON gives a →HOMILY at least on Sundays and feast days. Then, again only on Sundays and feast days, the congregation professes its common faith in the →CREED, followed by the intercessions. The second part of Holy Mass begins with the preparation of the gifts, which concludes with the Offertory prayer. The high point of the Eucharistic celebration is the Eucharistic Prayer, which is introduced by the Preface and the →SANCTUS. Now the gifts of bread and wine are transformed into the Body and Blood of Christ. The Eucharistic Prayer concludes, finally, in the →DOXOLOGY, which makes the transition to the Lord's Prayer. Then comes the prayer for peace, the →AGNUS DEI, the breaking of the bread, and the distribution of the holy Gifts to the faithful, which often is done only under the form of the Body of Christ. Holy Mass ends with meditation, thanksgiving, a concluding prayer, and a blessing by the priest. [1348–1355]

The →KYRIE:

Celebrant   Lord, have mercy!
Response   Lord, have mercy!
C. Christ, have mercy!
R. Christ, have mercy!
C. Lord, have mercy!
R. Lord, have mercy!

C. *Kyrie eleison!*   **R.** *Kyrie eleison!*
C. *Christe eleison!*   **R.** *Christe eleison!*
C. *Kyrie eleison!*   **R.** *Kyrie eleison!*

? COMMUNION
(from Latin *communio* = fellowship): By Communion, we mean receiving the Body and Blood of Christ in the transformed (consecrated) gifts of bread and wine. This occurs as a rule during Holy Mass, but also on certain occasions outside of Mass (for instance, when Holy Communion is brought to the sick). Communion only under the species of bread is also a full communion with Christ.

? KYRIE ELEISON
(Greek = Lord, have mercy): The *Kyrie eleison,* an ancient cry of homage to gods and rulers, was applied very early to Christ; around the year 500 it was carried over from the Greek liturgy, without translating it, into the Roman and Western liturgy.

GLORIA
(Latin = honor):
The joyful song of the
angels heard by the
shepherds (Lk 2:14) on
Christmas night serves
as the introduction to
an ancient Christian
hymn that has existed
in this form since the
ninth century, in which
the praise of God is sung
with solemnity.

ALLELUIA
("Let us praise the
Lord!"; composed of the
Hebrew *halal* = praise
ye!, glorify!, and the
divine name *YHWH*): This
exclamation, which oc-
curs twenty-four times in
the Psalms, is used in the
Mass as an acclamation
greeting the Word of the
Lord in the Gospel.

HOMILY
(from Greek
homilein = to exhort
someone, speak to him
as a peer, converse with
him): Homily is another
word for sermon. Within
the Eucharistic liturgy,
the preacher has the task
of proclaiming the Good
News (Greek *evangelion*)
and helping the faithful
and encouraging them to
recognize and accept the
practical →

The → GLORIA:

Glory to God in the highest,
and on earth peace to people of good will.
We praise you, we bless you,
we adore you, we glorify you,
we give you thanks for your great glory,
Lord God, heavenly King,
O God, almighty Father.
Lord Jesus Christ, Only Begotten Son,
Lord God, Lamb of God, Son of the Father,
you take away the sins of the world,
have mercy on us;
you take away the sins of the world,
receive our prayer;
you are seated at the right hand of the Father,
have mercy on us.
For you alone are the Holy One,
you alone are the Lord,
you alone are the Most High,
Jesus Christ,
with the Holy Spirit,
in the glory of God the Father.

Gloria in excelsis Deo
et in terra pax hominibus bonae voluntatis.
Laudamus te, benedicimus te,
adoramus te, glorificamus te,
gratias agimus tibi propter magnam gloriam tuam,
Domine Deus, Rex caelestis,
Deus Pater omnipotens,
Domine Fili unigenite, Iesu Christe,
Domine Deus, Agnus Dei,
Filius Patris,
qui tollis peccata mundi, miserere nobis;
qui tollis peccata mundi,
suscipe deprecationem nostram.
Qui sedes ad dexteram Patris, miserere nobis.
Quoniam tu solus Sanctus,
tu solus Dominus,
tu solus Altissimus, Iesu Christe,
cum Sancto Spiritu:
in gloria Dei Patris. Amen.

The → SANCTUS:

Holy, Holy, Holy Lord God of hosts.
Heaven and earth are full of your glory.
Hosanna in the highest.
Blessed is he who comes in the name of the Lord.
Hosanna in the highest.

Sanctus, Sanctus, Sanctus Dominus Deus Sabaoth.
Pleni sunt caeli et terra gloria tua.
Hosanna in excelsis.
Benedictus qui venit in nomine Domini.
Hosanna in excelsis.

The → AGNUS DEI:

Lamb of God, you take away the sins of the world,
have mercy on us.
Lamb of God, you take away the sins of the world,
have mercy on us.
Lamb of God, you take away the sins of the world,
grant us peace.

Agnus Dei, qui tollis peccata mundi, miserere nobis.
Agnus Dei, qui tollis peccata mundi, miserere nobis.
Agnus Dei, qui tollis peccata mundi, dona nobis pacem.

215 *Who leads the celebration of the Eucharist?*

**Actually Christ himself acts in every celebration
of the Eucharist. The → BISHOP or the → PRIEST
represents him. [1348]**

It is the → CHURCH'S belief that the celebrant stands at
the altar *in persona Christi capitis* (Latin = in the person
of Christ, the Head). This means that priests do not
merely act in Christ's place or at his command; rather,
on the basis of their ordination, Christ himself, as Head
of the Church, acts through them. → 249–254

216 *In what way is Christ there when the Eucharist
is celebrated?*

**Christ is mysteriously but really present in the
→ SACRAMENT of the → EUCHARIST. As often as the**

→ consequences of the
Word of God that they
have just heard. During
Holy Mass the homily is
reserved to the priest
or deacon; in other set-
tings, Christian laity may
also preach.

? SANCTUS
(Latin = holy): The
Sanctus is one of the
most ancient parts of
the Mass. It originated
in the eighth century
b.c. (!) and can never
be omitted. The song is
composed of the cry of
the angels in Isaiah 6:3
and a greeting in Psalm
118:26 that is applied to
the presence of Christ.

**? TRANSSUBSTAN-
TIATION**
(from Latin *trans* =
through, and *substantia*
= essence, substance):
with this concept the
Church explains how
Jesus can be present
under the appearance
of the gifts of bread and
wine in the Eucharist.
Whereas the "sub-
stances" (meaning the
"essences") of bread and
wine are changed by the
working →

→ of the Holy Spirit at the words of consecration into the Body and Blood of Christ, their outward "species" or forms remain the same. Jesus Christ is really but invisibly present in what looks like bread and wine as long as the appearances of bread and wine are preserved.

For as often as you eat this bread and drink the chalice, you proclaim the Lord's death until he comes.

1 Cor 11:26

→ **CHURCH** fulfills Jesus' command, "Do this in remembrance of me" (1 Cor 11:24), breaks the bread and offers the chalice, the same thing takes place today that happened then: Christ truly gives himself for us, and we truly gain a share in him. The unique and unrepeatable sacrifice of Christ on the Cross is made present on the altar; the work of our redemption is accomplished. [1362–1367]

217 *What happens in the Church when she celebrates the Eucharist?*

Every time the Church celebrates the → **EUCHARIST**, she stands before the source from which she herself constantly springs anew. By "eating" the Body of Christ, the Church becomes the Body of Christ, which is just another name for the Church. In the sacrifice of Christ, who gives himself to us, body and soul, there is room for our whole life. We can unite everything—our work and our sufferings, our joys— with Christ's sacrifice. If we offer ourselves in this way, we are transformed: We become pleasing to God and like good, nourishing bread for our fellowmen. [1368–1372, 1414]

Again and again we grumble about the → CHURCH, as though she were just an association of more or less good people. In reality the Church is what happens daily in a mysterious way at the altar. God gives himself to each one of us individually, and he wants to transform us through → COMMUNION with him. Once we are transformed, we are supposed to transform the world. Everything else that the Church is besides that is secondary. → 126, 171, 208

218 *What is the right way to honor the Lord present in the bread and wine?*

Because God is truly present in the consecrated species of bread and wine, we must preserve the sacred gifts with the greatest reverence and worship our Lord and Redeemer in the Most Blessed Sacrament. [1378–1381, 1418]

If there are consecrated hosts left over after the celebration of Holy → EUCHARIST, they are kept in sacred vessels in the tabernacle. Since the Most Blessed Sacrament is present in them, the → TABERNACLE is one of the most venerable places in every church. We genuflect before any tabernacle. Certainly, anyone who is really following Christ will recognize him in the poorest of the poor and serve him in them. But he will also find time to spend in adoration before the tabernacle and offer his love to our Eucharistic Lord.

219 *How often must a Catholic Christian participate in the celebration of the Eucharist?*

A Catholic Christian is obliged to attend Holy Mass on all Sundays and holy days of obligation. Anyone who is really seeking Jesus' friendship responds as often as possible to Jesus' personal invitation to the feast. [1389, 1417]

Actually, for a genuine Christian, "Sunday duty" is just as inappropriate an expression as "kiss duty" would be for someone who was truly in love. No one can have a living relationship with Christ without going to the place where he is waiting for us. Therefore, from ancient times the celebration of Mass has been the

TABERNACLE
(Latin *tabernaculum* = hut, tent): In a way reminiscent of the Old Testament Ark of the Covenant, the tabernacle developed in the Catholic Church as a prominent, richly ornamented place for preserving the Most Blessed Sacrament (Christ in the form of bread).

MONSTRANCE
(Latin *monstrare* = to show): a sacred object used to display Christ in the form of consecrated bread on special occasions for adoration by the faithful.

DOXOLOGY
(Greek *doxa* = glory): A doxology is the solemn, formulaic, laudatory conclusion of a prayer, for instance, the conclusion of the Eucharistic Prayer, which reads: *Through him, and with him, and in him, to you, O God, almighty Father, in the unity of the Holy Spirit, is all honor and glory, for ever and ever.* →

→ Often doxologies are addressed to the Holy Trinity, for instance, *Glory be to the Father, and to the Son, and to the Holy Spirit, as it was in the beginning, is now, and ever shall be, world without end,* the formula that usually concludes a Christian prayer.

Lord, I am not worthy to have you come under my roof; but only say the word, and my servant will be healed.

Mt 8:8

An adaptation of these words that the centurion spoke to Jesus is recited before receiving Holy Communion: "Lord, I am not worthy that you should enter under my roof, but only say the word and my soul shall be healed."

Whoever, therefore, eats the bread or drinks the cup of the Lord in an unworthy manner will be guilty of profaning the body and blood of the Lord. Let a man examine himself, and so eat of the bread and drink of the cup.

1 Cor 11:27–28

"heart of Sunday" and the most important appointment in the week.

220 What sort of preparation do I need in order to be able to receive Holy Eucharist?

Someone who would like to receive Holy → EUCHARIST must be Catholic. If he has a serious sin on his conscience, he must first make a confession. Before approaching the altar, one should be reconciled with his neighbors. [1389, 1417]

Until a few years ago, the practice was to eat nothing for at least three hours before Mass; that was how people prepared to encounter Christ in Holy → COMMUNION. Today the → CHURCH requires at least one hour of fasting. Another sign of reverence is to wear one's finest clothing—after all, we have a rendezvous with the Lord of the world.

221 How does Holy Communion change me?

Every Holy → COMMUNION unites me more deeply with Christ, makes me a living member of the Body of Christ, renews the graces that I received in Baptism and → CONFIRMATION, and fortifies me for the battle against sin. [1391–1397, 1416]

222 May the Eucharist be administered to non-Catholic Christians also?

Holy → COMMUNION is the expression of the unity of the Body of Christ. To belong to the Catholic → CHURCH, one must be baptized in her, share her faith, and live in union with her. It would be a contradiction if the Church were to invite to Communion people who do not (yet) share the faith and life of the Church. It would damage the credibility of the sign of the → Eucharist. [1398–1401]

Individual Orthodox Christians may ask to receive Holy Communion at a Catholic liturgy, because they share the Eucharistic faith of the Catholic Church, although their Church is not yet in full communion with the Catholic Church. In the case of members of other

Christian "ecclesial communities" or denominations, Holy Communion may be administered to an individual if there is a grave necessity and evidence of faith in the Real Presence in the Eucharist. Joint celebrations of the Eucharist / Lord's Supper by Catholics and Protestants are the goal and the wish of all ecumenical efforts; to anticipate them, however, without having established the reality of the Body of Christ in one faith and in the one Church is dishonest and therefore not allowed. Other ecumenical liturgies, in which Christians of various denominations pray together, are good and are also desired by the Catholic Church.

223 *In what way is the Holy Eucharist an anticipation of eternal life?*

Jesus promised his disciples, and us with them, that we will one day sit at table with him. Therefore every Holy Mass is a "memorial of the blessed Passion" (Eucharistic Prayer I, called the Roman Canon), the fullness of grace, and a pledge of future glory. [1402–1405]

✧ CHAPTER TWO ✧
The Sacraments of Healing

The Sacrament of Penance and Reconciliation

224 *Why did Christ give us the sacrament of Penance and the Anointing of the Sick?*

Christ's love is shown in the fact that he seeks the lost and heals the sick. That is why he gave us the → SACRAMENTS of healing and restoration, in which we are freed from sin and strengthened in our physical and spiritual weakness. [1420–1421] → 67

225 *What names are there for the sacrament of Penance?*

The sacrament of Penance is also called the → SACRAMENT of Reconciliation, of forgiveness, of conversion, or of confession. [1422–1424, 1486]

> Our sharing in the Body and Blood of Christ has no other purpose than to transform us into that which we receive.

POPE ST. LEO THE GREAT
(ca. 400–461)

> We break the one bread that provides the medicine of immortality, the antidote for death, and the food that makes us live forever in Jesus Christ.

ST. IGNATIUS OF ANTIOCH
(?–107/117)

> There [in your kingdom] we hope to enjoy forever the fullness of your glory, when you will wipe away every tear from our eyes. For seeing you, our God, as you are, we shall be like you for all the ages and praise you without end.

Eucharistic Prayer III

"For the Son of man came to seek and to save the lost."

Lk 19:10

226 *But we have Baptism, which reconciles us with God; why then do we need a special sacrament of Reconciliation?*

Baptism does snatch us from the power of sin and death and brings us into the new life of the children of God, but it does not free us from human weakness and the inclination to sin. That is why we need a place where we can be reconciled with God again and again. That place is confession.[1425–1426]

It does not seem like a modern thing to go to confession; it can be difficult and may cost a great deal of effort at first. But it is one of the greatest graces that we can receive again and again in our life—it truly renews the soul, completely unburdens it, leaving it without the debts of the past, accepted in love, and equipped with new strength. God is merciful, and he desires nothing more earnestly than for us, too, to lay claim to his mercy. Someone who has gone to confession turns a clean, new page in the book of his life. → 67–70

227 *Who instituted the sacrament of Penance?*

Jesus himself instituted the sacrament of Penance when he showed himself to his apostles on Easter day and commanded them, "Receive the Holy Spirit. If you forgive the sins of any, they are forgiven; if you retain the sins of any, they are retained" (Jn 20:22a–23). [1439, 1485]

Nowhere did Jesus express more beautifully what happens in the sacrament of Penance than in the parable of the Prodigal Son: We go astray, we are lost and can no longer cope. Yet our Father waits for us with great, indeed, infinite longing; he forgives us when we come back; he takes us in again, forgives our sins. Jesus himself forgave the sins of many individuals; it was more important to him than working miracles. He regarded this as the great sign of the dawning of the kingdom of God, in which all wounds are healed and all tears are wiped away. Jesus forgave sins in the power of

the Holy Spirit, and he handed that power on to his → APOSTLES. We fall into the arms of our heavenly Father when we go to a → PRIEST and confess.
→ 314, 524

228 Who can forgive sins?

God alone can forgive sins. Jesus could say "Your sins are forgiven" (Mk 2:5) only because he is the Son of God. And → PRIESTS can forgive sins in Jesus' place only because Jesus has given them that authority. [1441–1442]

Many people say, "I can go directly to God; why do I need a priest?" God, though, wants it otherwise. We rationalize our sins away and like to sweep things under the rug. That is why God wants us to tell our sins and to acknowledge them in a personal encounter. Therefore, the following words from the Gospel are true of priests: "If you forgive the sins of any, they are forgiven; if you retain the sins of any, they are retained" (Jn 20:23).

229 What prepares a person for repentance?

The insight into one's personal guilt produces a longing to better oneself; this is called contrition. We arrive at contrition when we see the contradiction between God's love and our sin. Then we are full of sorrow for our sins; we resolve to change our life and place all our hope in God's help. [1430–1433, 1490]

The reality of sin is often repressed. Some people even think that guilt feelings should be dealt with in a merely psychological way. But genuine guilt feelings are important. It is like driving an automobile: When the speedometer indicates that the speed limit has been exceeded, the speedometer is not responsible, but the driver is. The closer we come to God, who is all light, the clearer our dark sides come to light also. Yet God is not a light that burns but, rather, light that heals. That is why repentance impels us to go into the Light in which we will be completely healed. → 312

What is repentance? A great sorrow over the fact that we are the way we are.

MARIE VON EBNER-ESCHENBACH
(1830–1916, Austrian writer)

Some saints described themselves as terrible criminals because they saw God, they saw themselves—and they saw the difference.

BL. TERESA OF CALCUTTA
(1910–1997)

Penance is the second Baptism, the baptism of tears.

ST. GREGORY NAZIANZEN
(330–390)

 Love covers a multitude of sins.

1 Pet 4:8

230 *What is penance?*

Penance is making restitution or satisfaction for a wrong that has been committed. Penance must not take place exclusively in my head; I must express it in acts of charity and in solidarity with others. One does penance also by praying, fasting, and supporting the poor spiritually and materially. [1434–1439]

Penance is often misunderstood. It has nothing to do with low self-esteem or scrupulosity. Penance is not brooding over what a bad person I am. Penance frees and encourages us to make a new start.

231 *What are the two basic elements required for the forgiveness of a Christian's sins to occur in the sacrament of Penance?*

What is required for the forgiveness of sins is the person who undergoes conversion and the → PRIEST who in God's name gives him absolution from his sins.

232 *What must I bring to a confession?*

Essential elements of every confession are an examination of conscience, contrition, a purpose of amendment, confession, and penance. [1450–1460; 1490–1492; 1494]

The *examination of conscience* should be done thoroughly, but it can never be exhaustive. No one can be absolved from his sin without real *contrition*, merely on the basis of "lip-service". Equally indispensable is the *purpose of amendment*, the resolution not to commit that sin again in the future. The sinner absolutely must declare the sin to the confessor and, thus, *confess* to it. The final essential element of confession is the *atonement* or *penance* that the confessor imposes on the sinner to make restitution for the harm done.

> A sign of sincere repentance is avoiding the occasion of sin.
>
> ST. BERNARD OF CLAIRVAUX (1090–1153)

233 What sins must be confessed?

Under normal circumstances, all serious sins that one remembers after making a thorough examination of conscience and that have not yet been confessed can be forgiven only in individual sacramental confession. [1457]

Of course there will be reluctance before making a confession. Overcoming it is the first step toward interior healing. Often it helps to think that even the → POPE has to have the courage to confess his failings and weaknesses to another priest—and thereby to God. Only in life-or-death emergencies (for instance, during an airstrike in wartime or on other occasions when a group of people are in danger of death) can a priest administer "general absolution" to a group of people without the personal confession of sins beforehand. However, afterwards, one must confess serious sins in a personal confession at the first opportunity. → 315–320

ABSOLUTION (from Latin *absolvere* = to loosen, acquit): The absolution of the priest is the sacramental forgiveness of one or more sins after the penitent's confession of sins. The formula of absolution reads:

> God, the merciful Father, by the death and Resurrection of his Son has reconciled the world to himself and sent the Holy Spirit for the forgiveness of sins. Through the ministry of the Church may he give you pardon and peace. And I absolve you from your sins, in the name of the Father, and of the Son, and of the Holy Spirit.

234 When is a Catholic obliged to confess his serious sins? How often should one go to confession?

Upon reaching the age of reason, a Catholic is obliged to confess his serious sins. The Church

> It is not correct to think we must live like this, so that we are never in need of pardon. We must accept our frailty but keep on going, not giving up but moving forward and becoming converted ever anew through the sacrament of Reconciliation for a new start, and thus grow and mature in the Lord by our communion with him.

POPE BENEDICT XVI,
February 17, 2007

> We put off our conversion again and again until death, but who says that we will still have the time and strength for it then?

ST. JOHN VIANNEY
(1786–1859)

urgently advises the faithful to do this at least once a year. At any rate one must go to confession before receiving Holy →COMMUNION if one has committed a serious sin. [1457]

By "the age of reason", the Church means the age at which one has arrived at the use of reason and has learned to distinguish between good and bad.
→ 315–320

235 *Can I make a confession even if I have not committed any serious sins?*

Confession is a great gift of healing that brings about closer union with the Lord, even if, strictly speaking, you do not have to go to confession.[1458]

In Taizé, at Catholic conferences, at World Youth Day celebrations – everywhere, you see young people being reconciled with God. Christians who take seriously their decision to follow Jesus seek the joy that comes from a radical new beginning with God. Even the saints went to confession regularly, if possible. They needed it in order to grow in humility and charity, so as to allow themselves to be touched by God's healing light even in the inmost recesses of their souls.

236 Why are priests the only ones who can forgive sins?

No man can forgive sins unless he has a commission from God to do so and the power given by him to ensure that the forgiveness he promises the penitent really takes place. The → BISHOP, in the first place, is appointed to do that and, then, his helpers, the ordained → PRIESTS. [1461–1466, 1495]

→ 150, 228, 249–250

237 Are there sins that are so serious that not even the average priest can forgive them?

There are sins in which a man turns completely away from God and at the same time, because of the seriousness of the deed, incurs → EXCOMMUNICATION. When a sin results in "excommunication", absolution can be granted only by the → BISHOP or a → PRIEST delegated by him, and, in a few cases, only by the → POPE. In danger of death, any priest can absolve from every sin and excommunication. [1463]

For example, a bishop who, without the Pope's authorization, consecrates another priest to be a bishop automatically excludes himself from sacramental communion; the Church simply acknowledges this fact. The purpose of "excommunication" is to correct the sinner and to lead him back to the right path.

238 May a priest later repeat something he has learned in confession?

No. Under no circumstances. The secrecy of the confessional is absolute. Any → PRIEST who would tell another person something he had learned in the confessional would be excommunicated. Even to the police, the priest cannot say or suggest anything. [1467]

There is hardly anything that priests take more seriously than the seal of the confessional. There are priests who have suffered torture for it and have gone to their deaths. Therefore, you can speak candidly and unreservedly to a priest and confide in him with great

> Candor toward a brother must not be mistaken for confession. The latter is made to the Lord of heaven and earth in the presence of a man who is authorized to hear it.
>
> BROTHER ROGER SCHUTZ
> (1915–2005)

> The closest thing to a father confessor is probably a bartender.
>
> PETER SELLERS
> (1925–1980, British actor)

? EXCOMMUNI-CATION
(from Latin *ex* = out of and *communicatio* = participation, communion): the exclusion of a Catholic Christian from the sacraments.

> Love Jesus! Have no fear! Even if you had committed all the sins in this world, Jesus repeats these words to you: Your many sins are forgiven, because you loved much.
>
> ST. PADRE PIO OF PIETRELCINA
> (1887–1968, one of the most popular saints of Italy)

peace of mind, because his only job at that moment is to be entirely "the ear of God".

239 *What are the positive effects of confession?*

Confession reconciles the sinner with God and the Church. [1468–1470, 1496]

The second after absolution is like a shower after playing sports, like the fresh air after a summer storm, like waking up on a sunlit summer morning, like the weightlessness of a diver …. As the lost son was received back by his father with open arms, so "reconciliation" means: we are at peace with God again.

The Sacrament of the Anointing of the Sick

240 *How was "sickness" interpreted in the Old Testament?*

In the Old Testament sickness was often experienced as a severe trial, against which one could protest but in which one could also see God's hand. In the prophets the thought appears that sufferings are not just a curse and not always the consequence of personal sin, that by patiently bearing sufferings one can also be there for others. [1502]

241 *Why did Jesus show so much interest in the sick?*

Jesus came in order to show God's love. He often did this in places where we feel especially threatened: in the weakening of our life through sickness. God wants us to become well in body and soul and, therefore, to believe and to acknowledge the coming of God's kingdom. [1503–1505]

Sometimes a person has to become sick in order to recognize what we all—healthy or sick—need more than anything else: God. We have no life except in him. That is why sick people and sinners can have a special instinct for the essential things. Already in the → NEW TESTAMENT it was precisely the sick people who sought the presence of Jesus; they tried "to touch him, for power came forth from him and healed them all" (Lk 6:19). → 91

242 Why should the Church take special care of the sick?

Jesus shows us: Heaven suffers with us when we suffer. God even wants to be rediscovered in "the least of these my brethren" (Mt 25:40). That is why Jesus designated care of the sick as a central task for his disciples. He commands them, "Heal the sick" (Mt 10:8), and he promises them divine authority: "In my name they will cast out demons; ... they will lay their hands on the sick, and they will recover" (Mk 16:17–18). [1506–1510]

One of the distinctive characteristics of Christianity has always been that the elderly, the sick, and the needy are central to it. Mother Teresa, who cared for those who were dying in the gutters of Calcutta, is only one in a long series of Christian women and men who have discovered Christ precisely in those who were marginalized and avoided by others. When Christians are really Christian, a healing influence goes out from them. Some even have the gift of healing others physically in the power of the Holy Spirit (the charism of healing, → CHARISM).

243 For whom is the sacrament of the Anointing of the Sick intended?

The → SACRAMENT of the Anointing of the Sick can be received by any Catholic whose health is in a critical state. [1514–1515, 1528–1529]

One can receive the Anointing of the Sick several times in one's life. Therefore it makes sense for young people to ask for this sacrament also, if, for example, they are about to undergo a serious operation. On such occasions many Catholics combine the Anointing of the Sick with a (general) confession; in case the operation fails, they want to go to meet God with a clear conscience.

> " I would prefer even the worst possible Christian world to the best pagan world, because in a Christian world there is room for those for whom no pagan world ever made room: cripples and sick people, the old and the weak. And there was more than room for them: there was love for those who seemed and seem useless to the pagan and the godless world.

HEINRICH BÖLL
(1917-1985, German writer)

> " Care for the sick must have priority over everything else: They should be served as though they were really Christ.

ST. BENEDICT OF NURSIA
(ca. 480–547)

> " And we make one more promise that no other man makes, for we promise to be servants and slaves to our lords, the sick.

Rule for the Military Hospitaller Order of St. John of Jerusalem of Rhodes and of Malta (= "Order of Malta")

> Is any among you sick? Let him call for the elders of the Church, and let them pray over him, anointing him with oil in the name of the Lord.
>
> Jas 5:14

> Even though I walk through the valley of the shadow of death, I fear no evil; for you are with me.
>
> Ps 23:4

244 *How is the Anointing of the Sick administered?*

The essential ritual by which the → SACRAMENT of the Anointing of the Sick is administered consists of an anointing of the forehead and hands with holy oil, accompanied by prayers. [1517–1519, 1531]

245 *How does the Anointing of the Sick work?*

The Anointing of the Sick imparts consolation, peace, and strength and unites the sick person, in his precarious situation and his sufferings, with Christ in a profound way. For the Lord experienced our fears and bore our pains in his body. For many people the Anointing of the Sick brings about physical healing. But if God should decide to call someone home to himself, he gives him in the Anointing of the Sick the strength for all the physical and spiritual battles on his final journey. In any case, the Anointing of the Sick has the effect of forgiving sins. [1520–1523, 1532]

Many sick people are afraid of this → SACRAMENT and put it off until the last minute because they think it is a sort of death sentence. But the opposite is true: the Anointing of the Sick is a sort of life insurance. A Christian who is caring for a sick person should relieve him of any false fear. Most people in serious danger sense intuitively that nothing is more important for them at the moment than to embrace immediately and unconditionally the One who overcame death and is life itself: Jesus, the Savior.

> 99
> Through this holy anointing may the Lord in his love and mercy help you with the grace of the Holy Spirit. ... May the Lord who frees you from sin save you and raise you up.
>
> From the Rite of the Anointing of the Sick

246 *Who can administer the Anointing of the Sick?*

Administering the Anointing of the Sick is reserved to bishops and priests, for it is Christ who acts through them by virtue of their ordination. [1516, 1530]

247 What is meant by "Viaticum"?

Viaticum means the last Holy →Communion that a person receives before dying. [1524–1525]

Rarely is Communion so vitally necessary as in the moment when a person sets out on the path that completes his earthly life: In the future he will have only as much life as he has in union (= communion) with God.

He who eats my flesh and drinks my blood has eternal life, and I will raise him up at the last day.

Jn 6:54

◇ CHAPTER THREE ◇
The Sacraments of Communion and Mission

248 What are the names of the sacraments that serve to build up communion in the Church?

Someone who is baptized and confirmed can receive moreover a special mission in the Church in two special sacraments and thus be enlisted in the service of God: Holy Orders and Matrimony. [1533–1535]

The two → SACRAMENTS have something in common: They are directed *to the good of others*. No one is ordained just for himself, and no one enters the married state merely for his own sake. The sacrament of Holy Orders and the sacrament of Matrimony are supposed to build up the People of God; in other words, they are a channel through which God pours out love into the world.

I will bless you … so that you will be a blessing.

Gen 12:2b

Only Christ [is] truly priest. But the others are his ministers.

ST. THOMAS AQUINAS
(1225–1274)

The Sacrament of Holy Orders

249 What happens in Holy Orders?

The man who is ordained receives a gift of the Holy Spirit that gives him a sacred authority that is conferred upon him by Christ through the bishop. [1538]

Being a → PRIEST does not mean just assuming an office or a ministry. Through Holy Orders a priest receives as a gift a definite power and a mission for his brothers and sisters in faith. → 150, 215, 228, 236

Priestly ordination is administered as a means of salvation, not for an individual man, but rather for the whole Church.

ST. THOMAS AQUINAS
(1225–1274)

250 *How does the Church understand the sacrament of Holy Orders?*

The priests of the Old Covenant saw their duty as mediating between heavenly and earthly things, between God and his people. Since Christ is the "one mediator between God and men" (1 Tim 2:5), he perfected and *ended* that priesthood. After Christ there can be an ordained priesthood only *in* Christ, *in* Christ's sacrifice on the Cross, and *through* a calling and apostolic mission from Christ.
[1539–1553, 1592]

A Catholic → PRIEST who administers the → SACRAMENTS acts not on the basis of his own power or moral perfection (which unfortunately he often lacks), but rather "in persona Christi". Through his ordination, the transforming, healing, saving power of Christ is grafted onto him. Because a priest has nothing of his own, he is above all a *servant*. The distinguishing characteristic of every authentic priest, therefore, is humble astonishment at his own vocation. → 215

251 *What are the degrees of the sacrament of Holy Orders?*

The sacrament of Holy Orders has three degrees:
→ BISHOP *(episcopate)*, → PRIEST *(presbyterate)*,
→ DEACON *(diaconate)*. [1554, 1593] → 140

252 *What happens in episcopal ordination?*

In episcopal ordination the fullness of the sacrament of Holy Orders is conferred upon a → PRIEST. He is ordained a successor of the → APOSTLES and enters the college of bishops. Together with the other bishops and the → POPE, he is from now on responsible for the entire Church. In particular the Church appoints him to the offices of teaching, sanctifying, and governing. [1555–1559]

The episcopal ministry is the real pastoral ministry in the Church, for it goes back to the original witnesses to Jesus, the apostles, and continues the pastoral ministry of the apostles that was instituted by Christ.

The Pope, too, is a → BISHOP, but the first among them and the head of the college. → 92, 137

253 How important for a Catholic Christian is his bishop?

A Catholic Christian feels that he is under an obligation to his → BISHOP; the bishop is appointed for him, too, as Christ's representative. Moreover, the bishop, who exercises his pastoral ministry together with → PRIESTS and → DEACONS as his ordained assistants, is the visible principle and the foundation of the local Church (diocese). [1560–1561]

254 What happens in priestly ordination?

In priestly ordination the → BISHOP calls down God's power upon the candidates for ordination. It imprints upon the souls of these men an indelible seal that can never be lost. As a collaborator with his bishop, the → PRIEST will proclaim the Word of God, administer the → SACRAMENTS, and, above all, celebrate the Holy → EUCHARIST. [1562–1568]

During the celebration of a Holy Mass, the actual ordination of priests begins when the candidates are called by name. After the bishop's homily, the future priest promises obedience to the bishop and his successors. The actual ordination takes place through the imposition of the bishop's hands and his prayer. → 215, 236, 259

255 What happens in diaconal ordination?

In diaconal ordination the candidate is appointed to a special service within the sacrament of Holy Orders. For he represents Christ as the one who came, "not to be served but to serve, and to give his life as a ransom for many" (Mt 20:28). In the liturgy of ordination we read: "As a minister of the Word, of the altar, and of charity, [the → DEACON] will make himself a servant to all."

You must all follow the lead of the bishop, as Jesus Christ followed that of the Father; follow the presbyterate as you would the apostles; reverence the deacons as you would God's commandment. Let no one do anything touching the Church apart from the bishop.

ST. IGNATIUS OF ANTIOCH (d. 107)

The priest continues [Christ's] work of redemption on earth.

ST. JOHN VIANNEY (1786–1859)

DEACON
The deacon (Greek diakonos = servant) is the first degree in the sacrament of Holy Orders in the Catholic Church. As the name itself implies, a deacon is involved especially in charitable work (diakonia), yet he also teaches and catechizes, proclaims the Gospel, preaches at Mass, and assists during the liturgy.

The original model of the deacon is the martyr St. Stephen. When the → APOSTLES in the original Church of Jerusalem saw that they were overwhelmed by their many charitable duties, they appointed seven men "to serve tables", whom they then ordained. The first mentioned is Stephen: "full of grace and power", he accomplished much for the new faith and for the poor in the Christian community. Over the centuries the diaconate became merely a degree of Holy Orders on the way to the presbyterate, but today it is once again an independent vocation for both celibates and married men. On the one hand, this is supposed to reemphasize service as a characteristic of the Church; on the other hand, it helps the priests, as in the early Church, by establishing an order of ministers who take on particular pastoral and social duties of the Church. Diaconal ordination, too, makes a lifelong, irrevocable mark on the ordained man. → 140

256 *Who can receive the sacrament of Holy Orders?*

A baptized, Catholic man who is called by the Church to be a → DEACON, → PRIEST, or → BISHOP can be validly ordained to that ministry. [1577–1578]

257 *Is it demeaning to women that only men may receive the sacrament of Holy Orders?*

The rule that only men may receive Holy Orders in no way demeans women. In God's sight, man and woman have the same dignity, but they have different duties and → CHARISMS. The Church sees herself as bound by the fact that Jesus chose *men* exclusively to be present at the Last Supper for the institution of the priesthood. Pope John Paul II declared in 1994 "that the Church has no authority whatsoever to confer priestly ordination on women and that this judgment is to be definitively held by all the Church's faithful".

Like no one else in antiquity, Jesus provocatively affirmed the value of women, bestowed his friendship on them, and protected them. Women were among his followers, and Jesus highly valued their faith. Moreover, the first witness to the Resurrection was a woman. That is why Mary Magdalene is called "the apostle of the → APOSTLES". Nevertheless, the ordained priesthood (and consequently pastoral ministry) has always been conferred on men. In male priests the Christian community was supposed to see a representation of Jesus Christ. Being a priest is a special service that also makes demands on a man in his gender-specific role as male and father. It is, however, not some form of masculine superiority over women. As we see in Mary, women play a role in the Church that is no less central than the masculine role, but it is feminine. Eve became the mother of all the living (Gen 3:20). As "mothers of all the living", women have special gifts and abilities. Without their sort of teaching, preaching, charity,→ SPIRITUALITY, and guidance, the Church would be "paralyzed on one side". Whenever men in the Church use their priestly ministry as an instrument of power or do not allow opportunities to women, they offend against charity and the Holy Spirit of Jesus. → 64

? CELIBACY
Celibacy (from Latin *caelebs* = a single, unmarried person) is the personal commitment of a person to live in the unmarried state "for the sake of the kingdom of heaven". In the Catholic Church this promise is lived out especially by people in religious orders (who take religious vows) and by the clergy (who make a promise of celibacy).

" Does the Catholic Church know what a radical reversal of values she would introduce [by abolishing celibacy]? The celibacy of priests, the folly of the Gospel, has preserved a hidden reality within it. The Church has thereby directed herself toward the invisible, toward the mystery of Christ.

BROTHER ROGER SCHUTZ

---

258 *Why does the Church require priests and bishops to live a celibate life?*

Jesus lived as a celibate and in this way intended to show his undivided love for God the Father. To follow Jesus' way of life and to live in unmarried chastity "for the sake of the kingdom of heaven" (Mt 19:12) has been since Jesus' time a sign of love, of undivided devotion to the Lord, and of a complete willingness to serve. The Roman Catholic Church requires this way of life of its bishops and priests, while the Eastern Catholic Churches demand it only of their bishops. [1579–1580, 1599]

Celibacy, says Pope Benedict, cannot mean "remaining empty in love, but rather must mean allowing oneself to be overcome by a passion for God". A → PRIEST who lives as a celibate should be fruitful inasmuch as he represents the fatherly character of God and Jesus.

Like living stones be yourselves built into a spiritual house, to be a holy priesthood, to offer spiritual sacrifices acceptable to God through Jesus Christ.

1 Pet 2:5

I am created to do or to be something for which no one else is created: I have a place in God's counsels, in God's world, which no one else has.

BL. JOHN HENRY NEWMAN
(1801–1890)

One drop of love is more than an ocean of understanding.

BLAISE PASCAL
(1588–1651)

The Pope goes on to say, "Christ needs priests who are mature and manly, capable of exercising a true spiritual fatherhood."

259 *How is the universal priesthood of all the faithful different from the ordained priesthood?*

Through Baptism Christ has made us into a kingdom of "priests to his God and Father" (Rev 1:6). Through the universal priesthood, every Christian is called to work in the world in God's name and to bring →BLESSINGS and grace to it. In the Upper Room during the Last Supper and when he commissioned the →APOSTLES, however, Christ equipped some with a sacred authority to serve the faithful; these ordained priests represent Christ as pastors (shepherds) of his people and as head of his Body, the Church. [1546–1553, 1592]

Using the same word, → "PRIEST", for two related things that nevertheless "differ essentially and not only in degree" (Second Vatican Council, LG 10, 2) often leads to misunderstandings. On the one hand, we should observe with joy that all the baptized are "priests" because we live in Christ and share in everything he is and does. Why, then, do we not call down a permanent blessing on this world? On the other hand, we must rediscover God's gift to his Church, the ordained priests, who represent the Lord himself among us.
→ 138

The Sacrament of Marriage

260 *Why did God dispose man and woman for each other?*

God disposed man and woman for each other so that they might be "no longer two but one" (Mt 19:6). In this way they are to live in love, be fruitful, and thus become a sign of God himself, who is nothing but overflowing love. [1601–1605]
→ 64, 400, 417

261 *How does the sacrament of Matrimony come about?*

The → SACRAMENT of Matrimony comes about through a promise made by a man and a woman before God and the Church, which is accepted and confirmed by God and consummated by the bodily union of the couple. Because God himself forms the bond of sacramental marriage, it is binding until the death of one of the partners. [1625–1631]

The man and the woman mutually administer the sacrament of Matrimony. The → PRIEST or the → DEACON calls down God's → BLESSING on the couple and, furthermore, witnesses that the marriage comes about under the right circumstances and that the promise is comprehensive and is made publicly. A marriage can come about only if there is *marital consent,* that is, if the man and the woman enter marriage of their own free will, without fear or coercion, and if they are not prevented from marrying by other natural or ecclesiastical ties (for example, an existing marriage, a vow of celibacy).

> How can I ever express the happiness of a marriage joined by the Church ...? How wonderful the bond between two believers, now one in hope, one in desire, one in discipline, one in the same service, ... undivided in spirit and flesh, truly two in one flesh. Where the flesh is one, one also is the spirit.
>
> TERTULLIAN
> (160–after 220, Latin ecclesiastical writer)

262 *What is necessary for a Christian, sacramental marriage?*

A sacramental marriage has three necessary elements: (a) free consent, (b) the affirmation of a life-long, exclusive union, and (c) openness to children. The most profound thing about a Christian marriage, however, is the couple's knowledge: "We are a living image of the love between Christ and the Church." [1644–1654, 1664]

MONOGAMY, POLYGAMY

(from the Greek *monos* = one, *polys* = many, and *gamos* = marriage): marriage to one person or marriage to several persons at once. Christianity forbids polygamy, which is also punished by the state as the crime of "bigamy" (Greek *bi* = two).

The requirement of *unity* and *indissolubility* is directed in the first place against → POLYGAMY, which Christianity views as a fundamental offense against charity and human rights; it is also directed against what could be called "successive polygamy", a series of non-binding love affairs that never arrive at one, great, irrevocable commitment. The requirement of *marital fidelity* entails a willingness to enter a lifelong union, which excludes affairs outside the marriage. The requirement of *openness to fertility* means that the Christian married couple are willing to accept any children that God may send them. Couples who remain childless are called by God to become "fruitful" in some other way. A marriage in which one of these elements is excluded at the marriage ceremony is not valid.

263 *Why is marriage indissoluble?*

Marriage is triply indissoluble: first, because the essence of love is mutual self-giving without reservation; second, because it is an image of God's unconditional faithfulness to his creation; and third, because it represents Christ's devotion to his Church, even unto death on the Cross.
[1605, 1612–1617, 1661]

At a time when 50 percent of marriages in many places end in divorce, every marriage that lasts is a great sign—ultimately a sign for God. On this earth, where so much is *relative*, people ought to believe in God, who alone is *absolute*. That is why everything that is not relative is so important: someone who speaks the truth *absolutely* or is *absolutely* loyal. Absolute fidelity in marriage is not so much a human achievement as it is a testimony to the faithfulness of God, who is there even when we betray or forget him in so many ways. To be married in the Church means to rely more on God's help than on one's own resources of love.

> Someone who loves a neighbor allows him to be as he is, as he was, and as he will be.
>
> MICHEL QUOIST
> (1921-1997, French priest and author)

> To love a person means to see him as God intended him.
>
> FYODOR M. DOSTOYEVSKY
> (1821–1881)

> To love someone means to be the only one to see a miracle that is invisible to others. .
>
> FRANCOIS MAURIAC
> (1885-1979)

> Husbands, love your wives, as Christ loved the Church and gave himself up for her, that he might sanctify her, having cleansed her by the washing of water with the word. ... Even so husbands should love their wives as their own bodies.
>
> Eph 5:25–26, 28

If we are faithful, he [Jesus Christ] remains faithful—for he cannot deny himself.

2 Tim 2:13

❞❞ Christ has no hands but ours to do his work today.

ANONYMOUS,
14th century

 Cast all your anxieties on him, for he cares about you.

1 Pet 5:7

264 *What threatens marriages?*

What really threatens marriages is sin; what renews them is forgiveness; what makes them strong is prayer and trust in God's presence. [1606–1608]

Conflict between men and women, which sometimes reaches the point of mutual hatred in marriages, of all places, is not a sign that the sexes are incompatible; nor is there such a thing as a genetic disposition to infidelity or some special psychological disability for lifelong commitments. Many marriages, however, are endangered by a lack of communication and consideration. Then there are economic and societal problems. The decisive role is played by the reality of sin: envy, love of power, a tendency to quarrel, lust, infidelity, and other destructive forces. That is why forgiveness and reconciliation, in confession as well, is an essential part of every marriage.

265 *Are all people called to marriage?*

Not everyone is called to marriage. Even people who live alone can have fulfillment in life. To many of them Jesus shows a special way; he invites them to remain unmarried "for the sake of the kingdom of heaven" (Mt 19:12). [1618–1620]

Many people who live alone suffer from loneliness, which they perceive only as a lack and a disadvantage. Yet a person who does not have to care for a spouse or a family also enjoys freedom and independence and has time to do meaningful and important things that a married person would never get to. Maybe it is God's will that he should care for people for whom no one else cares. Not uncommonly God even calls such a person to be especially close to him. This is the case when one senses a desire to renounce marriage "for the sake of the kingdom of heaven". Of course a Christian vocation can never mean despising marriage or sexuality. Voluntary celibacy can be practiced only *in* love and *out* of love, as a powerful sign that God is more important than anything else. The unmarried person renounces a sexual relationship but not love; full of longing he goes out to meet Christ the bridegroom who is coming (Mt 25:6).

266 How is a Church wedding celebrated?

As a rule a wedding must take place publicly. The bride and bridegroom are questioned as to their intention to marry. The → PRIEST or the → DEACON blesses their rings. The bride and bridegroom exchange rings and mutually promise "to be true in good times and in bad, in sickness and in health" and vow to each other: "I will love you and honor you all the days of my life." The celebrant ratifies the wedding and administers the → BLESSING. [1621–1624, 1663]

Here are some excerpts from one form of the Rite of Catholic Marriage: **Celebrant:** N. and N., have you come here freely and without reservation to give yourselves to each other in marriage?" **Bride and bridegroom:** "Yes." **Celebrant:** "Will you love and honor each other as man and wife for the rest of your lives?" **Bride and bridegroom:** "Yes." The celebrant then asks the bride and bridegroom together the following questions. "Will you accept children lovingly from God and bring them up according to the law of Christ and his Church?" **Bride and bridegroom:** "Yes."

267 What should be done if a Catholic wants to marry a non-Catholic Christian?

Church approval must be obtained for the wedding. This is because a so-called "mixed" (that is, interdenominational) marriage requires from both partners a special fidelity to Christ, so that the scandal of Christian division, which has still not been remedied, does not continue in miniature and perhaps even lead to giving up the practice of the faith. [1633–1637]

"Where you go I will go, and where you lodge I will lodge; your people shall be my people, and your God my God; where you die I will die, and there will I be buried. May the Lord do so to me and more also if even death parts me from you."

Ruth 1:16–17

Difference of confession between the spouses does not constitute an insurmountable obstacle for marriage, when they succeed in placing in common what they have received from their respective communities, and learn from each other the way in which each lives in fidelity to Christ.

CCC, 1634

DISPENSATION
A dispensation in Catholic canon law is an exemption from a Church law. The authority competent to issue a dispensation is the local bishop or the Apostolic See.

268 Can a Catholic Christian marry a person from another religion?

For Catholic believers, to enter into and live in marriage with a person who belongs to another → RELIGION can cause difficulties for their own faith and for their future children. Given her responsibility for the faithful, the Church has therefore established the impediment of disparity of religion. Such a marriage can therefore be contracted validly only if a → DISPENSATION from this impediment is obtained before the wedding. The marriage is not sacramental. [1633–1637]

269 May a husband and wife who are always fighting get a divorce?

The Church has great respect for the ability of a person to keep a promise and to bind himself in lifelong fidelity. She takes people at their word. Every marriage can be endangered by crises. Talking things over together, prayer (together), and often therapeutic counseling as well can open up ways out of the crisis. Above all, remembering that in a sacramental marriage there is always a third party to the bond—Christ—can kindle hope again and again. Someone for whom marriage has become unbearable, however, or who may even be exposed to spiritual or physical violence, may divorce. This is called a "separation from bed and board", about which the Church must be notified. In these cases, even though the common life is broken off, the marriage remains valid. [1629, 1649]

Indeed, there are also cases in which the crisis in a marriage ultimately goes back to the fact that one spouse or both was not eligible at the time of the wedding or did not fully consent to the marriage. Then the marriage is invalid in the canonical (legal) sense. In such cases an annulment procedure can be introduced at the diocesan tribunal. → 424

270 What is the Church's stance on people who are divorced and remarried?

She accepts them lovingly, following Jesus' example. Anyone who divorces after being married in the Church and then during the lifetime of the spouse enters into a new union obviously contradicts Jesus' clear demand for the indissolubility of marriage. The Church cannot abolish this demand. This retraction of fidelity is contrary to the → EUCHARIST, in which it is precisely the irrevocable character of God's love that the Church celebrates. That is why someone who lives in such a contradictory situation is not admitted to Holy → COMMUNION. [1665, 2384]

Far from treating all specific cases alike, Pope Benedict XVI speaks about "painful situations" and calls on pastors "to discern different situations carefully, in order to be able to offer appropriate spiritual guidance to the faithful involved" (Apostolic Exhortation *Sacramentum caritatis,* 29).

271 What does it mean to say that the family is a "Church in miniature"?

What the Church is on a large scale, the family is on a small scale: an image of God's love in human fellowship. Indeed, every marriage is perfected in openness to others, to the children that God sends, in mutual acceptance, in hospitality and being for others. [1655–1657]

Nothing in the early Church fascinated people more about the "New Way" of the Christians than their "domestic churches". Often someone "believed in the Lord, together with all his household; and many ... believed and were baptized" (Acts 18:8). In an unbelieving world, islands of living faith were formed, places of prayer, mutual sharing, and cordial hospitality. → ROME, Corinth, Antioch, the great cities of antiquity, were soon permeated with domestic churches that were like points of light. Even today families in which Christ is at home are the leaven that renews our society. → 368

→ or spiritual director, dedication to the life of charity, works of penance, and commitment to the education of their children. (paragraph 29)

BENEDICT XVI,
Sacramentum Caritatis

99 No one is without a family in this world: the Church is a home and family for everyone, especially those who "labor and are heavy laden".

POPE JOHN PAUL II (1920–2005), Apostolic Exhortation *Familiaris consortio*

99 If you want someone to become Christian, let him live for a year in your house.

ST. JOHN CHRYSOSTOM (349/350–407)

EXORCISM
Exorcism (Greek *exorkismós* = summoning out) is a prayer by virtue of which a person is protected from the evil one or delivered from the evil one.

❧ CHAPTER FOUR ❧
Other Liturgical Celebrations

272 *What are sacramentals?*

Sacramentals are sacred signs or sacred actions in which a blessing is conferred.
[1667–1672, 1677–1678]

Examples of sacramentals are holy water, the consecration of a bell or an organ, the blessing of a house or an automobile, the blessing of throats on the feast of St. Blaise, receiving ashes on Ash Wednesday, palm branches on Palm Sunday, the Easter candle, and the blessing of produce on the feast of the Assumption of the Blessed Virgin Mary.

273 *Does the Church still practice exorcism?*

At every Baptism a so-called simple → EXORCISM is performed, a prayer in which the person being baptized is taken away from the devil and is strengthened against the "principalities and powers" that Jesus overcame. Major exorcism is a prayer offered by Jesus' authority and in his strength through which a baptized Christian is delivered from the influence and power of the devil; the Church rarely uses this prayer, and only after the most rigorous examination. [1673]

The depiction of "exorcisms" in Hollywood films for the most part does not reflect the truth about Jesus and the Church. It was often reported about Jesus that he drove out demons. He had power over evil principalities and powers and could deliver men from them. To the apostles Jesus gave "authority over unclean spirits, to cast them out, and to heal every disease and every infirmity" (Mt 10:1). The Church does the same today whenever an authorized → PRIEST pronounces the prayer of exorcism over a person who requests it. First, however, the possibility must be excluded

that the phenomenon is *psychological* in nature (a psychiatrist is competent in such matters). An exorcism wards off *spiritual* temptation and oppression and delivers from the power of the evil one. → 90–91

→ actions and "purify" this tradition so that it may become part of the life of the Church today.

POPE BENEDICT XVI,
February 22, 2007

274 *How important is so-called "popular piety"?*

Popular piety, which is expressed in veneration for →RELICS, processions, pilgrimages, and devotions, is an important way in which the faith becomes inculturated. It is good as long as it is in and of the Church, leads to Christ, and does not try to "earn" heaven by works, apart from God's grace. [1674–1676]

RELICS
Relics (from Latin *relictum* = remains) are remnants of the bodies of saints or else objects that the saints used during their lifetime.

275 *Is it permissible to venerate relics?*

The veneration of relics is a natural human need, a way of showing respect and reverence to the persons who are venerated. →RELICS of saints are properly venerated when the faithful praise God's work in people who have devoted themselves completely to God. [1674]

99 Unwaveringly, the Church marches forward on her pilgrim way between the world's persecutions and God's consolations.

ST. AUGUSTINE
(354–430)

276 *What is the purpose of a pilgrimage?*

Someone who goes on a pilgrimage "prays with his feet" and experiences with all his senses that his entire life is one long journey to God. [1674]

In ancient Israel people made pilgrimages to the Temple in Jerusalem. Christians adopted this custom. And so this developed, especially in the Middle Ages, into a regular pilgrimage movement to the holy places (above all to Jerusalem and to the tombs of the apostles in Rome and Santiago de Compostela). Often people went on pilgrimage so as to do penance, and sometimes their actions were affected by the false notion that one had to justify oneself before God by tormenting and punishing oneself. Today pilgrimages are experiencing a unique revival. People are looking for the peace and the strength that come from those grace-filled localities. They are tired of going it alone; they want to get out of the rut of the daily routine, get rid of some ballast, and start moving toward God.

277 *What are the Stations of the Cross?*

Following Jesus on his Way of the Cross by praying and meditating on the fourteen Stations is a very ancient devotion in the Church, which is practiced especially in Lent and Holy Week. [1674–1675]

The fourteen Stations of the Cross are:

1. Jesus is condemned to death.

2. Jesus takes up his Cross.

3. Jesus falls the first time.

4. Jesus meets his sorrowful Mother.

5. Simon of Cyrene helps Jesus carry the Cross.

6. Veronica wipes the face of Jesus.

7. Jesus falls the second time.

8. Jesus meets the women of Jerusalem.

9. Jesus falls the third time.

10. Jesus is stripped of his garments.

11. Jesus is nailed to the Cross.

12. Jesus dies on the Cross.

13. Jesus is taken down from the Cross and presented to his sorrowful Mother.

14. Jesus is laid in the tomb.

→ hands to see that it be not one inch too large and not one ounce too heavy for you. He has blessed it with His holy Name, anointed it with His consolation, taken one last glance at you and your courage, and then sent it to you from heaven, a special greeting from God to you, an alms of the all-merciful love of God.

ST. FRANCIS OF SALES (1567–1622)

99 We are not at all separated from one another [by death], because we all run the same course and we will find one another again in the same place.

SIMEON OF THESSALONICA (d. 1429, theologian and mystic)

278 *What is the purpose of a Christian funeral?*

A Christian funeral is a service performed by the Christian community for the benefit of its dead. It expresses the sorrow of the survivors, yet it always has a Paschal character. Ultimately, we die in Christ so as to celebrate with him the feast of the Resurrection. [1686–1690]

PART THREE

How We Are to Have Life in Christ

"Apart from me you can do nothing."

Jn 15:5

Let nothing trouble you / Let nothing frighten you
Everything passes / God never changes
Patience obtains all
Whoever has God
Wants for nothing
God alone is enough.

ST. TERESA OF AVILA
(1515–1582)

So God created man in his own image; in the image of God he created him.

Gen 1:27

When God disappears, men and women do not become greater; indeed, they lose the divine dignity, their faces lose God's splendor. In the end, they turn out to be merely products of a blind evolution and, as such, can be used and abused. This is precisely what the experience of our epoch has confirmed for us.

POPE BENEDICT XVI,
August 15, 2005

◇ SECTION ONE ◇
Why We Are Put on Earth, What We Are Supposed to Do, And How God's Holy Spirit Helps Us to Do It

279   Why do we need faith and the sacraments in order to live a good, upright life?

If we were to rely only on ourselves and our own strength, we would not get far in our attempts to be good. Through faith we discover that we are God's children and that God makes us strong. When God gives us his strength, we call this "grace". Especially in the sacred signs that we call the → SACRAMENTS, God gives us the ability actually to do the good that we want to do. [1691–1695]

Since God saw our misery, he "delivered us from the dominion of darkness" (Col 1:13) through his Son, Jesus Christ. He granted us the opportunity to make a new start in fellowship with him and to walk the path of love. → 172–178

◇ CHAPTER ONE ◇
The Dignity of the Human Person

280   What reasons do Christians give for human dignity?

Every person, from the first moment of his life in the womb, has an inviolable dignity, because from all eternity God willed, loved, created, and redeemed that person and destined him for eternal happiness. [1699–1715]

If human dignity were based solely on the successes and accomplishments of individuals, then those who are weak, sick, or helpless would have no dignity. Christians believe that human dignity is, in the first place, the result of God's respect for us. He looks at every person and loves him as though he were the only creature in the world. Because God has looked

upon even the least significant child of Adam, that person possesses an infinite worth, which must not be destroyed by men. → 56–65

281 *Why do we yearn for happiness?*

God has placed in our hearts such an infinite desire for happiness that nothing can satisfy it but God himself. All earthly fulfillment gives us only a foretaste of eternal happiness. Above and beyond that, we should be drawn to God. [1718–1719, 1725]
→ 1–3

282 *Does Sacred Scripture speak about a way to happiness?*

We become happy by trusting in Jesus' words in the Beatitudes. [1716–1717]

The Gospel is a promise of happiness to all people who wish to walk in God's ways. Especially in the Beatitudes (Mt 5:3–12), Jesus has told us specifically that eternal blessedness (→ BLESSING) is based on our following his example and seeking peace with a pure heart.

283 What are the Beatitudes?

**Blessed are the poor in spirit,
for theirs is the kingdom of heaven.**

**Blessed are those who mourn,
for they shall be comforted.**

**Blessed are the meek,
for they shall inherit the earth.**

**Blessed are those who hunger and thirst for
righteousness, for they shall be satisfied.**

**Blessed are the merciful,
for they shall obtain mercy.**

**Blessed are the pure in heart,
for they shall see God.**

**Blessed are the peacemakers,
for they shall be called sons of God.**

**Blessed are those who are persecuted for
righteousness' sake, for theirs is the kingdom of
heaven.**

**Blessed are you when men revile you and persecute
you and utter all kinds of evil against you falsely on
my account. Rejoice and be glad, for your reward is
great in heaven, for so men persecuted the prophets
who were before you. (Mt 5:3–12)**

284 Why are the Beatitudes so important?

**Those who yearn for the kingdom of God look to
Jesus' list of priorities: the Beatitudes.
[1716-1717, 1725-1726]**

From Abraham on, God made promises to his people.
Jesus takes them up, extends their application to
heaven, and makes them the program for his own
life: the Son of God becomes poor so as to share our
poverty; he rejoices with those who rejoice and weeps
with those who weep (Rom 12:15); he employs no
violence but rather turns the other cheek (Mt 5:39); he
has mercy, makes peace, and thereby shows us the sure
way to heaven.

" For he alone is
the way that is worth
following,
the light that is worth
lighting,
the life that is worth
living,
and the love that is
worth loving.

BL. TERESA OF CALCUTTA
(1910–1997)

" To will all that God
wills, and always to will
it, on all occasions and
without reservations, is
the kingdom of God that
is completely within.

FRANÇOIS FÉNELON
(1651–1715)

285 What is eternal happiness?

Eternal happiness is seeing God and being taken up into God's happiness. [1720-1724, 1729]

In God the Father, the Son, and the Holy Spirit there is unending life, joy, and communion. To be taken up into it will be an incomprehensible, infinite happiness for us men. This happiness is the pure gift of God's grace, for we men can neither bring it about ourselves nor comprehend it in its magnitude. God would like us to decide in favor of our happiness; we should choose God freely, love him above all things, do good and avoid evil insofar as we are able. → 52, 156–158

286 What is freedom and what is it for?

Freedom is the God-given power to be able to act of one's own accord; a person who is free no longer acts under the influence of someone else. [1730–1733, 1743–1744]

God created us as free men and wills our freedom so that we might decide wholeheartedly in favor of the good, indeed for the greatest "good"—in other words, for God. The more we do what is good, the freer we become. → 51

287 But doesn't "freedom" consist of being able to choose evil as well?

Evil is only apparently worth striving for, and deciding in favor of evil only apparently makes us free. Evil does not make us happy but rather deprives us of what is truly good; it chains us to something futile and in the end destroys our freedom entirely. [1730–1733, 1743–1744]

We see this in addiction: Here a person sells his freedom to something that appears good to him. In reality he becomes a slave. Man is freest when he is always able to say Yes to the good; when no addiction, no compulsion, no habit prevents him from choosing and doing what is right and good. A decision in favor of the good is always a decision leading toward God. → 51

288 *Is man responsible for everything he does?*

Man is responsible for everything he does consciously and voluntarily.
[1734–1737, 1745–1746]

No one can be held (fully) responsible for something he did under coercion, out of fear, ignorance, under the influence of drugs or the power of bad habits. The more a person knows about the good and practices the good, the more he moves away from the slavery of sin (Rom 6:17; 1 Cor 7:22). God desires that such free persons should (be able to) take responsibility for themselves, for their environment, and for the whole earth. But all of God's merciful love is also for those who are not free; every day he offers them an opportunity to allow themselves to be set free for freedom.

289 *Must we allow a person to use his free will, even when he decides in favor of evil?*

For a person to be able to use his freedom is a fundamental right based on his human dignity. An individual's freedom can be curtailed only if the exercise of his freedom is detrimental to human dignity and the freedom of others. [1738, 1740]

Freedom would be no freedom at all if it were not the freedom to choose even what is wrong. It would violate the dignity of a man if we did not respect his freedom. One of the central duties of the State is to protect the liberties of all its citizens (freedom of religion, of assembly, and association, freedom of opinion, freedom to choose one's occupation, and so on). The freedom of one citizen is the limit to the freedom of another.

> The good man is free, even if he is a slave. The evil man is a slave, even if he is a king.
>
> ST. AUGUSTINE
> (354–430)

> The way to the goal begins on the day when you assume full responsibility for your actions.
>
> DANTE ALIGHIERI
> (1265-1321, Italian poet, author of the *Divine Comedy*)

> The martyrs of the early Church died for their faith in that God who was revealed in Jesus Christ, and for this very reason they also died for freedom of conscience and the freedom to profess one's own faith—a profession that no State can impose but which, instead, can only be claimed with God's grace in freedom of conscience. A missionary Church known for proclaiming her message to all peoples must necessarily work for the freedom of the faith.
>
> POPE BENEDICT XVI,
> December 22, 2005

For you did not receive the spirit of slavery to fall back into fear, but you have received the spirit of sonship. When we cry, "Abba! Father!" it is the Spirit himself bearing witness with our spirit that we are children of God.

Rom 8:15

290 How does God help us to be free men?

Christ wants us to be "set free for freedom" (see Gal 5:1) and to become capable of brotherly love. That is why he sends us the Holy Spirit, who makes us free and independent of worldly powers and strengthens us for a life of love and responsibility.
[1739–1742, 1748]

The more we sin, the more we think only about ourselves and the less well we can develop freely. In sinning we also become more inept at doing good and practicing charity. The Holy Spirit, who has come down into our hearts, gives us a heart that is filled with love for God and mankind. We avail ourselves of the Holy Spirit as the power that leads us to inner freedom, opens our hearts for love, and makes us better instruments for what is good and loving.

→ 120, 310–311

291 How can a person tell whether his action is good or bad?

A person is capable of distinguishing good actions from bad ones because he possesses reason and a conscience, which enable him to make clear judgments. [1749–1754, 1757–1758]

The following guidelines make it easier to distinguish good actions from bad ones: (1) *What I do* must be good; a good intention alone is not enough. Bank robbery is always bad, even if I commit that crime with the good intention of giving the money to poor people. (2) Even when what I do is truly good, if I perform the good action with a *bad intention,* it makes the whole action bad. If I walk an elderly woman home and help her around the house, that is good. But if I do it while planning a later break-in, that makes the whole action something bad. (3) The *circumstances* in which someone acts can diminish his responsibility, but they cannot change at all the good or bad character of an action. Hitting one's mother is always bad, even if the mother has previously shown little love to the child.
→ 295–297

292 May we do something bad so that good can result from it?

No, we may never deliberately do something evil or tolerate an evil so that good can result from it. Sometimes there is no other course of action but to tolerate a lesser evil in order to prevent a greater evil. [1755–1756, 1759–1761]

The end does not justify the means. It cannot be right to commit infidelity so as to stabilize one's marriage. It is just as wrong to use embryos for stem cell research, even if one could thereby make medical breakthroughs. It is wrong to try to "help" a rape victim by aborting her child.

293 Why did God give us "passions" or emotions?

We have passions so that through strong emotions and distinct feelings we might be attracted to what

In the Christian tradition, "conscience", "con-scientia", means "with knowledge": that is, [we] ourselves, our being is open and can listen to the voice of being itself, the voice of God.... In the depths of our being, not only can we listen to the needs of the moment, to material needs, but we can also hear the voice of the Creator himself and thus discern what is good and what is bad.

POPE BENEDICT XVI,
July 24, 2007

His conscience is man's most secret core and his sanctuary. There he is alone with God whose voice echoes in his depths.

Second Vatican Council, GS

If a man is truly to will what is good, he must be willing to do everything for that good or be willing to suffer anything for that good.

SØREN KIERKEGAARD
(1813–1855)

> There is good without evil, but there is nothing evil without good.

ST. THOMAS AQUINAS
(1225–1274)

is right and good and repelled from what is evil and bad. [1762–1766, 1771–1772]

God made man in such a way that he can love and hate, desire or despise something, be attracted by some things and afraid of others, be full of joy, sorrow, or anger. In the depths of his heart man always loves good and hates evil—or what he considers to be such.

> Virtue is what one does passionately; vice is what one cannot stop doing because of passion.

ST. AUGUSTINE
(354–430)

294 *Is someone a sinner if he experiences strong passions within himself?*

No, passions can be very valuable. They are designed to lead to and reinforce good actions; only when they are disordered do the passions contribute to evil. [1767–1770, 1773–1775]

Passions that are ordered to the good become *virtues*. They then become the motive force of a life of fighting for love and justice. Passions that overpower a person, rob him of his freedom and entice him to evil, we call *vice*. → 396

295 What is conscience?

Conscience is the inner voice in a man that moves him to do good under any circumstances and to avoid evil by all means. At the same time it is the ability to distinguish the one from the other. In the conscience God speaks to man. [1776–1779]

Conscience is compared with an inner voice in which God manifests himself in a man. God is the one who becomes apparent in the conscience. When we say, "I cannot reconcile that with my conscience", this means for a Christian, "I cannot do that in the sight of my Creator!" Many people have gone to jail or been executed because they were true to their conscience.

→ 120, 290–292, 312, 333

296 Can someone be compelled to do something that is against his conscience?

No one may be compelled to act against his conscience, provided he acts within the limits of the →COMMON GOOD. [1780–1782, 1798]

Anyone who overlooks the conscience of a person, ignores it and uses coercion, violates that person's dignity. Practically nothing else makes man more human than the gift of being able personally to distinguish good from evil and to choose between them. This is so even if the decision, seen in an objective light, is wrong. Unless man's conscience has been incorrectly formed, the inner voice speaks in agreement with what is generally reasonable, just, and good in God's sight.

297 Can a person form his conscience?

Yes, in fact he must do that. The conscience, which is innate to every person endowed with reason, can be misled and deadened. That is why it must be formed into an increasingly fine-tuned instrument for acting rightly. [1783–1788, 1799–1800]

The first school of conscience is self-criticism. We have the tendency to judge things to our own advantage. The

> 99 If ... we feel responsibility, are ashamed, are frightened, at transgressing the voice of conscience, this implies that there is One to whom we are responsible, before whom we are ashamed, and whose claims upon us we fear.
>
> BL. JOHN HENRY NEWMAN (1801–1890)

> 99 Anything that is done against conscience is a sin.
>
> ST. THOMAS AQUINAS (1225–1274)

> 99 To do violence to people's conscience means to harm them seriously, to deal an extremely painful blow to their dignity. In a certain sense it is worse than killing them.
>
> BL. JOHN XXIII (1881–1963, the Pope who convoked the Second Vatican Council)

> 99 In the formation of their consciences, the Christian faithful ought carefully to attend to the sacred and certain doctrine of the Church. For the church is, by the will of Christ, the teacher of the truth.
>
> Second Vatican Council, DH

> 99 Christians have a great help for the formation of conscience in the Chruch and her Magisterium.
>
> BL. JOHN PAUL II, *Veritatis splendor*

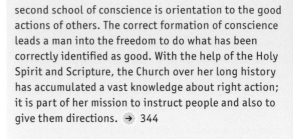
second school of conscience is orientation to the good actions of others. The correct formation of conscience leads a man into the freedom to do what has been correctly identified as good. With the help of the Holy Spirit and Scripture, the Church over her long history has accumulated a vast knowledge about right action; it is part of her mission to instruct people and also to give them directions. → 344

298 Is someone who in good conscience acts wrongly guilty in God's sight?

No. If a person has thoroughly examined himself and arrived at a certain judgment, he must in any case follow his inner voice, even at the risk of doing something wrong. [1790–1794, 1801–1802]

God does not blame us for the objective harm that results from a wrong judgment of conscience, provided that we ourselves are not responsible for having a badly formed conscience. While it is quite true that ultimately one must follow one's conscience, it must likewise be kept in mind that people have swindled, murdered, tortured, and betrayed others on the basis of what they wrongly suppose to be their conscience.

299 What is meant by a "virtue"?

A virtue is an interior disposition, a positive habit, a passion that has been placed at the service of the good. [1803, 1833]

"You, therefore, must be perfect, as your heavenly Father is perfect" (Mt 5:48). That means that we must change on our way to God. By our human abilities we can do that only in fits and starts. With his grace God supports the *human virtues* and gives us, above and beyond that, the so-called *supernatural virtues* (→ 305), which help us to come closer to God and live more securely in his light. → 293–294

300 Why do we have to work to form our character?

We must work at forming our character so that we can freely, joyfully, and easily accomplish what is good. A firm faith in God, in the first place, helps us to do this, but also the practice of the *virtues*, which means developing within ourselves, with God's help, firm dispositions, not giving ourselves over to disorderly passions, and directing our faculties of intellect and will more and more consistently toward the good. [1804–1805, 1810–1811, 1834, 1839]

The most important virtues are: prudence, justice, fortitude, temperance. These are also called the "cardinal virtues" (from Latin *cardo* = hinge, or from *cardinalis* = principal).

301 How does a person become prudent?

A person becomes prudent by learning to distinguish what is essential from what is non-essential, to set the right goals and to choose the best means of attaining them. [1806, 1835]

The virtue of prudence directs all the other virtues. For prudence is the ability to recognize what is right. After all, someone who wants to lead a good life must know what the "good" is and recognize its worth. Like the merchant in the Gospel "who, on finding one pearl of great value, went and sold all that he had and bought it" (Mt 13:46). Only a prudent person can apply the virtues of justice, fortitude, and moderation so as to do good.

302 How does one act justly?

One acts justly by always making sure to give to God and to one's neighbor what is due to them. [1807, 1836]

The guiding principle of justice is: "To each his due". A child with a disability and a highly gifted child must be encouraged in different ways so that each may fulfill his potential. Justice is concerned with equity and longs to see people get that to which they are entitled. We must

> To live well is nothing other than to love God with all one's heart, with all one's soul, and with all one's efforts; from this it comes about that love is kept whole and uncorrupted (through temperance). No misfortune can disturb it (and this is fortitude). It obeys only [God] (and this is justice) and is careful in discerning things, so as not to be surprised by deceit or trickery (and this is prudence).

ST. AUGUSTINE
(354–430)

> Prudence has two eyes, one that foresees what one has to do, the other that examines afterward what one has done.

ST. IGNATIUS LOYOLA
(1491–1556)

> Justice without mercy is unloving; mercy without justice is degrading.

FRIEDRICH VON BODELSCHWINGH
(1831-1910 Lutheran theologian and founder of the Bethel Hospitals)

allow justice to govern our relations with God also and give him what is his: our love and worship.

303 What does it mean to have fortitude?

Someone who practices fortitude perseveres in his commitment to the good, once he has recognized it, even if in the extreme case he must sacrifice even his own life for it. [1809, 1837] → 295

304 Why is it virtuous to be moderate?

Moderation is a virtue because immoderate behavior proves to be a destructive force in all areas of life. [1809, 1838]

Someone who is immoderate abandons himself to the rule of his impulses, offends others by his inordinate desires, and harms himself. In the → NEW TESTAMENT words like "sobriety" and "discretion" stand for "moderation".

305 What are the three supernatural virtues?

The supernatural virtues are faith, hope, and charity. They are called "supernatural" because they have their foundation in God, are directly related to God, and are for us men the way by which we can reach God directly. [1812–1813, 1840]

306 Why are faith, hope, and charity virtues?

Faith, hope, and charity, too, are genuine powers—bestowed by God, of course—that a person can develop and consolidate with the grace of God so as to obtain "the abundant life" (see Jn 10:10). [1812–1813, 1840–1841]

307 *What is faith?*

Faith is the power by which we assent to God, acknowledge his truth, and commit ourselves personally to him. [1814–1816, 1842]

Faith is the path created by God leading to the truth that is God himself. Because Jesus is "the way, and the truth, and the life" (Jn 14:6), this faith cannot be merely an attitude or "confidence" about something or other. On the one hand, the faith has definite contents, which the Church professes in the → CREED (= profession of faith), and it is her duty to safeguard them. Anyone who wants to accept the gift of faith, in other words, anyone who wants to believe, acknowledges this faith, which has been preserved constantly through the ages and in many different cultures. On the other hand, part of faith is a trusting relationship to God with heart and mind, with all one's emotional strength. For faith becomes effective only through charity, practical love (see Gal 5:6). Whether someone really believes in the God of love is shown, not in his solemn affirmations, but rather in charitable deeds.

 He who says "I know him" but disobeys his commandments is a liar, and the truth is not in him.

1 Jn 2:4

 "Every one who acknowledges me before men, I also will acknowledge before my Father who is in heaven."

Mt 10:32

Likewise the Spirit helps us in our weakness; for we do not know how to pray as we ought, but the Spirit himself intercedes for us with sighs too deep for words.

Rom 8:26

If I have all faith, so as to remove mountains, but have not love, I am nothing.

1 Cor 13:2

God is love, and he who abides in love abides in God, and God abides in him.

1 Jn 4:16

" The most important hour is always the present; the most significant person is precisely the one who is sitting across from you right now; the most necessary work is always love.

MEISTER ECKHART
(ca. 1260–1328)

308 *What is hope?*

Hope is the power by which we firmly and constantly long for what we were placed on earth to do: to praise God and to serve him; and for our true happiness, which is finding our fulfillment in God; and for our final home: in God. [1817–1821, 1843]

Hope is trusting in what God has promised us in creation, in the prophets, but especially in Jesus Christ, even though we do not yet see it. God's Holy Spirit is given to us so that we can patiently hope for the Truth. → 1-3

309 *What is charity?*

Charity is the power by which we, who have been loved first by God, can give ourselves to God so as to be united with him and can accept our neighbor for God's sake as unconditionally and sincerely as we accept ourselves. [1822–1829, 1844]

Jesus places love above all laws, without however abolishing the latter. Therefore St. Augustine rightly says, "Love, and do what you will." Which is not at all as easy as it sounds. That is why charity, love, is the greatest virtue, the energy that inspires all the other virtues and fills them with divine life.

310 *What are the seven gifts of the Holy Spirit?*

The seven gifts of the Holy Spirit are wisdom, understanding, counsel, fortitude, knowledge, piety, and fear of the Lord. With these the Holy Spirit "endows" Christians, in other words, he grants them particular powers that go beyond their natural aptitudes and gives them the opportunity to become God's special instruments in this world. [1830–1831, 1845]

We read in one of Paul's letters: "To one is given through the Spirit the utterance of wisdom, and to another the utterance of knowledge according to the same Spirit, to another faith by the same Spirit, to another gifts of healing by the one Spirit, to another

the working of miracles, to another prophecy, to another the ability to distinguish between spirits, to another various kinds of tongues, to another the interpretation of tongues" (1 Cor 12:8–10).
→ 113–120

311 What are the fruits of the Holy Spirit?

The → FRUITS OF THE HOLY SPIRIT are charity, joy, peace, patience, kindness, goodness, generosity, gentleness, faithfulness, modesty, self-control, and chastity (cf. Gal 5:22–23). [1832]

In the → "FRUITS OF THE HOLY SPIRIT" the world can see what becomes of people who let themselves be adopted, led, and completely formed by God. The fruits of the Holy Spirit show that God really plays a role in the life of Christians. → 120

312 How does a person know that he has sinned?

A person knows that he has sinned through his conscience, which accuses him and motivates him to confess his offenses to God. [1797, 1848]
→ 229, 295–298

313 Why must a sinner turn to God and ask him for forgiveness?

Every sin destroys, obscures, or denies what is good; God, however, is all-good and the author of all good. Therefore every sin goes against God (also) and must be set right again through contact with him. [1847]
→ 224–239

314 How do we know that God is merciful?

In many passages in Sacred Scripture God shows that he is merciful, especially in the parable of the merciful father (Lk 15) who goes out to meet his prodigal son, accepts him unconditionally, and celebrates his return and their reconciliation with a joyful banquet. [1846, 1870]

Truly, truly, I say to you, he who believes in me will also do the works that I do; and greater works than these will he do, because I go to the Father.

Jn 14:12

Draw your strength simply from your joy in Jesus. Be happy and peaceful. Accept whatever he gives. And give whatever he takes, with a big smile.

BL. TERESA OF CALCUTTA (1910–1997) to her coworkers

If we say we have no sin, we deceive ourselves, and the truth is not in us.

1 Jn 1:8

If we confess our sins, he is faithful and just, and will forgive our sins and cleanse us from all unrighteousness.

1 Jn 1:9

Never doubt God's mercy!

ST. BENEDICT OF NURSIA (ca. 480–547, Founder of Western monasticism)

Already in the → OLD TESTAMENT God says through the prophet Ezekiel: "I have no pleasure in the death of the wicked, but that the wicked turn from his way and live" (Ezek 33:11). Jesus is sent "to the lost sheep of the house of Israel" (Mt 15:24), and he knows that "Those who are well have no need of a physician, but those who are sick" (Mt 9:12). Therefore he eats with tax collectors and sinners, and then toward the end of his earthly life he even interprets his death as an initiative of God's merciful love: "This is my blood of the covenant, which is poured out for many for the forgiveness of sins" (Mt 26:28). → 227, 524

315 What is a sin in the first place?

A sin is a word, deed, or intention by which man deliberately and voluntarily offends against the true order of things, as God's loving providence has arranged them. [1849–1851, 1871–1872]

To sin means more than to violate some rules about which men have agreed. Sin turns freely and deliberately against God's love and ignores him. Sin is ultimately "love of oneself even to contempt of God" (St. Augustine), and in the extreme case the sinful creature says, "I want to be like God" (see Gen 3:5). Just as sin burdens me with guilt, wounds me, and by its consequences ruins me, so too it poisons and damages the world in which I live. It becomes possible to recognize sin and its seriousness by drawing near to God. → 67, 224–239

316 How can we distinguish serious sins (mortal sins) from less serious (venial) sins?

Serious sin destroys the divine power of love in a person's heart, without which there can be no eternal beatitude. Hence it is also called mortal sin. Serious sin breaks with God, whereas venial sin only strains the relationship with him. [1852–1861, 1874]

A serious sin cuts a person off from God. One requirement for such a sin is that it be opposed to an important value, for instance, directed against *life*, against marriage, or *God* (for example, murder, blasphemy, adultery, and so on) and that it be committed with full knowledge and full consent. Venial sins are opposed to secondary values or are committed without full knowledge of their seriousness or without full consent of the will. Such sins disrupt the relationship with God but do not sever it.

317 How can a person be delivered from a serious sin and reunited with God?

In order to heal the break with God that is caused by a serious sin, a Catholic Christian must be reconciled with God through confession. [1856] → 224 -239

318 What are vices?

Vices are negative habits that deaden and dull the conscience, incline a person to evil, and habitually prepare him for sin. [1865–1867]

Human vices are found in connection with the capital sins of pride, avarice, envy, anger, lust, gluttony, and sloth (or acedia, spiritual boredom).

319 Are we responsible for the sins of other people?

No, we are not responsible for other people's sins, unless we are guilty of misleading or seducing another person to sin or of cooperating in it or of encouraging someone else to sin or of neglecting to offer a timely warning or our help. [1868]

320 Is there such a thing as structures of sin?

Structures of sin exist only in a manner of speaking. A sin is always connected with an individual person, who knowingly and willingly agrees to something evil. [1869]

Nevertheless, there are societal situations and institutions that are so contradictory to God's commandments that we speak about "structures of sin"—yet these, too, are the consequence of personal sins.

> " I have just produced expensive ashes: I have burned a five-hundred-franc note. Oh, that is not as bad as if I had committed a venial sin.
>
> ST. JOHN VIANNEY (1786–1859)

> " If there were no forgiveness of sins in the Church, there would be no hope for eternal life and eternal deliverance. Let us thank God, who gave his Church such a great gift.
>
> ST. AUGUSTINE (354–430)

> " And so both virtue and vice are in our power. For when the deed is in our power, so is the omission, and when we can say No, we can also say Yes.
>
> ARISTOTLE (382–322 b.c., along with Plato, the greatest philosopher in antiquity)

> The greatest gift that man can have this side of heaven is to be able to get along well with the people with whom he lives.

BL. EGIDIO OF ASSISI
(?–1262, one of the closest companions of St. Francis of Assisi)

> Even if you are not afraid to fall alone, how do you presume that you will rise up alone? Consider: two together can accomplish more than one alone.

ST. JOHN OF THE CROSS
(1542–1591)

> Each of us is the result of a thought of God. Each of us is willed, each of us is loved, each of us is necessary.

POPE BENEDICT XVI
at his inauguration

321 *Can a Christian be a radical individualist?*

No, a Christian can never be a radical individualist, because man is by nature designed for fellowship. [1877–1880, 1890–1891]

Every person has a mother and a father; he receives help from others and is obliged to help others and to develop his talents for the benefit of all. Since man is God's "image", in a certain way he reflects God, who in his depths is not alone but triune (and thus life, love, dialogue, and exchange). Finally, love is the central commandment for all Christians; through it we profoundly belong together and are fundamentally dependent on one another. "You shall love your neighbor as yourself" (Mt 22:39).

322 *What is more important, society or the individual?*

In God's sight every individual matters in the first place as a person and only then as a social being. [1881, 1892]

Society can never be more important than the individual person. Men may never be means to a societal end. Nevertheless, social institutions such as the State and the family are necessary for the individual; they even correspond to his nature.

323 *How can the individual be integrated into society in such a way that he nevertheless can develop freely?*

The individual can develop freely in society if the "principle of subsidiarity" is observed. [1883–1885, 1894]

The principle of subsidiarity, which was developed as part of → CATHOLIC SOCIAL TEACHING, states: What individuals can accomplish by their own initiative and efforts should not be taken from them by a higher authority. A greater and higher social institution must not take over the duties of a subordinate organization and deprive it of its competence. Its purpose, rather, is to intervene in a subsidiary fashion (thus offering help) when individuals or smaller institutions find that a task is beyond them.

324 *On what principles does a society build?*

Every society builds on a hierarchy of values that is put into practice through justice and love. [1886–1889, 1895–1896]

No society can last unless it is based on a clear orientation toward values that are reflected in a just ordering of relationships and an active implementation of this justice. Thus man may never be made into a means to an end of societal action. Every society needs constant conversion from unjust structures. Ultimately this is accomplished only by love, the greatest social commandment. It respects others. It demands justice. It makes conversion from inequitable conditions possible. → 449

325 *What is the basis for authority in society?*

Every society relies on a legitimate authority to ensure that it is orderly, cohesive, and smooth-running and to promote its development. It is in keeping with human nature, as created by God, that men allow themselves to be governed by legitimate authority. [1897–1902, 1918–1919, 1922]

? CATHOLIC SOCIAL TEACHING / SOCIAL PRINCIPLES
The Church's teaching about the ordering of life in society and about the attainment of individual and social justice. Its four central principles are: personhood, the common good, solidarity, and subsidiarity.

99 Today's justice is yesterday's charity; today's charity is tomorrow's justice.

BL. ÉTIENNE-MICHEL GILLET
(1758–1792, priest and martyr)

99 The Church values the democratic system inasmuch as it ensures the participation of citizens in making political choices and guarantees to the governed the possibility both of electing and holding accountable those who govern them and of replacing them through peaceful means when appropriate.

POPE JOHN PAUL II
(1920–2005), Encyclical *Centesimus annus*

? THE COMMON GOOD

The common good is the good that is shared by all in common. It includes "the sum total of social conditions which allow people, either as groups or as individuals, to reach their fulfillment more fully and more easily" (*Gaudium et spes*).

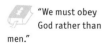
Of course an authority in society must never originate in the raw usurpation of power but must have legitimacy under law. Who rules and what form of government is appropriate are left to the will of the citizens. The Church is not committed to particular forms of government but only says that they must not contradict the → COMMON GOOD.

326 *When does an authority act legitimately?*

An authority acts legitimately when it works for the sake of the → COMMON GOOD and applies just methods of attaining the goals thereof.
[1903–1904, 1921]

The people in a State must be able to rely on the fact that they live under a "government of laws", which has rules that are binding for all. No one is obliged to obey laws that are arbitrary and unjust or that contradict the natural moral order. In that case there is a right, or in some circumstances even the duty, to resist.

327 *How can the common good be promoted?*

The → COMMON GOOD follows wherever the fundamental rights of the person are respected and men can freely develop their intellectual and religious potential. The common good implies that men can live in society with freedom, peace, and security. In an age of globalization, the common good must also acquire a worldwide scope and allow for the rights and duties of all mankind.
[1907–1912, 1925, 1927]

The → COMMON GOOD is best served where the good of the individual person and of the smaller units of society (for instance, the family) is central. The individual and the smaller social unit need to be protected and promoted by the stronger power of State institutions.

328 *What can the individual contribute to the common good?*

Working for the → COMMON GOOD means assuming responsibility for others. [1913–1917, 1926]

The common good must be the business of everyone. This happens first of all when men get involved in their particular surroundings—family, neighborhood, workplace—and take responsibility. It is important also to exercise social and political responsibility. Someone who assumes this sort of responsibility, however, wields power and is always in danger of misusing that power. Therefore, everyone in a position of responsibility is called upon to engage in an ongoing process of conversion, so that he can exercise that responsibility for others in lasting justice and charity.

329 *How does social justice come about in a society?*

Social justice comes about where the inalienable dignity of every person is respected and the resulting rights are safeguarded and championed without reservation. Among these is also the right to active participation in the political, economic, and cultural life of the society. [1928–1933, 1943–1944]

The basis of all justice is respect for the inalienable dignity of the human person, "whose defense and promotion have been entrusted to us by the Creator, and to whom the men and women at every moment of history are strictly and responsibly in debt" (Pope John Paul II, Encyclical *Sollicitudo rei socialis,* published 1987). Human rights are an immediate consequence of human dignity, and no State can abolish or change them. States and authorities that trample these rights underfoot are unjust regimes and lose their authority. A society is not perfected by laws, however, but rather by love of neighbor, which makes it possible for everyone to "look upon his neighbor (without any exception) as 'another self'" (GS 27, 1). → 280

330 *To what extent are all men equal in God's sight?*

All men are equal in God's sight insofar as all have the same Creator, all were created in the same image of God with a rational soul, and all have the same Redeemer. [1934–1935, 1945]

Because all men are equal in God's sight, every person possesses the same dignity and has a claim to the same

No one can claim, as Cain did, that he is not responsible for the fate of his brother.

Pope John Paul II
(1920–2005)

Respect the good reputation of your enemies.

ST. JOHN VIANNEY
(1786–1859)

"As you did it to one of the least of these my brethren, you did it to me."

Mt 25:40

There is not, never has been, and never will be a single person for whom Christ did not suffer.

Council of Quiercy, a.d. 853

[All] men are to deal with their fellows in justice and civility.

Second Vatican Council,
Dignitatis humanae [DH]

God says: I have willed that one should need another and that all should be my ministers in distributing the graces and gifts they have received from me.

ST. CATHERINE OF SIENA
(1347–1380)

Nothing that you have not given away will be really yours.

C. S. LEWIS
(1898–1963)

"He who has two coats, let him share with him who has none; and he who has food, let him do likewise."

Lk 3:11

The Creator has inscribed on our being the "natural law", which is the reflection in our hearts of his plan for creation, as the guide and inner standard for our life.

POPE BENEDICT XVI,
May 27, 2006

human rights. Hence every kind of social, racist, sexist, cultural, or religious discrimination against a person is an unacceptable injustice.

331 *Why is there nevertheless injustice among men?*

All men have the same dignity, but not all of them meet with the same living conditions. In cases where injustice is man-made, it contradicts the Gospel. In cases where men have been endowed by God with different gifts and talents, God is asking us to rely on one another: in charity one should make up for what the other lacks. [1936–1938, 1946–1947]

There is a kind of inequality among men that does not come from God but rather originates in societal conditions, especially in the unjust distribution of raw

materials, land, and capital worldwide. God expects us to remove from the world everything that is plainly contrary to the Gospel and disregards human dignity. Yet there is another sort of inequality among men that is quite in keeping with God's will: inequality in talents, initial conditions, and opportunities. These are an indication that being human means being there for others in charity so as to share and to promote life.
→ 61

332 How is the solidarity of Christians with other people expressed?

Christians are committed to just societal structures. Part of this is universal access to the material, intellectual, and spiritual goods of this world. Christians also make sure that the dignity of human work is respected, which includes a just wage. Handing on the faith is also an act of solidarity with all mankind. [1939–1942, 1948]

Solidarity is the practical hallmark of a Christian. Practicing solidarity is not just a command of reason. Jesus Christ, our Lord, identified completely with the poor and the lowly (Mt 25:40). To refuse solidarity with them would be to reject Christ.

PRINCIPLE OF SOLIDARITY
(from Latin *solidus* = thick, firm, strong): a principle of Catholic social teaching that aims at strengthening community and promoting a "civilization of love" (Pope John Paul II).

333 Is there a natural law that everyone can know?

If people are to do good and avoid evil, certainty about what is good or evil must be inscribed within them. In fact there is such a moral law that is, so to speak, "natural" to men and can be known in principle by every person by reason. [1949–1960, 1975, 1978–1979]

The natural moral law is valid for everyone. It tells men what fundamental rights and duties they have and thus forms the real foundation for life together in the family, in society, and in the State. Because our natural knowledge is often troubled by sin and human weakness, a person needs God's help and his → REVELATION in order to stay on the right path.

NATURAL MORAL LAW
"In all cultures there are examples of ethical convergence, some isolated, some interrelated, as an expression of the one human nature, willed by the Creator; the tradition of ethical wisdom knows this as the natural law" (Pope Benedict XVI, Encyclical *Caritas in veritate*).

334 What connection is there between the "natural moral law" and the Law of the Old Covenant?

The Law of the Old Covenant expresses truths that by nature are evident to human reason yet are now proclaimed and authenticated as God's Law. [1961–1963, 1981]

335 What significance does the Law of the Old Covenant have?

In the Law (the Torah), and its centerpiece, the Ten Commandments (the → DECALOGUE), the will of God is manifested to the people of Israel; following the Torah is for Israel the central way to salvation. Christians know that we can tell by the Law what ought to be done. They also know, however, that it is not the Law that saves us. [1963–1964, 1981–1982]

Every man has the experience of finding that something good is, so to speak, "prescribed". But one does not have the strength to accomplish it; it is too difficult; one feels "helpless" (see Rom 8:3 and Rom 7:14–25). One sees the Law and feels that one has been handed over to sin. And so precisely through the Law it becomes clear how urgently we rely on inner strength in order to fulfill the Law. That is why the Law, as good and important as it is, only prepares the way for faith in the saving God. → 349

336 How did Jesus deal with the Law of the Old Covenant?

"Do not think", says Jesus in the Sermon on the Mount, "that I have come to abolish the law and the prophets; I have come not to abolish them but to fulfil them" (Mt 5:17). [1965–1972, 1977, 1983–1985]

Jesus, being a faithful Jew, lived according to the ethical ideas and requirements of his time. But on a series of issues he departed from a literal, merely formal interpretation of the Law.

337 How are we saved?

No man can save himself. Christians believe that they are saved by God, who for this purpose sent his Son Jesus Christ into the world. For us salvation means that we are freed by the Holy Spirit from the power of sin and have been brought back from the realm of death to a life without end, a life in God's presence. [1987–1995, 2017–2020]

Paul observes: "All have sinned and fall short of the glory of God" (Rom 3:23). Sin cannot exist in the presence of God, who is justice and goodness through and through. If sin is worth nothing, what about the sinner, then? In his love, God found a way by which he destroys sin but saves the sinner. He makes him "right" again, that is to say, righteous or *just*. That is why from ancient times salvation has also been called *justification*. We are not made just by our own power. A man can neither forgive his own sins nor rescue himself from death. For that, God has to act on our behalf—out of mercy, not because we could deserve or merit it. In Baptism, God grants us "the righteousness of God through faith in Jesus Christ" (Rom 3:22). Through the Holy Spirit, who is poured out into our hearts, we take part in the death and Resurrection of Christ—we die to sin and are born to new life in God. The divine gifts of faith, hope, and charity come over us and make us able to live in the light and to obey God's will.

338 What is grace?

By grace we mean God's free, loving gift to us, his helping goodness, the vitality that comes from him. Through the Cross and Resurrection, God devotes himself entirely to us and communicates himself to us in grace. Grace is everything God grants us, without our deserving it in the least. [1996–1998, 2005, 2021]

"Grace", says Pope Benedict XVI, "is being looked upon by God, our being touched by his love." Grace is not a thing, but rather God's communication of himself to men. God never gives less than himself. In grace we are in God.

JUSTIFICATION A central concept from the "doctrine about grace". It means the restoration of the right relation between God and man. Since only Jesus Christ achieved this right relation ("righteousness"), we can come again into God's presence only if we are "justified" by Christ and, so to speak, enter into his intact relationship with God. To believe, therefore, means to accept the righteousness of Jesus for oneself and one's life.

For by grace you have been saved through faith; and this is not your own doing, it is the gift of God—not because of works, lest any man should boast.

Eph 2:8–9

God never gives less than himself.

ST. AUGUSTINE (354–430)

339 What does God's grace do to us?

God's grace brings us into the inner life of the Holy Trinity, into the exchange of love between Father, Son, and Holy Spirit. It makes us capable of living in God's love and of acting on the basis of this love. [1999–2000, 2003–2004, 2023–2024]

Grace is infused in us from above and cannot be explained in terms of natural causes *(supernatural grace)*. It makes us—especially through Baptism—children of God and heirs of heaven *(sanctifying or deifying grace)*. It bestows on us a permanent disposition to do good *(habitual grace)*. Grace helps us to know, to will, and to do everything that leads us to what is good, to God, and to heaven *(actual grace)*. Grace comes about in a special way in the sacraments, which according to the will of our Savior are the preeminent places for our encounter with God *(sacramental grace)*. Grace is manifested also in special gifts of grace that are granted to individual Christians (→ CHARISMS) or in special powers that are promised to those in the state of marriage, the ordained state, or the religious state *(graces of state)*.

340 How is God's grace related to our freedom?

God's grace is freely bestowed on a person, and it seeks and summons him to respond in complete freedom. Grace does not compel. God's love wants our free assent. [2001–2002, 2022]

One can also say No to the offer of grace. Grace, nevertheless, is not something external or foreign to man; it is what he actually yearns for in his deepest freedom. In moving us by his grace, God anticipates man's free response.

341 Can someone earn heaven by good works?

No. No man can gain heaven merely by his own efforts. The fact that we are saved is God's grace, pure and simple, which nevertheless demands the free cooperation of the individual. [2006–2011, 2025–2027]

Although it is grace and faith through which we are saved, nevertheless, our good works ought to show the love produced by God's action in us.

342 *Are we all supposed to become "saints"?*

Yes. The purpose of our life is to be united with God in love and to correspond entirely to God's wishes. We should allow God "to live his life in us" (Mother Teresa). That is what it means to be holy: a "saint". [2012–2016, 2028–2029]

Every man asks himself the question: Who am I and why am I here, how do I find myself? Faith answers: Only in → HOLINESS does man become that for which God created him. Only in holiness does man find real harmony between himself and his Creator. Holiness, however, is not some sort of self-made perfection; rather, it is union with the incarnate love that is Christ. Anyone who gains new life in this way finds himself and becomes holy.

 As he who called you is holy, be holy yourselves in all your conduct; since it is written, "You shall be holy, for I am holy."

1 Pet 1:15–16

Holiness is not the luxury of a few people, but a simple duty for you and me.

BL. TERESA OF CALCUTTA (1910–1997)

◇ CHAPTER THREE ◇
The Church

343 *How does the Church help us to lead a good, responsible life?*

In the Church we are baptized. In the Church we receive the faith that the Church has preserved intact down through the centuries. In the Church we hear the living Word of God and learn how we must live if we want to please God. Through the →SACRAMENTS that Jesus entrusted to his disciples, the Church builds us up, strengthens, and consoles us. In the Church there is the blazing fire of the saints, by which our hearts are kindled. In the Church the Holy →EUCHARIST is celebrated, in which Christ's sacrifice and strength are renewed for us in such a way that, united with him, we become his Body and live by his strength. Despite all her human weaknesses, apart from the Church no one can be a Christian. [2030–2031, 2047]

344 *Why does the Church also make declarations about ethical questions and about matters of personal conduct?*

Believing is a path. One learns how to stay on this path, in other words, how to act rightly and to lead a good life, only by following the instructions in the Gospel. The teaching authority (→ MAGISTERIUM) of the Church must remind people also about the demands of the natural moral law. [2032–2040, 2049–2051]

There are not two truths. What is humanly right cannot be wrong from the Christian perspective. And what is right according to Christianity cannot be humanly wrong. That is why the Church must teach comprehensively about moral issues.

345 *What are the "Five Precepts of the Church"?*

(1) You shall attend Mass on Sunday and holy days of obligation and abstain from work or activities

that offend against the character of the day.
(2) You shall receive the sacrament of Penance at least once a year. (3) You shall receive the →EUCHARIST at least during the Easter season. (4) You shall observe the prescribed seasons of fasting and days of abstinence (Ash Wednesday and Good Friday). (5) You shall contribute to the material support of the Church. [2042–2043]

346 *What is the purpose of the precepts of the Church, and how binding are they?*

The "Five Precepts of the Church" with their minimum requirements are supposed to remind us that one cannot be a Christian without making a moral effort, without participating personally in the sacramental life of the Church, and without union with her in solidarity. They are obligatory for every Catholic Christian. [2041, 2048]

347 *Why is "not practicing what you preach" such a serious deficiency in a Christian?*

Agreement between one's life and one's witness is the first requirement for proclaiming the Gospel. Not practicing what you profess is therefore →HYPOCRISY, a betrayal of the Christian duty to be "salt of the earth" and "light of the world". [2044–2046]

Paul was the one who reminded the Church in Corinth: "You show that you are a letter from Christ ... written not with ink but with the Spirit of the living God, not on tablets of stone but on tablets of human hearts" (2 Cor 3:3). Christians themselves, not the things they say, are Christ's "letters of recommendation" (2 Cor 3:2) to the world.

> Nothing may have priority over the liturgy.

ST. BENEDICT OF NURSIA
(ca. 480–547)

? HYPOCRISY
Implies a double standard in the morality that one practices publicly or implicitly. Externally a hypocritical person advocates goals and values that he does not respect privately. "Little children, let us not love in word or speech but in deed and in truth" (1 Jn 3:18).

> The world is full of people who preach water and drink wine.

GIOVANNI GUARESCHI
(1908–1968, Italian author of *The Little World of Don Camillo*)

> Christ does not want admirers but followers.

SØREN KIERKEGAARD
(1813–1855)

> Most people do not suspect what God could make out of them if they would only place themselves at his disposal.

ST. IGNATIUS LOYOLA
(1491–1556)

The Ten Commandments as printed nearby are not found in precisely that form in Sacred Scripture; the text is based on two biblical sources: Ex 20:2–17 and Deut 5:6–21. Centuries ago the two sources were summarized for instructional purposes, and the Ten Commandments were presented to the faithful in the present form of the catechetical tradition.

348 *"Teacher, what ... must I do to have eternal life?" (Mt 19:16)*

Jesus says, "If you would enter life, keep the commandments" (Mt 19:17). Then he adds, "and come, follow me" (Mt 19:21). [2052–2054, 2075–2076]

Christianity is more than a correct life and keeping the commandments. Being a Christian is a living relationship to Jesus. A Christian unites himself deeply and personally with the Lord and with him sets out on the way that leads to true life.

349 *What are the Ten Commandments?*

1. **I am the Lord your God: you shall not have strange Gods before me.**
2. **You shall not take the name of the Lord your God in vain.**
3. **You shall keep holy the Lord's day.**
4. **Honor your father and your mother.**
5. **You shall not kill.**
6. **You shall not commit adultery.**
7. **You shall not steal.**
8. **You shall not bear false witness against your neighbor.**
9. **You shall not covet your neighbor's wife.**
10. **You shall not covet your neighbor's goods.**

350 Are the Ten Commandments a random list?

No. The Ten Commandments form a unity. One commandment refers to another. You cannot arbitrarily toss out individual commandments. Someone who breaks one commandment is violating the whole Law. [2069, 2079]

What is remarkable about the Ten Commandments is that all of human life is included within them. Indeed, we men are related at the same time to God (Commandments 1–3) and to our fellow men (Commandments 4–10); we are religious and social beings.

351 Aren't the Ten Commandments outmoded?

No, the Ten Commandments are by no means the product of a particular time. They express man's fundamental obligations toward God and neighbor, which are always and everywhere valid. [2070–2072]

The Ten Commandments are commandments of reason just as they are also part of the binding → REVELATION of God. They are so fundamentally binding that no one can be dispensed from keeping these commandments.

❦ CHAPTER ONE ❦
"You Shall Love the Lord Your God
with All Your Heart, and with All Your Soul,
and with All Your Mind"

THE FIRST COMMANDMENT:
I am the Lord, your God. You shall not have strange Gods before me.

352 What is the meaning of the commandment, "I am the Lord, your God" (Ex 20:2)?

Because the Almighty has revealed himself to us as our God and Lord, we must not place anything above him or consider anything more important or give any other thing or person priority over him. To know God

DECALOGUE
("Ten Words", from Greek *deka* = ten and *logos* = word). The Ten Commandments are the central summary of the basic rules of human behavior in the Old Testament. Jews and Christians both look to this fundamental text for orientation.

We love, because he first loved us.

1 Jn 4:19

Where is God? How can we love him? It is not enough to say, "My God, I love you!" We love God in this world by giving something up, by giving something away. Of course I can eat the sugar myself, but I can also give it away.

BL. TERESA OF CALCUTTA (1910–1997)

and to serve and worship him has absolute priority in our life. [2083–2094, 2133–2134]

God expects us to give him our full *faith;* we should place all our *hope* in him and direct all the strength of our *love* toward him. The commandment to love God is the most important of all commandments and the key to all the others. That is why it stands at the beginning of the Ten Commandments.

353 *Why do we worship God?*

We worship God because he exists and because reverence and worship are the appropriate response to his revelation and his presence. "You shall worship the Lord your God and him only shall you serve" (Mt 4:10). [2095–2105, 2135–2136]

Worshipping God, however, is also beneficial to men, for it frees them from servitude to the powers of this world. When God is no longer worshipped and when he is no longer thought to be Lord over life and death, others assume that position and put human dignity at risk. → 485

354 Can people be forced to believe in God?

No. No one may force others to believe, not even one's own children, just as no one may be forced to be an unbeliever. A person can make the decision to believe only in complete freedom. Christians, however, are called to help other people, by word and example, to find the way to faith.
[2104–2109, 2137]

Pope John Paul II said, "Proclaiming Christ and bearing witness to him, when done in a way that respects consciences, does not violate freedom. Faith demands a free adherence on the part of man, but at the same time faith must also be offered to him" (Encyclical *Redemptoris missio,* 1990, no. 8).

355 "You shall not have strange Gods before me." What does that mean?

This commandment forbids us:
- **to adore other gods and pagan deities or to worship an earthly idol or to devote oneself entirely to some earthly good (money, influence, success, beauty, youth, and so on)**
- **to be superstitious, which means to adhere to esoteric, magic, or occult or New Age practices or to get involved with fortune telling or spiritualism, instead of believing in God's power, providence, and → BLESSINGS**
- **to provoke God by word or deed**
- **to commit a → SACRILEGE**
- **to acquire spiritual power through corruption and to desecrate what is holy through trafficking (simony). [2110–2128, 2138–2140]**

356 Is esotericism as found, for example in New Age beliefs, compatible with the Christian faith?

No. → ESOTERICISM ignores the reality of God. God is a personal Being; he is love and the origin of life, not

> We should fear God out of love and not love him out of fear.

ST. FRANCIS DE SALES
(1567–1622)

> We impose our faith on no one. Such proselytism is contrary to Christianity. Faith can develop only in freedom. But we do appeal to the freedom of men and women to open their hearts to God, to seek him, to hear his voice.

POPE BENEDICT XVI,
September 10, 2006

PROSELYTISM
(from Greek *proserchomai* = to arrive): the exploitation of the intellectual or physical poverty of others to draw them over to one's own faith.

SACRILEGE
(from Latin *sacrilegium* = plundering of a temple): the theft, profanation, or desecration of something sacred.

some cold cosmic energy. Man was willed and created by God, but man himself is not divine; rather, he is a creature that is wounded by sin, threatened by death, and in need of redemption. Whereas most proponents of esotericism assume that man can redeem himself, Christians believe that only Jesus Christ and God's grace redeem them. Nor are nature and the cosmos God (as → PANTHEISM claims). Rather, the Creator, even though he loves us immensely, is infinitely greater and unlike anything he has created. [2110–2128]

Many people today practice yoga for health reasons, enroll in a → MEDITATION course so as to become more calm and collected, or attend dance workshops so as to experience their bodies in a new way. These techniques are not always harmless. Often they are vehicles for doctrines that are foreign to Christianity. No reasonable person should hold an irrational world view, in which people can tap magical powers or harness mysterious spirits and the "initiated" have a secret knowledge that is withheld from the "ignorant". In ancient Israel, the surrounding peoples' beliefs in gods and spirits were exposed as false. God alone is Lord; there is no god besides him. Nor is there any (magical) technique by which one can capture or charm "the divine", force one's wishes on the universe, or redeem oneself. Much about these esoteric beliefs and practices is → SUPERSTITION or → OCCULTISM.

357 Is atheism always a sin against the First Commandment?

→ If someone intentionally and explicitly denies God, he sins against the first commandment. However, his responsibility may be seriously impaired, as when, for example, he has learned nothing about God or has examined the question about God's existence conscientiously and cannot believe. [2127–2128]

The line between being unable to believe and being unwilling to believe is not clear. The attitude that simply dismisses faith as unimportant, without having examined it more closely, is often worse than well-considered → ATHEISM. → 5

358 Why does the Old Testament forbid images of God, and why do we Christians no longer keep that commandment?

In order to protect the mystery of God and to set the people of Israel apart from the idolatrous practices of the pagans, the First Commandment said, "You shall not make for yourself a graven image" (Ex 20:4). However, since God himself acquired a human face in Jesus Christ, the prohibition against images was repealed in Christianity; in the Eastern Church, → ICONS are even regarded as sacred. [2129–2132, 2141]

The knowledge of the patriarchs of Israel that God surpasses everything (→ TRANSCENDENCE) and is much greater than anything in the world lives on today in Judaism as in Islam, where no image of God is or ever was allowed. In Christianity, in light of Christ's life on earth, the prohibition against images was mitigated from the fourth century on and was abolished at the Second Council of Nicaea (787). By his Incarnation, God is no longer absolutely unimaginable; after Jesus we can picture what he is like: "He who has seen me has seen the Father" (Jn 14:9). → 9

? **PANTHEISM**
(Greek *pan* = all, *theos* = God): the world view that nothing exists except God; accordingly, everything that exists is God, and God is everything that exists. This doctrine is incompatible with the Christian faith.

" Unbelievers are the most credulous of all.

BLAISE PASCAL
(1588–1651)

? **OCCULTISM**
(Latin *occultus* = hidden, secret): a collective term for teachings and practices through which man supposedly acquires power over his destiny, matter, and surroundings. Examples of occult practices are Ouija boards, astrology, and clairvoyance.

? **ATHEISM**
(Greek *theos* = God): the view that God does not exist. A general term for various forms of denying God's existence in theory or in practice.

AGNOSTICISM
(Greek *gnosis* = knowledge): the view that God cannot be known. A general term for a position that leaves open the question about God's existence because it supposedly cannot be decided or because God cannot be known with certainty.

TRANSCENDENT
(from Latin *transcendere* = to go beyond): surpassing sensory experience; other-worldly.

ICON
(from Greek *eikon* = image): An icon is a sacred image in the Eastern Church that is painted according to venerable patterns by an artist who is praying and fasting; it is supposed to produce a mystical union between the observer and what is depicted (Christ, angels, saints).

Blessed be the name of the Lord from this time forth and for evermore!

Ps 113:2

THE SECOND COMMANDMENT:
You Shall Not Take the Name of the Lord Your God in Vain.

359 *Why does God want us to "hallow" his name (that is, keep it holy)?*

To tell someone your name is a sign of trust. Since God has told us his name, he makes himself recognizable and grants us access to him through this name. God is absolute truth. Someone who calls Truth himself by his name but uses it to testify to a lie sins seriously. [2142–2155, 2160–2164]

One must not pronounce the name of God irreverently. For we know him only because he has entrusted himself to us. The Holy Name, after all, is the key to the heart of the Almighty. Therefore it is a terrible

DANIELE

or to make false promises in his name. The Second Commandment is therefore also a commandment that protects "holiness" in general. Places, things, names, and people who have been touched by God are "holy". Sensitivity to what is holy is called reverence.
→ 31

MONIQUE

360 *What is the meaning of the Sign of the Cross?*

Through the Sign of the Cross we place ourselves under the protection of the Triune God. [2157, 2166]

At the beginning of the day, at the beginning of a prayer, but also at the beginning of important undertakings, a Christian makes the Sign of the Cross over himself and thus starts his business "in the name of the Father and of the Son and of the Holy Spirit". We are surrounded on all sides by the Triune God; calling upon him by name sanctifies the things we set out to do; it obtains → BLESSINGS for us and strengthens us in difficulties and temptations.

361 *What does it mean for a Christian to be baptized with a particular name?*

"In the name of the Father and of the Son and of the Holy Spirit", the person is baptized with a name. The name and the face are ultimately what make a person unique, even in God's sight. "Fear not, for I have redeemed you; I have called you by name, you are mine" (Is 43:1). [2158]

Christians treat the name of a person reverently, because the name is profoundly connected with that person's identity and dignity. From time immemorial Christians have selected names for their children from the list of the saints; they do so in the belief that the patron saint is an example for them and will intercede with God for them in a special way. → 201

HELEN

Reverence is the pole on which the world turns.

JOHANN WOLFGANG VON GOETHE
(1749–1832, German poet)

Let us not be ashamed to profess the Crucified One; let us confidently seal our forehead with our fingers, let us make the Sign of the Cross on everything, on the bread we eat and over the cup we drink. Let us make this sign as we come and go, before sleeping, when we lie down and when we arise, while traveling and while resting.

ST. CYRIL OF JERUSALEM
(ca. 313–386/387)

"I will not blot his name out of the book of life; I will confess his name before my Father and before his angels."

Rev 3:5

ROGER · JANE · FERNANDO · GIULIANO · BENJAMIN · LISA
FELICITAS · FELIPE · MARY · FERNANDO · LEONARD · FRIDA · GIACOMO
TRISTAN · MARTIN · CARLOS · JUANITA · BÉLA · THORBEN · GABRIEL · BRANDON
BRUNO · JEREMY · SOPHIE · EMILIA · ESTEBAN · JORGE
JOHANNES · TAMARA · JESSICA · ALONZO · CLARK · DOROTHÉE

> Remember the sabbath day, to keep it holy ... In it you shall not do any work, you, or your son, or your daughter, your manservant, or your maidservant, or your cattle, or the sojourner who is within your gates.
>
> Ex 20:8, 10

SABBATH
(Hebrew, approximately "break for rest"): the Jewish day of rest commemorating the seventh day of creation and the Exodus from Egypt. It begins on Friday evening and ends on Saturday evening. In Orthodox Judaism it is observed with a host of rules for maintaining the Sabbath rest.

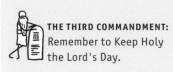

THE THIRD COMMANDMENT:
Remember to Keep Holy the Lord's Day.

362 Why do Jews celebrate the Sabbath?

The → SABBATH is for the people of Israel the great sign commemorating God, the Creator and Redeemer. [2168–2172, 2189]

The → SABBATH recalls in the first place the seventh day of creation, when God "rested, and was refreshed" (Ex 31:17), this, so to speak, authorizes all men to interrupt their work and replenish their energies. Even slaves were supposed to be allowed to observe the Sabbath. This recalls the second great commemorative sign, the liberation of Israel from slavery in Egypt: "You shall remember that you [yourself] were a servant in the land of Egypt ... " (Dt 5:15). The Sabbath is therefore a feast of human freedom; on the Sabbath all breathe freely; on it the division of the world into masters and slaves is abolished. In traditional Judaism this day of freedom and rest is also a sort of foretaste of the world to come. → 47

363 How does Jesus deal with the Sabbath?

Jesus observes the → SABBATH, but at the same time he deals with it very liberally, as one who has complete command over it: "The sabbath was made for man, not man for the sabbath" (Mk 2:27). [2173]

The fact that Jesus claims the right to heal on the Sabbath and to interpret the Sabbath laws mercifully poses a dilemma for his Jewish contemporaries: Either Jesus is the Messiah sent by God, which makes him "Lord even of the sabbath" (Mk 2:28), or else he is merely a man, in which case his actions on the Sabbath are a sin against the Law.

364 Why do Christians replace the Sabbath with Sunday?

Christians replaced the celebration of the Sabbath with the celebration of Sunday because Jesus Christ rose from the dead on a Sunday. The "Lord's Day", however, does include elements of the Sabbath. [2174–2176, 2190–2191]

The Christian Sunday has three essential elements: (1) It recalls the creation of the world and communicates the festive splendor of God's goodness to the passage of time. (2) It recalls the "eighth day of creation", when the world was made new in Christ (thus a prayer from the Easter Vigil says: "You have wonderfully created man and even more wonderfully restored him."). (3) It includes the theme of rest, not just to sanctify the interruption of work, but to point even now toward man's eternal rest in God.

365 How do Christians make Sunday "the Lord's day"?

A Catholic Christian attends Holy Mass on Sunday or on the vigil of Sunday. On that day he refrains from all work that would prevent him from worshipping God or disturb the festive, joyful, restful, and restorative character of the day. [2177–2186, 2192–2193]

Since Sunday is an Easter celebration that occurs each week, Christians from the earliest times have gathered together on that day to celebrate and thank their Redeemer and to reunite themselves with him and with others who are redeemed. So it is a central duty of every conscientious Catholic Christian to "keep holy" Sunday and the other holy days of the Church. One is exempted from it only by urgent family duties and important responsibilities in society. Because participation in the Sunday → EUCHARIST is fundamental for a Christian life, the Church explicitly declares that it is a serious sin to stay away from Sunday Mass without good reason. → 219, 345

> If pagans call it the "day of the sun", we willingly agree, for today the light of the world is raised, today is revealed the sun of justice with healing in his rays.
>
> ST. JEROME (347–419)

> That is the difference between animals and man: the latter has a Sunday outfit, too.
>
> MARTIN LUTHER (1483–1546)

> Without Sunday we cannot live.
>
> The Christian MARTYRS OF ABITENE, before they were executed in 304 by Emperor Diocletian because they had opposed his ban on the celebration of Sunday.

> People used to say: Give your soul a Sunday! Now they say: Give your Sunday a soul!
>
> PETER ROSEGGER (1843-1918, Austrian writer)

What does Sunday cost us? The very question is already a decisive attack on Sunday. For Sunday is Sunday precisely because it costs nothing and brings in nothing, in the economic sense. The question of what preserving it as a work-free day "costs" presupposes that we have already conceptually turned Sunday into a workday.

ROBERT SPAEMANN
(b. 1927, German
philosopher)

Honor your father and your mother, that your days may be long in the land which the Lord your God gives you.

Ex 20:12

 The Life of the parents is the book which the children read.

ST. AUGUSTINE
(354–430)

---

366 *Why is it important for the State to preserve Sunday?*

Sunday is a genuine service to the good of society, because it is a sign of opposition to the total absorption of man by the working world. [2188, 2192–2193]

Therefore in lands that have a Christian character, Christians not only demand the governmental preservation of Sunday, they also do not ask others to do work that they themselves do not want to do on Sunday. Everyone in creation should take part in this "breather".

❖ CHAPTER TWO ❖

"You Shall Love Your Neighbor as Yourself"

 THE FOURTH COMMANDMENT:
Honor your father
and your mother.

367 *To whom does the Fourth Commandment refer, and what does it require of us?*

The Fourth Commandment refers in the first place to one's physical parents, but also to the people to whom we owe our life, our well-being, our security, and our faith. [2196–2200, 2247–2248]

What we owe in the first place to our parents—namely love, gratitude, and respect—should also govern our relations to people who guide us and are there for us. There are many people who represent for us a God-given, natural, and good authority: foster or step-parents, older relatives and ancestors, educators, teachers, employers, superiors. In the spirit of the Fourth Commandment we should do them justice. In the broadest sense, this commandment applies even to our duties as citizens to the State. → 325

> The family is a necessary good for peoples, an indispensable foundation for society and a great and lifelong treasure for couples. It is a unique good for children, who are meant to be the fruit of the love, of the total and generous self-giving of their parents.

POPE BENEDICT XVI,
July 8, 2006

> The family that prays together, stays together.

FATHER PATRICK PEYTON, C.S.C.
Irish priest, promoter of the Rosary

> Tuberculosis and cancer are not the most terrible sicknesses. I think that a much more terrible sickness is to be unwanted and unloved.

BL. TERESA OF CALCUTTA
(1910–1997)

368 *What place does the family have in God's plan of creation?*

A man and a woman who are married to each other form, together with their children, a family. God wills that the love of the spouses, if possible, should produce children. These children, who are entrusted to the protection and care of their parents, have the same dignity as their parents. [2201–2206, 2249]

God himself, in the depths of the Trinity, is communion. In the human sphere, the family is the primordial image of communion. The family is the unique school of living in relationships. Nowhere do children grow up as well as in an intact family, in which they experience heartfelt affection, mutual respect, and responsibility for one another. Finally, faith grows in the family, too; the family is, the Church tells us, a miniature church, a "domestic church", the radiance of which should invite others into this fellowship of faith, charity, and hope.
→ 271

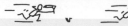

369 Why are families irreplaceable?

Every child is descended from one father and one mother and longs for the warmth and safety of a family so that he may grow up secure and happy. [2207–2208]

The family is the basic cell of human society. The values and principles that are lived out in the small circle of the family are what make solidarity in the life of larger society possible in the first place. → 516

> It is only the rock of total, irrevocable love between a man and a woman that can serve as the foundation on which to build a society that will become a home for all mankind.
>
> POPE BENEDICT XVI,
> May 11, 2006

370 Why should the State protect and promote families?

The welfare and future of a State depend on the ability of the smallest unit within it, the family, to live and develop. [2209–2213, 2250]

No State has the right to intrude on the basic cell of society, the family, by its regulations or to question its right to exist. No State has the right to define the family differently, for the family's commission comes from the Creator. No State has the right to deprive the family of its fundamental functions, especially in the area of education. On the contrary, every State has the duty to support families with its assistance and to ensure that its material needs are met. → 323

> If the family is in order, the State will be in order; if the State is in order, the great community of mankind will live in peace.
>
> LU BUWEI
> (ca. 300 b.c. – 236 b.c.,
> Chinese philosopher)

371 How does a child respect his parents?

A child respects and honors his parents by showing them love and gratitude. [2214–2220, 2251]

Children should be grateful to their parents in the first place because they received their life from the love of their parents. This gratitude establishes a lifelong relationship of love, respect, responsibility, and obedience, rightly understood. Especially in times of need, sickness, and old age, children should lovingly be there for their parents and care for them faithfully.

> With all your heart honor your father, and do not forget the birth pangs of your mother.... What can you give back to them that equals their gift to you?
>
> Sir 7:27–28

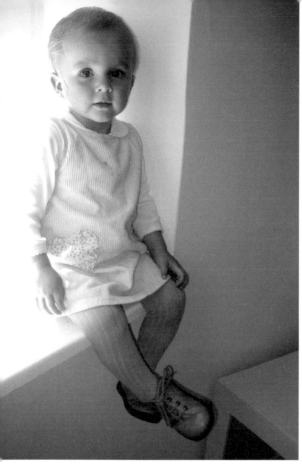

And they were bringing children to him, that he might touch them; and the disciples rebuked them. But when Jesus saw it he was indignant, and said to them, "Let the children come to me, do not hinder them; for to such belongs the kingdom of God."

Mk 10:13–14

" The fascination of children lies in this: that with each of them all things are remade, and the universe is put again upon its trial.

G. K. CHESTERTON
(1874–1936)

" Children ought to receive two things from their parents: roots and wings.

JOHANN WOLFGANG
VON GOETHE
(1749–1832)

372 *How do parents respect their children?*

God entrusted children to parents so that they might be steady, righteous examples for those children, that they might love and respect them and do everything possible so that their children can develop physically and spiritually. [2221–2231]

Children are a gift from God and not the property of the parents. Before they are their parents' children, they are God's children. The primary duty of parents is to present to their children the Good News and to communicate the Christian faith to them. → 374

> The younger ones should therefore honor the older ones, and the older ones should love the younger ones.

ST. BENEDICT OF NURSIA
(ca. 480–547)

> Love one another with brotherly affection; outdo one another in showing honor. Never flag in zeal, be aglow with the Spirit, serve the Lord.

Rom 12:10

373 How should a family live its faith together?

A Christian family should be a miniature church. All Christian family members are invited to strengthen one another in faith and to outdo one another in their zeal for God. They should pray for and with each other and collaborate in works of charity. [2226–2227]

Parents stand in for their children with their own faith, have them baptized, and serve as their models of faith. That means that parents should make it possible for their children to experience how valuable and beneficial it is to live in the familiar presence of the loving God. At some time, however, the parents, too, will learn from their children's faith and hear how God speaks through them, because the faith of young people is often accompanied by greater devotion and generosity and "because the Lord often reveals to a younger person what is better" (St. Benedict of Nursia, *Rule*, chap. 3, 3).

374 Why is God more important than the family?

Without relationship a person cannot live. Man's most important relationship is the one he has with God. This has priority over all human relationships, even family relationships. [2232–2233]

Children do not *belong* to the parents, nor do parents belong to their children. Every person belongs directly to God. Only to God is man bound absolutely and always. This is how we understand what Jesus said to those who are called: "He who loves father or mother more than me is not worthy of me; and he who loves son or daughter more than me is not worthy of me" (Mt 10:37). Therefore parents should place their children confidently into God's hands if the Lord calls them to the consecrated life in a religious order or to be a →
PRIEST. → 145

375 How is authority exercised correctly?

Authority is exercised properly when it is understood according to Jesus' example as service. It must never be arbitrary. [2234–2237, 2254]

Jesus showed us once and for all how authority should be exercised. He, the greatest authority, served others and took the last place. Jesus even washed the feet of his disciples (Jn 13:1–20). The authority of parents, teachers, educators, and superiors is given to them by God, not so that they can lord it over those who are entrusted to their care, but rather so that they might understand and exercise their duty of guiding and training as service. → 325

376 What duties do citizens have toward the State?

Every citizen has the duty to cooperate loyally with the civil authorities and to contribute to the → COMMON GOOD in truth, justice, freedom, and solidarity. [2238–2246]

A Christian, too, should love his homeland, defend it in various ways in times of need, and gladly offer to serve civil institutions. He should exercise the right to vote and even run for office and not shirk the duty to pay just taxes. Nevertheless, within the State the individual citizen remains a free man with fundamental rights; he has the right to offer constructive criticism of the State and its organs. The State is there for the people, not the individual for the State.

377 When must we refuse to obey the State?

No one may follow orders from the State that violate God's laws. [2242–2246, 2256–2257]

It was Peter who called us to practice only a relative obedience toward the State when he said, "We must obey God rather than men" (Acts 5:29). If a State should establish laws and procedures that are racist, sexist, or destructive of human life, a Christian is obliged in conscience to refuse to obey, to refrain from participation, and to offer resistance. → 379

Fathers, do not provoke your children, lest they become discouraged.

Col 3:21

"Whoever would be first among you must be your slave; even as the Son of man came not to be served but to serve, and to give his life as a ransom for many."

Mt 20:27–28

By birth I am an Albanian, by citizenship an Indian; I am a Catholic sister. By my mission I belong to the whole world, but my heart belongs to Jesus alone.

BL. TERESA OF CALCUTTA (1910–1997)

"Render therefore to Caesar the things that are Caesar's, and to God the things that are God's."

Mt 22:21

"You have heard that it was said to the men of old, 'You shall not kill; and whoever kills shall be liable to judgment.' But I say to you that every one who is angry with his brother shall be liable to judgment."

Mt 5:21–22

99 No one can under any circumstance claim for himself the right directly to destroy an innocent human being.

Vatican Instruction
Donum Vitae (1987)

99 The beginnings at first were merely a subtle shift in emphasis in the basic attitude of the physicians. It started with the acceptance of the attitude, basic in the euthanasia movement, that there is such a thing as life not worthy to be lived. This attitude in its early stages concerned itself merely with the severely and chronically sick. Gradually the sphere of those to be included in this category was enlarged to encompass the socially unproductive, the ideologically unwanted, the racially unwanted and finally all non-Germans. →

THE FIFTH COMMANDMENT:
You shall not kill.

378 Why is it not permissible to take one's own life or the lives of others?

God alone is Lord over life and death. Except in the case of legitimate self-defense of oneself or another, no one may kill another human being.
[2258–2262, 2318–2320]

An attack on life is a sacrilege committed against God. Human life is *sacred;* this means that it belongs to God; it is his property. Even our own life is only *entrusted* to us. God himself has given us the gift of life; only he may take it back from us. The Book of Exodus, translated literally, says "You shall not murder" (Ex 20:13).

379 What sorts of attacks on human life are forbidden by the Fifth Commandment?

Murder and acting as an accomplice to murder are forbidden. Killing unarmed civilians during a war is forbidden. The abortion of a human being, from the moment of conception on, is forbidden. Suicide, self-mutilation, and self-destructive behavior are forbidden. Euthanasia—killing the handicapped, the sick, and the dying—is also forbidden.
[2268–2283, 2322–2325]

Today people often try to get around the Fifth Commandment with seemingly humane arguments. But neither euthanasia nor abortion is a humane solution. That is why the Church is perfectly clear on these questions. Whoever participates in an abortion, forces a woman to undergo an abortion, or merely advises her to do so is automatically excommunicated—just as with other crimes against human life. If a psychologically ill person commits suicide, responsibility for the act of killing is often diminished and in many cases completely annulled. → 288

→ 288

---

380 Why is it permissible to tolerate the killing of another human being in the case of legitimate self-defense?

Someone who is actually attacking the lives of others may and must be stopped, if necessary by killing the attacker himself. [2263–2265, 2321]

Legitimate defense against aggression is not only a right; for someone who bears the responsibility for the lives of others it can even become a duty. Nevertheless, legitimate defense must not employ wrong, inappropriately harsh methods.

---

381 Why is the Church opposed to capital punishment?

The Church is committed to opposing the death penalty because it is "both cruel and unnecessary" (Pope John Paul II, St. Louis, January 27, 1999). [2266–2267]

Every legitimate State has in principle the right to punish crime appropriately. In *Evangelium vitae* (1995), the Pope does not say that the use of the death penalty is in every respect an unacceptable and illegitimate punishment. To take the life of a criminal is an extreme measure to which the State should resort only "in cases of absolute necessity". This necessity arises when the only way to protect human society is by killing the convicted criminal. But such cases, says Pope John Paul II, "are very rare, if not practically non-existent".

---

382 Is it permissible to offer assistance in dying?

To bring about death directly is always against the commandment "You shall not kill" (Ex 20:13). In contrast, to stand by and assist a dying person is humane and even obligatory. [2278–2279]

What really matters is whether a dying person is killed or allowed to die and thus accompanied. Someone who

---

→ But it is important to realize that the infinitely small wedged-in lever from which this entire trend of mind received its impetus was the attitude toward the nonrehabilitable sick.

LEO ALEXANDER
(1905-1985, Jewish American physician) on the Nazis' crime of euthanasia

A punishment imposed by the State must satisfy four criteria in order to be appropriate and just:
1. It should make amends for the crime.
2. The State intends thereby to restore public order and to provide for the security of its citizens.
3. The punishment should improve the guilty party.
4. The punishment corresponds to the seriousness of the crime.

People shouldn't die by the hand of another person, but holding the hand of another person.

FRANCIS CARDINAL
KÖNIG (1905–2004)

> The hospice movement, not the euthanasia movement, is the answer to our situation that respects human dignity. The forces of imagination and solidarity are mobilized to confront the gigantic problems that we are facing only when the cheap way out is relentlessly barred. When dying is not understood as part of life, that is the beginning of the civilization of death.

ROBERT SPAEMANN
(b. 1927)

> You shall not kill the embryo by abortion and shall not cause the newborn to perish.

Didache 2,2, third century

> Christians ...marry and have children like other people, but they do not expose newborns.

Letter to Diognetus
third century

> Abortion and infanticide are abominable crimes.

Second Vatican Council, GS

intentionally brings about the death of a dying person (euthanasia) breaks the Fifth Commandment. Someone who helps another person *in* the dying process obeys the commandment "Love your neighbor." In view of the certain impending death of a patient, it is therefore legitimate to withhold extraordinary or expensive medical procedures that are not proportionate to the expected outcome. The patient himself must make the decision to forgo "extraordinary" measures or must have stated this intention in an advance directive. If he is no longer capable of doing so, those who are legally entitled must represent the express or probable wishes of the dying person. Ordinary care of a dying person should never be discontinued; this is commanded by love of neighbor and mercy. Meanwhile it can be legitimate and in keeping with human dignity to use painkillers, even at the risk of shortening the

patient's life. The crucial thing is that the use of such medications must not aim at bringing about death, either as an end in itself or as a means of ending pain. → 393

383 Why is abortion unacceptable at any phase in the development of an embryo?

God-given human life is God's own property; it is sacred from the first moment of its existence and not under the control of any human being. "Before I formed you in the womb I knew you, and before you were born I consecrated you" (Jer 1:5). [2270–2274, 2322]

God alone is Lord over life and death. Not even "my" life belongs to me. Every child, from the moment of conception on, has a right to life. From his earliest beginnings an unborn human being is a separate person, and no one can infringe upon his rights, not the State, not the doctor, and not even the mother or father. The Church's clarity about this is not a lack of compassion; she means, rather, to point out the irreparable harm that is inflicted on the child who is killed in abortion and on his parents and on society as a whole. Protecting innocent human life is one of the noblest tasks of the State. If a State evades this responsibility, it undermines the foundations of a rule of law. → 323

384 Can a handicapped child be aborted?

No. Aborting a handicapped child is always a serious crime, even if it is done with the intention of sparing that person suffering later on. → 280

385 Can experiments be performed on living embryos and embryonic stem cells?

No. Embryos are human beings, because human life begins with the fusion of a sperm cell and an egg. [2275, 2323]

Everything you need to know about abortion is in the Fifth Commandment.

CHRISTOPH CARDINAL SCHÖNBORN (b. 1945)

God, give us the courage to protect every unborn life. For the child is God's greatest gift for the family, for a nation, and for the world.

BL. TERESA OF CALCUTTA (1910–1997), upon receiving the Nobel Peace Prize in 1979

If a human being is no longer safe in his mother's womb, where in the world can he be safe?

PHIL BOSMANS (b. 1922, Belgian priest and writer)

The diagnosis of disability in the unborn child cannot be a reason for abortion, because life with such a disability is also desired and appreciated by God, and here on earth no one can ever be sure that he or she will live without physical or spiritual limitations.

POPE BENEDICT XVI, September 28, 2006

Regarding embryos as biological material, "producing" them and then "using" their stem cells for purposes of research is absolutely immoral and falls under the commandment "You shall not kill." Research on adult stem cells is a different matter, since they cannot develop into human beings. Medical interventions on an embryo are justifiable only if they are made with the intention of healing, if the life and unimpaired development of the child are assured, and if the risks involved are not disproportionately great. → 292

386 *Why does the Fifth Commandment protect the physical and spiritual integrity of a human being as well?*

The right to life and human dignity form a unity; they are inseparably connected to each other. It is possible to put a person to death spiritually also. [2284–2287, 2326]

The commandment "You shall not kill" (Ex 20:13) applies to both physical and spiritual integrity. Every seduction and incitement to evil, every use of force is a serious sin, especially when it occurs in a relationship of dependency. The sin is especially evil when the dependence of children on adults is involved. This means not only *sexual abuse,* but also *spiritual seduction* by parents, → PRIESTS, teachers, or educators who lead their charges astray from values, and so on.

387 *How should we treat our body?*

The Fifth Commandment forbids also the use of violence against one's own body. Jesus expressly demands that we accept and love ourselves: "You shall love your neighbor as yourself" (Mt 22:39).

Self-destructive acts against one's own body ("body piercings", cutting and so on) are in most cases psychological reactions to experiences of abandonment and a lack of love; hence they call first and foremost for our sincere and loving response. Within the context of organ donation, it must be made clear, however, that there is no human right to destroy one's own God-given body. → 379

388 *How important is health?*

Health is an important value, but not an absolute one. We should treat our God-given body gratefully and carefully, but not be obsessed with it. [2288–2291]

Appropriate care for the health of its citizens is one of the fundamental obligations of the State, which must create living conditions in which sufficient food, sanitary housing, and basic medical care are available to all.

389 *Why is it a sin to take drugs?*

Using drugs is a sin because it is an act of self-destruction and thus an offense against the life that God has given us out of love. [2290–2291]

Every form of a person's dependence on legal substances (alcohol, medication, tobacco) and even more so on illegal drugs is an exchange of freedom for slavery; it damages the health and life of the person concerned and also does great harm to the people around him. Every time a person loses or forgets himself by becoming intoxicated, which can also include excessive eating and drinking, indulgence in sexual activity, or speeding with an automobile, he loses some of his human dignity and freedom and therefore sins against God. This should be distinguished from the reasonable, conscious, and moderate use of enjoyable things.
→ 286

390 *Is it permissible to experiment on a live human being?*

Scientific, psychological, or medical experiments on a live human subject are allowed only when the results that can be expected are important for human well-being and cannot be obtained otherwise. Everything, however, must take place with the free and informed consent of the subject in question. [2292–2295]

Their God is the belly, and they glory in their shame, with minds set on earthly things.

Phil 3:19

" One after the other they wheeled us out, powerless, helpless. Along the corridor in front of the door to the operating room we were anaesthetized by Dr. Schidlausky with an intravenous injection. Before going to sleep a thought flashed through my mind that I could no longer express: "But we are not guinea pigs." No, we were not guinea pigs. We were human beings!

WANDA POLTAWSKA
(b. 1921)

Moreover, the experiments must not be disproportionately risky. To make human beings the subjects of research against their will is a crime. The fate of the Polish resistance fighter Dr. Wanda Poltawska, a close confidant of Pope John Paul II, reminds us what was at stake then and still is now. During the Nazi period, Wanda Poltawska was a victim of criminal human experiments in the Ravensbrück concentration camp. Later Dr. Poltawska, a psychiatrist, advocated a reform of medical ethics and was among the founding members of the Pontifical Academy for Life.

391 *Is organ donation important?*

Donating organs can lengthen life or improve the quality of life, and therefore it is a genuine service to one's neighbor, provided no one is forced to do it. [2296]

It must be certain that the donor during his lifetime gave his free and deliberate consent and that he was not killed for the purpose of removing the organ(s). Donation by living donors is also possible, for example, in bone marrow transplants or in the donation of one kidney. Organ donation from a cadaver presupposes a certain determination of death and the consent of the donor during his lifetime or else of his representative.

" Christians have often denied the Gospel; yielding to a mentality of power, they have violated the rights of ethnic groups and peoples and shown contempt for their cultures and religious traditions: be patient and merciful towards us, and grant us your forgiveness!

POPE JOHN PAUL II
(1920–2005), Prayer for
Forgiveness in the Jubilee
Year 2000

392 *What sorts of acts violate the human right to bodily integrity?*

This right is violated by the use of violence, kidnapping and hostage taking, terrorism, torture, rape, and forced sterilization as well as by amputation and mutilation. [2297–2298]

These fundamental violations against justice, charity, and human dignity are not justified even when they are backed by government authority. Conscious of the historical guilt of Christians as well, the Church today fights against all use of physical or psychological force, especially against torture.

393 How do Christians assist someone who is dying?

Christians do not leave a dying person alone. They help him so that he can die in faith-filled trust, in dignity and peace. They pray with him and take care that the →SACRAMENTS are administered to him at the right time. [2299]

394 How do Christians treat the corpse of someone who has died?

Christians treat the corpse of a dead person respectfully and lovingly, realizing that God has called him to the resurrection of the dead. [2300–2301]

It is a traditional part of Christian funeral customs for the remains of a dead person to be buried in a dignified manner in the earth and for the grave to be decorated and tended. Today the Church also accepts other funeral arrangements (for instance, cremation), as long as they are not interpreted in a way contrary to the belief in the resurrection of the dead.

395 What is peace?

Peace is the consequence of justice and the sign of love put into action. Where there is peace, "every creature can come to rest in good order" (Thomas Aquinas). Earthly peace is the image of the peace of Christ, who reconciled heaven and earth. [2304–2305]

Peace is more than the absence of war, more than a carefully maintained balance of powers ("balance of terror"). In a state of peace, people can live securely with their legitimately earned property and freely exchange goods with one another. In peace the dignity

---

Development is the new name for peace.

POPE PAUL VI (1897–1978), Encyclical *Populorum progressio*

The effect of righteousness will be peace, and the result of righteousness, quietness and trust for ever.

Is 32:17

The birthday of the Lord is the birthday of peace.

POPE ST. LEO THE GREAT (ca. 400–461)

"Blessed are the peacemakers."

Mt 5:9

In my experience, every time people make an effort to live the Gospel as Jesus teaches us, everything begins to change: all aggressiveness, all fear and sadness then give way to peace and joy.

Belgian KING BAUDOUIN (1930–1993)

He is our peace.

Eph 2:14

"You have heard that it was said, 'You shall love your neighbor and hate your enemy.' But I say to you, Love your enemies and pray for those who persecute you."

Mt 5:43–44

And they shall beat their swords into plowshares, and their spears into pruning hooks; nation shall not lift up sword against nation, neither shall they learn war any more.

Mic 4:3

and the right of self-determination of individuals and of peoples are respected. In peace human coexistence is characterized by brotherly solidarity.

→ 66, 283–284, 327

396 How does a Christian deal with anger?

Paul says, "Be angry but do not sin; do not let the sun go down on your anger" (Eph 4:26). [2302–2304]

Anger is initially a natural emotion, a reaction to perceived injustice. If anger becomes hatred, however, and someone has ill-will toward his neighbor, this normal feeling becomes a serious offense against charity. All uncontrolled anger, especially thoughts of revenge, are detrimental to peace and destroy "the tranquility of order". → 294

397 What does Jesus think about nonviolence?

Jesus places a high value on nonviolent action. He commands his disciples: "Do not resist one who is evil. But if any one strikes you on the right cheek, turn to him the other also" (Mt 5:39). [2311]

He rebukes Peter, who wants to defend him with force: "Put your sword into its sheath" (Jn 18:11). Jesus does not call his disciples to take up weapons. He remains silent before Pilate. His way is to take the part of the victims, to go to the Cross, to redeem the world through love, and to call the peacemakers blessed. Therefore the Church, too, respects people who for reasons of conscience refuse to be part of the armed services but place themselves at the service of society in some other way. → 283–284

398 *Must Christians be pacifists?*

The Church strives for peace but does not preach radical pacifism. Indeed, no one can deny either the individual citizen or particular governments and alliances the fundamental right of armed self-defense. War is morally justifiable only as a last resort. [2308]

The Church unmistakably says No to war. Christians should do everything possible to avoid war before it starts: They oppose the stockpiling of arms and trafficking in weapons; they fight against racial, ethnic, and religious discrimination; they work to put an end to economic and social injustice and thus promote peace. → 283–284

399 *When is the use of military force allowed?*

The use of military force is possible only in an extreme emergency. There are several criteria for a "just war": (1) Authorization by the competent authority; (2) a just cause; (3) a just purpose; (4) war must be the last resort; (5) the methods used must be proportionate; (6) there must be a prospect of success. [2307–2309]

> War is not always inevitable. It is always a defeat for humanity.
>
> POPE JOHN PAUL II (1920–2005), January 13, 2003

> It is not power, but love that redeems us! This is God's sign: he himself is love. How often we wish that God would show himself stronger, that he would strike decisively, defeating evil and creating a better world. All ideologies of power justify themselves in exactly this way, they justify the destruction of whatever would stand in the way of progress and the liberation of humanity. We suffer on account of God's patience. And yet, we need his patience. God, who became a lamb, tells us that the world is saved by the Crucified One, not by those who crucified him. The world is redeemed by the patience of God. It is destroyed by the impatience of man.
>
> POPE BENEDICT XVI, April 24, 2005

Then the Lord God said, "It is not good that the man should be alone; I will make him a helper fit for him." ... Therefore a man leaves his father and his mother and clings to his wife, and they become one flesh.

Gen 2:18, 24

Set me as a seal upon your heart, as a seal upon your arm; for love is strong as death, jealousy is cruel as the grave. Its flashes are flashes of fire, a most vehement flame. Many waters cannot quench love, neither can floods drown it. If a man offered for love all the wealth of his house, it would be utterly scorned.

Song 8:6–7

Christianity snatched women from a condition that was the equivalent of slavery.

MADAME DE STAEL
(1766-1817, French author)

There is neither Jew nor Greek, there is neither slave nor free, there is neither male nor female; for you are all one in Christ Jesus.

Gal 3:28

THE SIXTH COMMANDMENT:
You shall not commit adultery.

400 *What does it mean to say that man is a sexual being?*

God created man as male and female. He created them for each other and for love. He created them with erotic desires and the ability to experience physical pleasure. He created them to transmit life. [2331–2333, 2335, 2392]

Being a man or being a woman is very deeply imprinted on the individual human person; it is a different way of feeling, a different way of loving, a different calling with respect to children, another way of believing. Because he intended that they should be there for each other and complement one another in love, God made man and woman different. That is why man and woman attract each other sexually and intellectually. When a husband and wife express their love for each other in bodily union, their love finds its deepest sensual expression. Just as God is creative in his love, so too man can be creative in love and give life to children.
→ 64, 260, 416–417

401 *Is there a priority of one sex over the other?*

No. God endowed men and women with identical dignity as persons. [2331, 2335]

Both men and women are human beings created in God's image and children of God redeemed by Jesus Christ. It is just as unchristian as it is inhumane to discriminate unjustly against someone because he is male or female. Equal dignity and equal rights, nevertheless, do not mean uniformity. The sort of egalitarianism that ignores the specific character of a man or a woman contradicts God's plan of creation.
→ 54, 260

402 What is love?

Love is the free self-giving of the heart. [2346]

To have a heart full of love means to be so pleased with something that one emerges from oneself and devotes oneself to it. A musician can devote himself to a masterpiece. A kindergarten teacher can be there wholeheartedly for her charges. In every friendship

there is love. The most beautiful form of love on earth, however, is the love between man and woman, in which two people give themselves to each other forever. All human love is an image of divine love, in which all love is at home. Love is the inmost being of the Triune God. In God there is continual exchange and perpetual self-giving. Through the overflowing of divine love, we participate in the eternal love of God. The more a person loves, the more he resembles God. Love should influence the whole life of a person, but it is realized with particular depth and symbolism when man and woman love one another in marriage and become "one flesh" (Gen 2:24). → 309

403 How is sexuality related to love?

Sexuality must not be separated from love; they must go together. The sexual encounter requires the framework of a true, dependable love. [2337]

> All the reasons in favor of the "subjec-tion" of woman to man in marriage must be understood in the sense of a "mutual subjection" of both "out of reverence for Christ".
>
> POPE JOHN PAUL II (1920–2005), Apostolic Let-ter *Mulieris dignitatem* (1988)

> Love is of God, and he who loves is born of God and knows God.
>
> 1 Jn 4:7

> One cannot live a trial life or die a trial death. One cannot love on a trial basis or accept a person on trial and for a limited time.
>
> POPE JOHN PAUL II (1920–2005), November 15, 1980

> Sexuality, by means of which man and woman give themselves to one another through the acts which are proper and exclusive to spouses, is by no means something purely biological, but concerns the innermost being →

PART THREE – HOW WE ARE TO HAVE LIFE IN CHRIST

218
219

[11] CHAPTER 2: YOU SHALL LOVE YOUR NEIGHBOR AS YOURSELF

→ of the human person as such. It is realized in a truly human way only if it is an integral part of the love by which a man and a woman commit themselves totally to one another until death. The total physical self-giving would be a lie if it were not the sign and fruit of a total personal self-giving.

POPE JOHN PAUL II, (1920–2005), Apostolic Exhortation *Familiaris Consortio*

99 Everything that makes a sexual encounter easy hastens at the same time its plunge into irrelevance.

PAUL RICOEUR (1913-2005 French philosopher)

CHASTITY
(from Latin *castus*, clean, pure, temperate): the virtue by which a person who is capable of passion deliberately and resolutely reserves his erotic desires for love and resists the temptation to find lewd images in the media or to use others as a means of achieving his own satisfaction.

When sexuality is separated from *love* and is sought only for the sake of satisfaction, one destroys the meaning of the sexual union of man and woman. Sexual union is the most beautiful bodily, sensual expression of love. People who look for sex without love are lying, because the closeness of their bodies does not correspond to the closeness of their hearts. Someone who does not take his own body language at its word does lasting damage to body and soul. Sex then becomes inhuman; it is degraded to a means of obtaining pleasure and degenerates into a commodity. Only committed, enduring love in marriage creates a space for sexuality that is experienced in a human way and brings lasting happiness.

404 *What is chaste love? Why should a Christian live a chaste life?*

A chaste love is a love that defends itself against all the internal and external forces that might destroy it. That person is chaste who has consciously accepted his sexuality and integrated it well into his personality. → CHASTITY and continence are not the same thing. Someone who has an active sex life in marriage must be chaste, too. A person acts chastely when his bodily activity is the expression of dependable, faithful love. [2238]

Chastity must not be confused with prudishness. A person who lives chastely is not the plaything of his lusts but, rather, lives his sexuality deliberately, motivated by love, and as an expression of that love. Unchaste behavior weakens love and obscures its meaning. The Catholic Church advocates a holistic-ecological approach to sexuality. This includes sexual pleasure, which is something good and beautiful; personal love; and fruitfulness, which means openness to having children. It is the understanding of the Catholic Church that these three aspects of sexuality belong together. Now if a man has one woman for sexual pleasure, a second to whom he writes love poetry, and a third with whom to have children, then he is exploiting all three and really loves none of them.

405 How can anyone live a chaste life? What can help?

Someone lives chastely when he is free to be loving and is not the slave of his drives and emotions. Anything, therefore, that helps one to become a more mature, freer, and more loving person and to form better relationships helps that person to love chastely, also.[2338–2345]

One becomes free to be loving through self-discipline, which one must acquire, practice, and maintain at every stage of life. It is helpful for me in this regard to obey God's commandments in all situations, to avoid temptations and any form of double life or → HYPOC-RISY, and to ask God for protection against temptations and to strengthen me in love. Being able to live out a pure and undivided love is ultimately a grace and a wonderful gift of God.

406 Does everybody have to be chaste, even married people?

Yes, every Christian should be loving and chaste, whether he is young or old, lives alone or is married. [2348–2349, 2394]

Not everyone is called to marriage, but everyone is called to love. We are destined to give our lives away; many do so in the form of marriage, others in the form of voluntary celibacy for the sake of the kingdom of heaven, others by living alone and yet being there for others. All human life finds its meaning in love. To be chaste means to *love with an undivided heart*. The unchaste person is torn and not free. Someone who loves authentically is free, strong, and good; he can devote himself in love. Thus Christ, who gave himself up completely for us and at the same time devoted himself completely to his Father in heaven, is a model of → CHASTITY, because he is the original model of strong love.

> I do not know yet whom I will marry. But I do not want to betray my future wife today.
>
> A student, when asked why he had never been in bed with a girlfriend

> Mastery of the moment is mastery over life.
>
> MARIE VON EBNER-ESCHENBACH

> Be sober, be watchful. Your adversary the devil prowls around like a roaring lion, seeking some one to devour.
>
> 1 Pet 5:8

> For this is the will of God, your sanctification: that you abstain from immorality; that each one of you know how to control his own body in holiness and honor, not in the passion of lust like heathens who do not know God.
>
> 1 Thess 4:3–5

407 *Why is the Church against premarital sexual relations?*

Because she would like to protect love. A person can give someone else no greater gift than himself . "I love you" means for both: "I want only you, I want all that you are, and I want to give myself to you forever!" Because that is so, we cannot, even with our bodies, really say "I love you" temporarily or on a trial basis. [2350, 2391]

Many people take their premarital relationships seriously. And yet there are two reservations involved that are incompatible with love: the "exit option" and the fear of a child. Because love is so great, so sacred, and so unique, the Church teaches young people the obligation to wait until they are married before they start to have sexual relations. → 425

408 *How can you live as a young Christian if you are living in a premarital relationship or have already had premarital relations?*

God loves us at every moment, in every "complicated" situation, even in a state of sin. God helps us to seek the whole truth about love and to find ways to live it more and more unambiguously and decisively.

In a conversation with a → PRIEST or a reliable, experienced Christian, young people can look for a way to live out their love with increasing integrity. They will learn that every life is a process and that, whatever has happened, they can make a new beginning with God's help.

409 *Is masturbation an offense against love?*

Masturbation is a grave offense against love, because it makes the excitement of sexual pleasure an end in itself and uncouples it from the holistic unfolding of love between a man and a woman. That is why "sex with yourself" is a contradiction in terms. [2352]

The Church does not demonize masturbation, but she warns against trivializing it. In fact many young people and adults are in danger of becoming isolated in their consumption of lewd pictures, films, and Internet services instead of finding love in a personal relationship. Loneliness can lead to a blind alley in which masturbation becomes an addiction. Living by the motto "For sex I do not need anyone; I will have it myself, however and whenever I need it" makes nobody happy.

→ now will make it easier for you later to show loving consideration for your future spouse.

POPE JOHN PAUL II (1920–2005), September 8, 1985 in Vaduz, Liechtenstein, to young people

410 What is meant by "fornication"?

Fornication (from Greek *porneia*) originally meant pagan sexual practice, for instance, temple prostitution. Later the term was applied to all forms of sexual activity outside of marriage. Today in English it generally refers to consensual sexual relations between an unmarried man and an unmarried woman. [2353]

Fornication is often based on seduction, lies, violence, dependency, and abuse. Fornication is therefore a serious offense against charity; it harms the dignity of the person and fails to recognize the meaning of human sexuality. Civil authorities have the duty to protect minors especially from fornication.

411 Why is prostitution a form of fornication?

In prostitution "love" becomes a commodity and the person is degraded to an object of pleasure. That is why prostitution is a serious offense against human dignity and a serious sin against charity. [2355]

Certainly those who profit from prostitution—human traffickers, pimps, clients—burden themselves with greater guilt than the women, men, children, and young people who sell their bodies, often under duress or in situations of dependence.

MASTURBATION (etymologically probably from the Latin prefix mas- = masculine and turbare = to move vehemently, to disturb). By masturbation is meant the deliberate stimulation of the genital organs in order to derive sexual pleasure.

To form an equitable judgment about the subjects' moral responsibility [with regard to masturbation] and to guide pastoral action, one must take into account the affective immaturity, force of acquired habit, conditions of anxiety, or other psychological or social factors that lessen, if not even reduce to a minimum, moral culpability.

CCC 2352

412 *Why is the production and consumption of pornography a sin against charity?*

Someone who misuses love by detaching human sexuality from the intimacy of a committed, loving relationship between two spouses and turns it into commercial goods sins seriously. Anyone who produces, buys, or consumes pornographic materials violates human dignity and seduces others to sin. [2523]

Pornography is a degenerate form of prostitution, for here too there is the suggestion that man can get "love" for money. Models and actors, producers and distributors are equally involved in this serious offense against charity and human dignity. Anyone who consumes pornographic materials, visits pornographic websites, or participates in pornographic events finds himself in the wider circle of prostitution and supports the dirty, billion-dollar business of selling sex.

413 *Why is rape a serious sin?*

Someone who rapes another person thoroughly and completely debases that person. He violently breaks into the deepest intimacy of another and wounds the victim at the core of his ability to love. [2356]

The rapist commits an outrage against *the very nature of love*. An essential part of sexual union is the fact that it is a gift that can only be given freely within the context of love. And so it is possible for rape to occur even within a marriage. The most despicable is rape within social, hierarchical, professional, or familial relationships of dependence, for instance, between parents and children or between teachers, educators, pastors, and those who are entrusted to their protection. → 386

414 *What does the Church say about using condoms to fight AIDS?*

Apart from the fact that condoms provide no absolutely safe protection against contagion, the Church rejects their use as a one-sided, mechanical method of fighting AIDS epidemics and advocates above all a new culture of human relationships and a change in social consciousness.

Only practicing fidelity and refraining from casual sexual contacts can provide lasting protection from AIDS and teach a holistic approach to love. Respect for the equal dignity of women and men, concern about the health of the family, responsibility in dealing with one's urges and desires, and also refraining (at appropriate times) from sexual union are all part of it. In the countries of Africa where societal campaigns have promoted such behavior, the rates of infection have decreased significantly. Besides that the Catholic Church does all she can to help people who are afflicted with AIDS.

415 *What is the Church's judgment on homosexuality?*

God created man as male and female and destined them for each other in a bodily way as well. The Church accepts without reservation those who experience homosexual feelings. They (persons who experience homosexual feelings) should not be unjustly discriminated against because of that. At the same time, the Church declares that all homosexual relations in any form are contrary to the order of creation. [2358–2359] → 65

> Those who remain silent are responsible.

ST. EDITH STEIN
(1891–1942, Jewish-Christian, philosopher and Carmelite, killed at Auschwitz)

> Blessed are the meek.

Mt 5:5

> Fidelity within marriage and abstinence outside it are the best ways to avoid infection and to halt the spread of the virus. Indeed, the values that flow from an authentic understanding of marriage and family life constitute the only sure foundation for a stable society.

POPE BENEDICT XVI,
December 14, 2006

Set me as a seal upon your heart, as a seal upon your arm; for love is strong as death, jealousy is cruel as the grave.
Its flashes are flashes of fire, a most vehement flame.
Many waters cannot quench love, neither can floods drown it.
If a man offered for love all the wealth of his house, it would be utterly scorned.

Song 8:6–7

416 What are the essential elements of Christian marriage?

(1) *Unity:* Marriage is a covenant that by its very nature brings about bodily, intellectual, and spiritual union between a man and a woman;
(2) *Indissolubility:* Marriage lasts "until death do us part";
(3) *Openness to offspring:* Every marriage must be open to children;
**(4) *Commitment to the spouse's welfare.*
[2360–2361, 2397–2398]**

If one of the two spouses deliberately excludes one of the four points listed above at the time of their wedding, the → SACRAMENT of Matrimony does not take place. → 64, 400

417 What significance does the sexual encounter have within marriage?

According to God's will, husband and wife should encounter each other in bodily union so as to be united ever more deeply with one another in love and to allow children to proceed from their love. [2362–2367]

In Christianity, the body, pleasure, and erotic joy enjoy a high status: "Christianity ... believes that matter is good, that God Himself once took on a human body, that some kind of body is going to be given to us even in Heaven and is going to be an essential part of our happiness, our beauty and our energy. Christianity has glorified marriage more than any other → RELIGION: and nearly all the greatest love poetry in the world has been produced by Christians. If anyone says that sex, in itself, is bad, Christianity contradicts him at once" (C. S. Lewis). Pleasure, of course, is not an end in itself. When the pleasure of a couple becomes self-enclosed and is not open to the new life that could result from it, it no longer corresponds to the nature of love.

Today, the need to avoid confusing marriage with other types of unions based on weak love is especially urgent. It is only the rock of total, irrevocable love between a man and a woman that can serve as the foundation on which to build a society that will become a home for all mankind.

POPE BENEDICT XVI,
May 11, 2006

" 'For this reason a man shall leave his father and mother and be joined to his wife, and the two shall become one [flesh].' So they are no longer two but one. What therefore God has joined together, let no man put asunder."

Mt 19:5–6 (citing Gen 2:24)

For everything created by God is good, and nothing is to be rejected if it is received with thanksgiving.

1 Tim 4:4

RESPONSIBLE PARENTHOOD
The Church affirms and defends a married couple's right, within the context of natural family planning, to determine by themselves the number of their children and the distance between the births.

418 *What is the significance of the child in a marriage?*

A child is a creature and a gift of God, which comes to earth through the love of his parents.
[2378, 2398]

True love does not desire a couple to be self-contained. Love opens up in the child. A child that has been conceived and born is not something "made", nor is he the sum of his paternal and maternal genes. He is a completely new and unique creature of God, equipped with his own soul. The child therefore does not belong to the parents and is not their property. → 368, 372

419 *How many children should a Christian married couple have?*

A Christian married couple has as many children as God gives them and as they can take responsibility for. [2373]

All children whom God sends are a grace and a great → BLESSING. That does not mean that a Christian couple is not supposed to consider how many children they can raise responsibly, given the health of each spouse and their economic or social situation. When a child comes "nevertheless", that child should be welcomed with joy and willingness and accepted with great love. By trusting in God, many Christian couples find the courage to have a large family.

420 *May a Christian married couple regulate the number of children they have?*

Yes, a Christian married couple may and should be responsible in using the gift and privilege of transmitting life. [2368–2369, 2399]

Sometimes social, psychological, and medical conditions are such that in the given circumstances an additional child would be a big, almost superhuman challenge for the couple. Hence there are clear criteria that the married couple must observe: Regulating births, in the first place, must not mean that the couple is avoiding conception as a matter of principle. Second, it must not mean avoiding children for selfish reasons. Third, it must not mean that external coercion is involved (if, for example, the State were to decide how many children a couple could have). Fourth, it must not mean that any and every means may be used.

421 Why are all methods of preventing the conception of a child not equally good?

The Church recommends the refined methods of self-observation and natural family planning (NFP) as methods of deliberately regulating conception. These are in keeping with the dignity of man and woman; they respect the innate laws of the female body; they demand mutual affection and consideration and therefore are a school of love. [2370–2372, 2399]

The Church pays careful attention to the order of nature and sees in it a deep meaning. For her it is therefore not a matter of indifference whether a couple manipulates the woman's fertility or instead makes use of the natural alternation of fertile and infertile days. It is no accident that → NATURAL FAMILY PLANNING is called natural: it is ecological, holistic, healthy, and an exercise in partnership. On the other hand, the Church rejects all artificial means of contraception—namely, chemical methods ("the Pill"), mechanical methods (for example, condom, intra-uterine device, or IUD), and surgical methods (sterilization)—since these attempt to separate the sexual act from its procreative potential and block the total self-giving of husband and wife. Such methods can even endanger the woman's health, have an abortifacient effect (= cause a very early abortion), and in the long run be detrimental to the couple's love life.

422 What can a childless couple do?

Married couples who suffer from infertility can accept any medical assistance that does not contradict the dignity of the human person, the rights of the child to be conceived, and the → HOLINESS of the → SACRAMENT of Matrimony. [2375, 2379]

? NATURAL FAMILY PLANNING (NFP)
A general term for methods of regulating conception that use the signs of the woman's fertility cycle and knowledge about the fertility of the man and woman together so as to achieve or avoid pregnancy.

" Pope John Paul II describes "contraception" (as opposed to "the regulation of births") as follows: "When couples [have] recourse to contraception ... they manipulate and degrade human sexuality—and with it themselves and their married partner—by altering its value of total self-giving. Thus the innate language that expresses the total reciprocal self-giving of husband and wife is overlaid, through contraception, by an objectively contradictory language, namely, →

There is no absolute right to have a child. Every child is a gift from God. Married couples to whom this gift has been denied, even though they have exhausted all permissible medical means of assistance, can take in foster children or adopt children or become socially involved in some other way, for instance, by caring for abandoned children.

423 What is the Church's judgment on surrogate motherhood and artificial fertilization?

All assistance in conceiving a child through research and medicine must stop when the common bond of parenthood is loosened and destroyed by the intrusion of a third person or when conception becomes a technological act outside of sexual union in marriage. [2374–2377]

Out of respect for human dignity, the Church cannot approve of the technologically assisted conception of a child through artificial insemination or fertilization. Every child has in God's plan the right to have a father and a mother, to know his parents, and if at all possible to grow up surrounded by their love. Artificial insemination and fertilization with the sperm of another man or the ovum of another woman (heterologous artificial insemination and fertilization) also destroys the spirit of marriage, in which husband and wife have the right to become a father or a mother only through the other spouse. But even homologous artificial insemination and fertilization (in which the sperm and the ovum come from the spouses) make a child the product of a technological procedure and does not allow it to originate from the loving union of a personal sexual encounter. If the child becomes a product, however, then that leads immediately to cynical questions about product quality and product liability. The Church also rejects pre-implantation diagnosis, which is carried out for the purpose of killing imperfect embryos. Surrogate motherhood, too, in which an artificially conceived embryo is implanted into another woman, is contrary to human dignity.

→ 280

424 What is adultery? Is divorce the appropriate response?

Adultery is committed when two people, at least one of whom is married to someone else, have sexual relations. Adultery is the fundamental betrayal of love, the violation of a covenant that was made in God's sight, and an injustice to one's neighbor. Jesus himself explicitly declared the indissolubility of marriage: "What therefore God has joined together, let not man put asunder" (Mk 10:9). Citing the original will of the Creator, Jesus abolished the toleration of divorce in the Old Covenant. [2353, 2364–2365, 2382–2384]

The encouraging promise of this message of Jesus is, "as children of your heavenly Father you are capable of lifelong love." Nevertheless, it is not easy to remain faithful to one's spouse for a lifetime. We must not condemn people whose marriages fail. Nevertheless, Christians who irresponsibly bring about divorce incur guilt. They sin against God's love, which is visible in marriage. They sin against the abandoned spouse and against abandoned children. Of course the faithful partner in a marriage that has become unbearable can move out of shared living accommodations. In some serious circumstances, it may be necessary to go through a civil divorce. In well-founded cases the Church can examine the validity of the marriage in an annulment proceeding. → 269

425 What does the Church have against "marriage without the certificate"?

For Catholics there is no marriage without a church wedding. In that ceremony Christ enters into a covenant with the husband and the wife and generously endows the couple with graces and gifts. [2390–2391]

Older individuals sometimes think they should advise young people to have nothing to do with ceremonies with vows. In their opinion, a marriage is just a rash attempt to combine incomes, perspectives, and good

" Fidelity is absolute anywhere at all or else it does not exist.

KARL JASPERS
(1883-1969, German philosopher)

" The root of the crisis of marriage and family lies in a false notion of freedom.

POPE JOHN PAUL II
(1920–2005)

" A ratified and consummated marriage between baptised persons cannot be dissolved by any human power or for any reason other than death.

CIC 1141 (Codex Iuris Canonici, Code of Canon Law of the Catholic Church)

Let what you say be simply ‚Yes' or ‚No'; anything more than this comes from the Evil One.

Mt 5:37

intentions while at the same time publicly making promises that cannot be kept. A Christian marriage is not a game, however, but rather the greatest gift God has devised for a man and a woman who love each other. God himself unites them at a depth that man could not achieve. Jesus Christ, who said, "Apart from me you can do nothing" (Jn 15:5), is present in a lasting way in the → SACRAMENT of Matrimony. He is the love in the love of the spouses. His strength is still there, even when the strength of the lovers seems to dry up. That is why the sacrament of Matrimony is anything but a piece of paper. It is like a divine and seaworthy vessel that the loving couple can board—a ship that the bride and groom know carries enough fuel to bring them with God's help to their longed-for destination. Whereas today many people say that there is nothing wrong with uncommitted premarital sex or extramarital relations, the Church invites us to resist this societal pressure clearly and forcefully.

> " I take you to be my wife/husband. I promise to be true to you in good times and in bad, in sickness and in health. I will love you and honor you all the days of my life.
>
> Vow formula in the sacrament of Matrimony

> " To have and not to give is in some cases worse than stealing.
>
> MARIE VON EBNER-ESCHENBACH
> (1830-1916, Austrian writer)

> " Though he was rich, yet for your sake he became poor, so that by his poverty you might become rich.
>
> 2 Cor 8:9

 THE SEVENTH COMMANDMENT:
You shall not steal.

426 *What is regulated by the Seventh Commandment: "You shall not steal" (Ex 20:15)?*

The Seventh Commandment not only forbids taking something away from another person, it also requires the just management and distribution of the earth's goods; it regulates the question of private property and the distribution of the proceeds from human work. The unjust distribution of raw materials is also indicted in this commandment. [2401]

In the first place, the Seventh Commandment actually forbids only taking someone else's property unlawfully. However, it also addresses the human endeavor to make just social arrangements in the world and to plan for its beneficial development. The Seventh Commandment says that we are obliged in faith to advocate the protection of the environment as part of creation and to conserve the earth's natural resources.

427 Why is there no absolute right to private property?

There is no absolute but only a relative right to private property because God created the earth and its goods for all mankind. [2402–2406, 2452]

Before parts of created reality can "belong" to individuals, because they have been obtained legally, inherited, or received as gifts, these owners must know that there is no property without social obligation. At the same time, the Church contradicts those who conclude from the social obligation associated with property that there should be no private property and that everything should belong to everybody, or to the State. The private owner who manages, tends, and increases a plot of land in keeping with the Creator's plan and divides the proceeds in such a way that each person gets what is his due is by all means acting according to the divine commission for creation.

428 What is theft, and what falls under the Seventh Commandment?

Theft is the unlawful appropriation of goods belonging to another. [2408–2409]

Appropriating someone else's goods unjustly is a sin against the Seventh Commandment even if the act cannot be indicted under civil law. What is unjust in God's sight is unjust. The Seventh Commandment, of course, applies not only to stealing, but also to the unfair withholding of a just wage, the keeping of found items that one could give back, and defrauding in general. The Seventh Commandment also pertains to the following: setting employees to work in inhumane conditions, not abiding by contracts into which one has entered, wasting profits without any consideration for social obligations, artificially driving prices up or down, endangering the jobs of colleagues for whom one is responsible, bribery and corruption, misleading dependent coworkers into illegal actions, doing shoddy work or demanding inappropriate remuneration, wasting or negligently managing public property, counterfeiting or falsifying accounting records, or tax evasion.

> The right to private property is not absolute and unconditional.
>
> PAUL VI,
> *Populorum progressio*

> When there is no property, there is no joy in giving, either; then no one can have the pleasure of helping his friends, the traveler, or the afflicted in their need.
>
> ARISTOTLE
> (382–322 b.c.)

In his social encyclical *Populorum progressio* (PP), Pope Paul VI established the central principle that "programs designed to increase productivity should have but one aim: to serve human nature" (PP 34). He rejects all notions of "profit as the chief spur to economic progress, free competition as the guiding norm of economics, and private ownership of the means of production as an absolute right, having no limits or concomitant social obligations."

PLAGIARISM
(from Latin *plagiarius* = kidnapper). Plagiarism is the unauthorized and concealed appropriation of someone else's intellectual property, which is made out to be one's own intellectual achievement.

Jesus praises the promise made by the tax collector Zacchaeus: "If I have defrauded any one of anything, I restore it fourfold" (Lk 19:8).

He who loves money will not be satisfied with money.

Eccles 5:10

429 *What rules apply to intellectual property?*

The misappropriation of intellectual property is theft also. [2408–2409]

Not just → PLAGIARISM is theft. The theft of intellectual property begins with copying other students' work in school, continues in the illegal taking of materials from the Internet, applies to the making of unauthorized copies or trafficking in pirated copies in various media, and extends to business dealings in stolen concepts and ideas. Every acquisition of someone else's intellectual property demands the free consent and appropriate remuneration of the author or inventor.

430 *What is meant by commutative justice?*

Commutative **justice regulates exchanges between persons in accordance with a strict respect for their rights. It makes sure that property rights are safeguarded, debts repaid, and freely contracted obligations are fulfilled, that reparation is made for injustice or damage, and that stolen goods are returned. [2411–2412]**

431 *Is it permissible to use tax dodges?*

Inventiveness in dealing with complex systems of taxation is morally unobjectionable. It is immoral to evade taxes or to commit tax fraud, in other words, to falsify, fail to report, or conceal facts so as to prevent a correct assessment of taxes due. [2409]

By paying taxes, citizens contribute, each according to his ability, so that the State can fulfill its duties. Therefore tax evasion is not a petty infraction. Taxes should be just and proportionate and should be levied by law.

432 *May a Christian speculate in the stock market or in Internet stocks?*

A Christian can speculate in the stock market or in Internet stocks, as long as he does so within the pa-

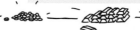

rameters of normal business practices for prudently investing one's own or someone else's money and does not thereby break any other commandments.

Speculating in stocks becomes immoral when dishonest means are used (for instance, insider information); when the transaction puts one's own or another's life savings at risk instead of insuring an income; when such speculation becomes an addiction, as with games of chance.

433 How should we treat property that belongs to everyone?

Vandalism and deliberately damaging public facilities and common property are forms of theft, and restitution must be made. [2409]

434 May a Christian make bets and play games of chance?

Betting and gambling are immoral and dangerous when the gambler risks his livelihood. It becomes even worse if he risks the livelihood of other people, especially of those who are entrusted to his care. [2413]

Morally speaking, it is a highly dubious practice to wager large sums on a game of chance while others lack the bare necessities of life. Betting and gambling, furthermore, can be addictive and enslave people.

435 Is it permissible to "buy" and "sell" human beings?

No human being, not even parts of a human being, may be turned into commodities, nor may a person make himself a commodity. Man belongs to God and has been endowed by him with freedom and dignity. Buying and selling people, as is common practice nowadays, and not only in prostitution, is a profoundly reprehensible act. [2414]

His money owns him instead of him owning his money.

ST. CYPRIAN OF CARTHAGE
(200–258, Church Father)

Every time you acquire and use an object, reflect that this is a product of human work and that if you consume, destroy, or damage it, you destroy that work and thus consume human life.

LEO TOLSTOY
(1818-1910, Russian novelist)

Trafficking in organs for transplantation and in embryos for the biotech industry or in children for purposes of adoption, the recruiting of child soldiers, prostitution—the age-old injustice of trafficking in human beings and slavery is reappearing everywhere. People are deprived of their freedom, their dignity, and their right of self-determination, even of their lives. Others reduce them to objects with which their owner can make a profit. Human trafficking in the strict sense should be distinguished from dealings between sports teams. Here, too, there is talk about "buying" and "selling" players, but of course these are transactions that presuppose the athletes' free consent.

→ 280

436 *How should we treat the environment?*

We fulfill God's commission with regard to creation when we care for the earth, with its biological laws, its variety of species, its natural beauty, and its dwindling resources, as a living space and preserve it, so that future generations also can live well on earth. [2415]

In the book of → GENESIS, God says, "Be fruitful and multiply, and fill the earth and subdue it; and have dominion over the fish of the sea and over the birds of the air and over every living thing that moves upon the earth" (Gen 1:28). Having "dominion over the earth" does not mean having an absolute right to dispose arbitrarily of animate and inanimate nature, animals, and plants. Because man is created in God's image, he should care for God's creation as a shepherd and steward. For the first book of the Bible also says, "The Lord God took the man and put him in the garden of Eden to till it and keep it" (Gen 2:15). → 42–50

437 How should we treat animals?

**Animals are our fellow creatures, which we should care for and in which we should delight, just as God delights in their existence.
[2416–2418, 2456–2457]**

Animals, too, are sentient creatures of God. It is a sin to torture them, to allow them to suffer, or to kill them uselessly. Nevertheless, man may not place love of animals above love of man.

438 Why does the Catholic Church have her own social teaching?

Because *all* men, as children of God, possess a unique dignity, the Church with her social teaching is committed to defending and promoting this human dignity for all men in the social sphere. She is not trying to preempt the legitimate freedom of politics or of the economy. When human dignity is violated in politics or economic practices, however, the Church must intervene. [2419–2420, 2422–2423]

"The joy and hope, the grief and anguish of the men of our time, especially of those who are poor or afflicted in any way, are the joy and hope, the grief and anguish of the followers of Christ as well" (Second Vatican Council, GS). In her social teaching, the Church makes this statement specific. And she asks: How can we take responsibility for the well-being and the just treatment of all, even of non-Christians? What is a just organization of human society, of political, economic, and social institutions supposed to look like? In her commitment to justice, the Church is guided by a love that emulates Christ's love for mankind.

439 How did the Church's social teaching develop?

→ CATHOLIC SOCIAL TEACHING was a response to the economic problems of the nineteenth century. Whereas industrialization had led to an increase in prosperity, the ones who profited from it were primarily factory owners, while many people sank into poverty as laborers with practically no

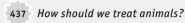 You are rightly committed to protecting the environment, plants, and animals. Say Yes even more decisively to human life, which in the hierarchy of creatures ranks far higher than all other created realities of the visible world.

POPE JOHN PAUL II
(1920–2005), September 8, 1985

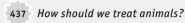 Charity is at the heart of the Church's social doctrine.

POPE BENEDICT XVI,
Encyclical *Caritas in Veritate*
[CiV]

You visit the earth and water it,
you greatly enrich it;
the river of God is full of water;
you provide their grain,
or so you have prepared it.
The pastures of the wilderness drip,
the hills gird themselves with joy,
the meadows clothe themselves with flocks,
the valleys deck themselves with grain,
they shout and sing together for joy.

Ps 65:9, 12–13

rights. From this experience Communism drew the conclusion that there was an irreconcilable opposition between *labor* and *capital,* which must be decided by class war. The Church, in contrast, advocated a just balance between the interests of the laborers and those of the factory owners. [2421]

The Church recommended that not only a few but everyone should benefit from the prosperity recently made possible by industrialization and competition. She therefore supported the development of labor unions and advocated protecting laborers from exploitation through legislation and government assurances and insuring them and their families against sickness and emergencies.

440 Are Christians obliged to become involved in politics and society?

It is a special duty of the Christian → LAITY people to become involved in politics, society, and commerce in the spirit of the Gospel: in charity, truth, and justice. → CATHOLIC SOCIAL TEACHING offers them clear guidance in this endeavor. [2442]

Partisan political activity is, however, incompatible with the ministry of bishops, → PRIESTS, and religious, who must be of service to everyone.

441 What does the Church say about democracy?

The Church supports democracy, because of all political systems it offers the best conditions for achieving equality before the law and safeguarding human rights. In order to do that, however, democracy must be more than mere majority rule. True democracy is possible only in a State ruled by law that recognizes the fundamental God given rights of all and defends them, if necessary, even against the will of the majority. [1922]

History teaches that even democracy offers no absolute protection from violations of human dignity and human rights. It always runs the risk of becoming a tyranny of the majority over a minority. Democracy depends on preconditions that it cannot guarantee in and of itself. That is why Christians in particular must make sure that the values indispensable to a democracy are not undermined.

442 What is the Church's stance on capitalism or the free-market economy?

Any form of capitalism that is not embedded in an established system of law runs the risk of detaching itself from the → COMMON GOOD and becoming a mere means for individuals to make profits. The Church rejects that decisively. On the other hand, she supports a free-market system which is at the service of man, prevents monopolies, and ensures that all are supplied with employment and vitally necessary goods. [2426]

→ CATHOLIC SOCIAL TEACHING evaluates all societal arrangements according to whether they serve the common good (→ COMMON GOOD), which means: to the extent that they enable "men, families, and associations more adequately and readily [to] attain their own perfection" (Second Vatican Council, GS). This is also true of commerce, which in the first place should be at the service of man.

443 What is the duty of managers and entrepreneurs?

Entrepreneurs and managers are concerned about the commercial success of their company. Besides their legitimate interests (including the profit motive), they also have a social responsibility to take into account the just concerns of their employees, suppliers, and customers, as well as of society as a whole, and also to be considerate of the environment. [2432]

444 What does the Church's social doctrine say about the topics of labor and unemployment?

To work is a duty that God has given to us. In a common effort we are supposed to look after and

> A democracy without values easily turns into open or thinly disguised totalitarianism.

POPE JOHN PAUL II, (1920–2005), Encyclical *Centesimus annus*

> Capitalism without humanity, solidarity, and justice has no morals and no future either.

REINHARD CARDINAL MARX (b. 1953; Archbishop of Munich and Freising)

> Locating resources, financing, production, consumption, and all the other phases in the economic cycle inevitably have moral implications. Thus every economic decision has a moral consequence.

POPE BENEDICT XVI, CiV

continue his work of creation. "The Lord God took the man and put him in the garden of Eden to till it and keep it" (Gen 2:15). For most people, work is the foundation of life. Unemployment is a serious misfortune that must be dealt with resolutely.

While today many people who would like to work find no jobs, there are also "workaholics" who work so much that they have no time left for God and their fellowmen. And while many people can scarcely feed themselves and their families with their wages, others earn so much that they can live a life of unimaginable luxury. Work is not an end in itself but should serve the development of a humane society. That is why → CATHOLIC SOCIAL TEACHING is committed to an economic order in which all men can collaborate actively and share in the prosperity that is achieved. It insists on a just wage that enables all to have a dignified existence, and it calls on the rich to practice the virtues of moderation, solidarity, and sharing. → 47, 332

445 *What is meant by the principle "labor before capital"?*

The Church has always taught "the principle of the priority of labor over capital" (Pope John Paul II, LE). Man owns money or capital as a thing. Labor,

in contrast, is inseparable from the person who performs it. That is why the basic needs of laborers have priority over the interests of capital.

The owners of capital and investors have legitimate interests, too, which must be protected. It is a serious injustice, however, when entrepreneurs and investors try to increase their own profits at the expense of the basic rights of their laborers and employees.

446 *What does the Church say about globalization?*

Globalization is in itself neither good nor bad; it is, rather, the description of a reality that must be shaped. "Originating within economically developed countries, this process by its nature has spread to include all economies. It has been the principal driving force behind the emergence from underdevelopment of whole regions, and in itself it represents a great opportunity. Nevertheless, without the guidance of charity in truth, this global force could cause unprecedented damage and create new divisions within the human family" (Pope Benedict XVI, CiV).

When we buy inexpensive jeans, we should not be indifferent to the conditions in which they were manufactured, to the question of whether or not the workers received a just wage. Everyone's fortune matters. No one's poverty should leave us indifferent. On the political level, there is a need for "a true world political authority" (Pope Benedict XVI, CiV [citing Bl. John XXIII, Encyclical *Pacem in terris*]) to help reach a compromise between the people in the rich nations and those in underdeveloped countries. Far too often the latter are still excluded from the advantages of economic globalization and have only burdens to bear.

447 *Is globalization exclusively a matter of politics and economics?*

There used to be the idea of a division of labor: economics should be concerned about increasing wealth, and politics should be concerned about distributing it justly. In the age of globalization, however, profits are obtained globally, while politics to a great extent

> Everything contained in the concept of capital in the strict sense is only a collection of things. Man, as the subject of work, and independently of the work that he does—man alone is a person.
>
> POPE JOHN PAUL II (1920–2005), LE

> It is disturbing to witness a globalization that exacerbates the conditions of the needy, that does not sufficiently contribute to resolving situations of hunger, poverty, and social inequality, that fails to safeguard the natural environment. These aspects of globalization can give rise to extreme reactions, leading to excessive nationalism, religious fanaticism, and even acts of terrorism.
>
> POPE JOHN PAUL II, (1920–2005), 2003

> As society becomes ever more globalized, it makes us neighbors but does not make us brothers. Reason, by itself, is capable of grasping the equality between men and of giving stability to their civic coexistence, but it cannot establish fraternity.

POPE BENEDICT XVI, CiV

> The economy in the global era seems to privilege the former logic, that of contractual exchange, but directly or indirectly it also demonstrates its need for the other two: political logic and the logic of the unconditional gift.

POPE BENEDICT XVI, CiV

> "Economy of Communion" was developed so that one day we will be able to give this example: a people in which no one is needy and no one is poor.

CHIARA LUBICH
(1920–2008; foundress of the Focolare Movement), 2001

is still limited within national boundaries. Therefore, what is needed today is not just the strengthening of transnational political institutions, but also the initiatives of individuals and social groups that are active economically in the poorer regions of the world, not primarily for the sake of profit, but rather out of a spirit of solidarity and love. The market and the State are necessary, but so is a strong civil society.

In a market, products and services are exchanged for goods having the same value. In many regions of this world, however, the people are so poor that they cannot offer anything in exchange and therefore continue to be left behind. So there is a need for economic initiatives that are defined, not by the "logic of exchange", but rather by the "logic of the unconditional gift" (Pope Benedict XVI, CiV). This means, not merely giving alms to the poor, but rather helping them to help themselves by opening up paths to economic freedom. There are Christian initiatives, for instance the "Economy of Communion" project of the Focolare Movement, which today involves more than 750 businesses worldwide. There are also non-Christian social entrepreneurs who, though profit-oriented, nevertheless work in the spirit of a "culture of giving" with the goal of alleviating poverty and marginalization.

448 *Are poverty and underdevelopment an inescapable fate?*

God has entrusted to us a rich earth that could offer all men sufficient food and living space. Yet there are whole regions, countries, and continents in which many people have scarcely the bare necessities for living. There are complex historical causes for this division in the world, but it is not irreformable. The rich countries have the moral obligation to help the underdeveloped nations out of poverty through developmental aid and the establishment of just economic and commercial conditions.

There are more than a billion people living on this earth who must make do with less than one dollar per day. They suffer from a lack of food and clean drinking water; most of them have no access to education or medical care. It is estimated that more than 25,000 people die every day from malnutrition. Many of them are children.

449 *What significance do the poor have for Christians?*

Love for the poor must be in every age the distinguishing mark of Christians. The poor deserve not just a few alms; they have a claim to justice. For Christians there is a special obligation to share their goods. Our example in love for the poor is Christ. [2443–2446] → 427

"Blessed are the poor in spirit, for theirs is the kingdom of heaven" (Mt 5:3)—that is the first sentence in Jesus' Sermon on the Mount. There is material, emotional,

> The hungry nations of the world cry out to the peoples blessed with abundance. And the Church, cut to the quick by this cry, asks each and every man to hear his brother's plea and answer it lovingly.
>
> PAUL VI, (1897–1978), Encyclical *Populorum progressio*

intellectual, and spiritual poverty. Christians must look after the needy of this earth with great consideration, love, and perseverance. After all, on no other point will they be evaluated by Christ so decisively as on their way of treating the poor: "As you did it to one of the least of these my brethren, you did it to me" (Mt 25:40). → 427

450 *What are the "corporal works of mercy"?*

To feed the hungry, give drink to the thirsty, clothe the naked, shelter the homeless, visit the sick and the imprisoned, and bury the dead.

451 *What are the "spiritual works of mercy"?*

The spiritual works of mercy are: to instruct the ignorant, to counsel the doubtful, comfort the sorrowful, admonish the sinner, bear wrongs patiently, forgive all injuries, and pray for the living and the dead.

THE EIGHTH COMMANDMENT:
You shall not bear false witness against your neighbor.

452 *What does the Eighth Commandment require of us?*

The Eighth Commandment teaches us not to lie. Lying means consciously and intentionally speaking or acting against the truth. Someone who lies deceives himself and misleads others who have a right to know the full truth of a matter.
[2464, 2467–2468, 2483, 2485–2486]

Every lie is an offense against justice and charity. Lying is a form of violence; it introduces the seed of division into a community and undermines the trust on which every human community is based.

453 *What does our relationship to the truth have to do with God?*

Living in respect for the truth means not only being true to oneself. More precisely it means being truthful, being true to God, for he is the source of all truth. We find the truth about God and about all of reality quite directly in Jesus, who is "the way, and the truth, and the life" (Jn 14:6).
[2465–2470, 2505]

Someone who really follows Jesus brings greater and greater truthfulness into his life. He eliminates all lies, falsehood, pretense, and ambiguity from his accomplishments in life and becomes transparent toward the truth. To believe means to become a witness to the truth.

454 *How strongly obligatory is the truth of the faith?*

Every Christian must give testimony to the truth and thereby follow after Christ, who before Pilate said, "For this I was born, and for this I have come into the world, to bear witness to the truth" (Jn 18:37).
[2472–2474]

You shall not bear false witness against your neighbor.

Ex 20:16

❝❞ Misusing words means despising people.

DAG HAMMARSKJÖLD
(1905–1961, Swedish U.N. General Secretary, mystic)

❝❞ I have only one vice: I lie.

A telling witticism

❝❞ Truth in this time is so obscured and lies so widespread that one cannot recognize the truth unless one loves it.

BLAISE PASCAL
(1588–1651)

❝❞ Indeed, Jesus Christ is the Personified Truth who attracts the world to himself. The truth radiating from Jesus is the splendor of truth. Every other truth is a fragment of the Truth that he is, and refers to him.

POPE BENEDICT XVI,
February 10, 2006

> Live in such a
way that you can die
tomorrow as a martyr.

CHARLES DE FOUCAULD
(he himself suffered
martyrdom in 1916)

MARTYR
(from Greek *martyr-ia* = witness, testimony):
A Christian martyr is a person who is ready to suffer violence or even to be killed for Christ, who is the truth, or for a con-scientious decision made on the basis of faith. This is precisely the opposite of Islamist suicide assas-sins. They do violence to themselves and others out of misinterpreted faith convictions and are therefore honored by radical Islamists as "martyrs".
The deacon Stephen was the first Christian martyr. On account of his commitment to the truth of the Gospel, he was stoned to death outside the gates of the city of Jerusalem between the years A.D. 36 and 40.

This can even mean that a Christian lays down his life out of fidelity to the truth and love for God and mankind. This ultimate form of commitment to the truth is called martyrdom.

455 *What does it mean to be truthful?*

Truthfulness means that one acts sincerely and speaks honestly. The truthful individual guards against double-dealing, misrepresentation, mali-cious deception, and hypocrisy. The worst form of untruthfulness is perjury. [2468, 2476]

A great evil in all communities is slander of other people and malicious gossip: A tells B "confidentially" something derogatory that C said about B.

456 *What should you do if you have lied to, deceived, or betrayed someone?*

Every offense against truth and justice, even if it has been forgiven, demands reparation. [2487]

If one cannot make amends publicly for a lie or false testimony, one must at least do whatever one can secretly. If one cannot compensate the injured party directly for the wrong, one is obliged in conscience to give him moral satisfaction, in other words, one must do his best so as to make at least symbolic reparation.

457 *Why does telling the truth require discretion?*

Communicating truth must be done prudently within the context of charity. Often the truth is wielded as a weapon and thus has a destructive rather than a constructive effect. [2488–2489, 2491]

When conveying information, we should think of the "three sieves" of Socrates: Is it true? Is it kind? Is it helpful? → DISCRETION is called for also in dealing with professional secrets. They should always be kept, ex-cept in special cases defined by strict criteria. Likewise, anyone who publicizes confidential communications that were made under the seal of secrecy commits a sin.

Everything we say must be true, but we need not say everything that is true.

458 *How confidential is the secret of the confessional?*

The secret of the confessional is sacred. It cannot be violated for any reason, however weighty. [2490]

A → PRIEST must not report even the most heinous crime. Not even what might seem like trifles can be revealed by the priest, even under torture. → 238

459 *What ethical responsibilities are connected with the communications media?*

Media producers have a responsibility toward media consumers. Above all they must truthfully inform. In both the gathering and the publication of real news, the rights and dignity of individuals must be observed. [2493–2499]

The means of social communication should contribute to the establishment of justice, freedom, and solidarity in the world. In actual fact, the media are not uncommonly used as weapons in ideological conflict, or else, in a quest for higher ratings, all ethical regulation of

? PERJURY
Perjury is reaffirming a false statement, whereby God is intentionally called to witness an untruth. It is a serious sin.

" Never repeat a rumor before you have verified it. And if it is true, hold your tongue all the more.

SELMA LAGERLÖF
(1858–1940, Swedish writer)

? DISCRETION
(from Latin *discernere* = distinguish): the ability to determine what one can say to whom and when.

the content is abandoned and the media are turned into instruments for seducing people and making them dependent.

? SOCIAL MEANS OF
COMMUNICATION

SOCIAL MEANS OF COMMUNICATION
Those media that are aimed not merely at individuals but at human society as a whole and influence it: the press, film, radio, television, the Internet, and so on.

460 *What dangers result from the media?*

Many people, especially children, think that whatever they see in the media is real. If in the name of entertainment violence is glorified, anti-social behavior is approved of, and human sexuality is trivialized, this is a sin both of those in the media who are responsible and also of those supervisory authorities that ought to put a stop to it.
[2496, 2512]

"Where your treasure is, there will your heart be also."

Mt 6:21

People who work in the media should always be aware of the fact that their productions have an educational effect. Young people must constantly examine themselves to determine whether they are able to use the media freely, with critical distance, or whether they have become addicted to particular media. Every person is responsible for his soul. Those who consume violence, hatred, and pornography in the media become spiritually deadened and do themselves harm.

461 How does art mediate between beauty and truth?

The true and the beautiful belong together, for God is the source of beauty and also the source of truth. Art, which is dedicated to the beautiful, is therefore a special path to the whole and to God. [2500–2503, 2513]

What cannot be said in words or expressed in thought is brought to light in art. It is "a freely given superabundance of the human being's inner riches" (CCC 2501). In a way that closely approximates God's creativity, inspiration and human skill are combined in the artist so as to give a valid form to something new, a previously unseen aspect of reality. Art is not an end in itself. It should uplift people, move them, improve them, and ultimately lead them to worship and thank God.

THE NINTH COMMANDMENT:
You shall not covet
your neighbor's wife.

462 Why does the Ninth Commandment forbid sexual desire?

The Ninth Commandment forbids, not desires per se, but rather disordered desires. The "covetousness" against which Sacred Scripture warns is the rule of impulses over the mind, the dominion of urges over the whole person, and the sinfulness that that causes. [2514, 2515, 2528, 2529]

The erotic attraction between man and woman was created by God and is therefore good; it is part of a person's sexual nature and biological constitution. It ensures that man and woman can unite with one another and descendants can spring from their love. The Ninth Commandment is meant to protect this union. The shelter of marriage and family must not be endangered through playing with fire, in other words, through reckless indulgence in the erotic energy that crackles between man and woman. That is why it is a good rule, especially for Christians: "Keep your hands off married men and women!" → 400–425

The author of beauty created them [the things of this world].

Wis 13:3

From the greatness and beauty of created things comes a corresponding perception of their Creator.

Wis 13:5

For me, perfection in art and in life springs from the biblical source.

MARC CHAGALL
(1887-1985, Russian painter)

Christians think God invented and made the universe—like a man making a picture or composing a tune.

C. S. LEWIS
(1898–1963)

Put to death therefore what is earthly in you: immorality, impurity, passion, evil desire, and covetousness, which is idolatry.

Col 3:5

"Blessed are the pure in heart, for they shall see God."

Mt 5:8

Now the works of the flesh are plain: immorality, impurity, licentiousness, idolatry, sorcery ... I warn you, as I warned you before, that those who do such things shall not inherit the kingdom of God.

Gal 5:19–21

Restore to me the joy of your salvation, and uphold me with a willing spirit. Then I will teach transgressors your ways, and sinners will return to you. Deliver me from bloodguilt, O God, O God of my salvation, and my tongue will sing aloud of your deliverance.

Ps 51:12–14

Act today in such a way that you do not need to blush tomorrow.

ST. JOHN BOSCO
(1815–1888)

Shame exists wherever there is a mystery.

FRIEDRICH NIETZSCHE
(1844–1900, German philosopher)

---

463 *How does one achieve "purity of heart"?*

The purity of heart required for love is achieved in the first place through union with God in prayer. When God's grace touches us, this also produces a path to pure, undivided human love. A chaste person can love with a sincere and undivided heart. [2520, 2532]

When we turn to God with a sincere intention, he transforms our hearts. He gives us the strength to correspond to his will and to reject impure thoughts, fantasies, and desires. → 404–405

464 *What good is shame?*

Shame safeguards a person's intimate space: his mystery, his most personal and inmost being, his dignity, but especially his capacity for love and sexual self-giving. It relates also to that which only love may see. [2521–2525, 2533]

Many young Christians live in an environment where it is taken for granted that everything should be on display and people are systematically trained to ignore feelings of shame. But shamelessness is inhuman. Animals experience no shame. In a human being, in contrast, it is an essential feature. It does not hide something inferior but rather protects something valuable, namely, the dignity of the person in his capacity to love. The feeling of shame is found in all cultures, although it assumes different forms. It has nothing to do with prudery or a repressive upbringing. A person is also ashamed of his sins and other things that would demean him if they were made generally known. Someone who offends another person's natural feeling of shame by words, glances, gestures, or actions robs him of his dignity. → 412-413

You shall not covet your neighbor's house; you shall not covet your neighbor's wife, or his manservant, or his maidservant, or his ox, or his donkey, or anything that is your neighbor's.

Ex 20:17

 "Take heed, and beware of all covetousness; for a man's life does not consist in the abundance of his possessions."

Lk 12,15

As rust consumes iron, so envy consumes the soul that is afflicted by it.

ST. BASIL THE GREAT (ca. 330–379) in his *Rule*

Hate no one. Do not be jealous. Do not act out of envy. Do not love quarreling. Flee arrogance.

ST. BENEDICT OF NURSIA (ca. 480–547) in his *Rule*

THE TENTH COMMANDMENT:
You shall not covet your neighbor's goods.

465 What attitude should a Christian take toward other people's property?

A Christian must learn to distinguish reasonable desires from those that are unreasonable and unjust and to acquire an interior attitude of respect for other people's property. [2534–2537, 2552]

Covetousness leads to greed, avarice, theft, robbery and fraud, violence and injustice, envy and immoderate desires to own what belongs to others.

466 What is envy, and how can you fight against it?

Envy is sadness and annoyance at the sight of another's well-being and the desire to acquire unjustly what others have. Anyone who wishes other people ill commits a sin. Envy decreases when we try to rejoice more and more in the accomplishments and gifts of others, when we believe in God's benevolent providence for ourselves as well, and when we set our hearts on true wealth, which consists of the fact that we already participate in God's life through the Holy Spirit. [2538–2540, 2553–2554]

467 Why does Jesus demand that we practice "poverty in spirit"?

"Though he was rich, yet for your sake he became poor, so that by his poverty you might become rich" (2 Cor 8:9). [2544–2547, 2555–2557]

Young people, too, experience inner emptiness. But experiencing this sort of poverty is not just something bad. I simply have to seek with my whole heart the one who can fill my emptiness and make wealth out of my

> Even God could not do anything for someone who left no room for him. One must be completely empty in order to let him in, so that he may do what he wants.

BL. TERESA OF CALCUTTA
(1910–1997)

 My soul waits for the Lord more than watchmen for the morning.

Ps 130:6

> In Scripture, to see is to possess ... Whoever sees God has obtained all the goods of which he can conceive.

ST. GREGORY OF NYSSA
(353–394, Doctor of the Church)

poverty. That is why Jesus says: "Blessed are the poor in spirit, for theirs is the kingdom of heaven" (Mt 5:3).
→ 283–284

468 *What should a person yearn for most?*

The ultimate and greatest longing of a person can only be for God. To see him, our Creator, Lord, and Redeemer, is unending blessedness.
[2548–2550, 2557] → 285

> God himself will be the goal of our desires; we shall contemplate him without end, love him without surfeit, praise him without weariness.

ST. AUGUSTINE
(354–430)

PART FOUR

How We Should Pray

> For me, prayer is a surge of the heart; it is a simple look turned toward heaven, it is a cry of recognition and of love, embracing both trial and joy.

ST. THÉRÈSE OF LISIEUX
(1873–1897)

> The desire to pray is already a prayer.

GEORGES BERNANOS
(1888-1948, French writer)

> Do what you can, and pray for what you cannot, and so God will grant you the ability to do it.

ST. AUGUSTINE
(354–430)

"They should seek God in the hope that they might feel after him and find him. Yet he is not far from each one of us."

Acts 17:27

⬥ SECTION ONE ⬥
Prayer in Christian life

469 *What is prayer?*

Prayer is turning the heart toward God. When a person prays, he enters into a living relationship with God. [2558–2565]

Prayer is the great gate leading into faith. Someone who prays no longer lives on his own, for himself, and by his own strength. He knows there is a God to whom he can talk. People who pray entrust themselves more and more to God. Even now they seek union with the one whom they will encounter one day face to face. Therefore, the effort to pray daily is part of Christian life. Of course, one cannot learn to pray in the same way one learns a technique. As strange as it sounds, prayer is a gift one obtains through prayer.

⬥ CHAPTER ONE ⬥
How to Pray: The Gift of God's Presence

470 *What prompts a person to pray?*

We pray because we are full of an infinite longing and God has created us men for himself: "Our hearts are restless until they rest in you" (St. Augustine). But we pray also because we need to; Mother Teresa says, "Because I cannot rely on myself, I rely on him, twenty-four hours a day." [2566–2567, 2591]

Often we forget God, run away from him and hide. Whether we avoid thinking about God or deny him—*he* is always there for us. He seeks us before we seek him; he yearns for us, he calls us. You speak with your conscience and suddenly notice that you are speaking with God. You feel lonely, have no one to talk with, and then sense that God is always available to talk. You are in danger and experience that a cry for help is answered by God. Praying is as human as breathing, eating, and loving. Praying purifies. Praying makes it possible to resist temptations. Praying strengthens us in our weakness. Praying removes fear, increases energy, and gives a second wind. Praying makes one happy.

> Praying does not mean listening to yourself speak; praying means calming down and being still and waiting until you hear God.

SØREN KIERKEGAARD
(1813–1855)

> Suddenly I experienced the silence like a presence. At the heart of this silence was the One who is himself silence, peace, and tranquility.

GEORGES BERNANOS
(1888–1948)

471 *Why is Abraham a model of prayer?*

Abraham listened to God. He was willing to set out for wherever God commanded and to do what God willed. By his listening and his readiness to make a new start, he is a model for our prayer.

Not many prayers of Abraham have been handed down. But wherever he went, he set up altars, places of prayer, to God. And so along the journey of his life he had many sorts of experiences with God, including some that tried and unsettled him. When Abraham saw that God was going to destroy the sinful city of Sodom, he pleaded for it. He even wrestled stubbornly with God. His plea for Sodom is the first great intercessory prayer in the history of the People of God.

Contemplata aliis tradere. (To contemplate and to give to others the fruits of contemplation.)

Motto of the Dominican Order

CONTEMPLATION
(from Latin *contemplare* = becoming absorbed in God's presence in prayer.) *Contemplation* (the interior, spiritual life) and *action* (the active life) are two sides of devotion to God. In Christianity the two belong inseparably together.

472 *How did Moses pray?*

From Moses we learn that "praying" means "speaking with God". At the burning bush God entered into a real conversation with Moses and gave him an assignment. Moses raised objections and asked questions. Finally God revealed to him his holy name. Just as Moses then came to trust God and enlisted wholeheartedly in his service, so we too should pray and thus go to God's school. [2574–2577]

The → BIBLE mentions Moses' name 767 times—so central is he as the liberator and lawgiver of the people of Israel. At the same time Moses was also a great intercessor for his people. In prayer he received his commission; from prayer he drew his strength. Moses had an intimate, personal relationship with God: "The

Lord used to speak to Moses face to face, as a man speaks to his friend" (Ex 33:11a). Before Moses acted or instructed the people, he withdrew to the mountain to pray. Thus he is the original example of contemplative prayer.

473 How are the Psalms important for our prayer?

The Psalms, along with the Our Father, are part of the Church's great treasury of prayers. In them the praise of God is sung in an ageless way.

There are 150 Psalms in the → OLD TESTAMENT. They are a collection of songs and prayers, some of them several thousand years old, which are still prayed today in the Church community—in the so-called Liturgy of the Hours. The Psalms are among the most beautiful texts in world literature and move even modern readers immediately by their spiritual power. → 188

474 How did Jesus learn to pray?

Jesus learned to pray in his family and in the synagogue. Yet Jesus broke through the boundaries of traditional prayer. His prayer demonstrates a union with his Father in heaven that is possible only to someone who is the Son of God. [2598–2599]

Jesus, who was God and man at the same time, grew up like other Jewish children of his time amid the rituals and prayer formulas of his people, Israel. Nevertheless, as the story of the twelve-year-old Jesus in the Temple demonstrated (Lk 2:41ff.), there was something in him that could not be learned: an original, profound, and unique union with God, his Father in heaven. Like all other men, Jesus hoped for another world, a hereafter, and prayed to God. At the same time, though, he was also part of that hereafter. This occasion already showed that one day people would pray to Jesus, acknowledge him as God, and ask for his grace.

475 How did Jesus pray?

Jesus' life was one single prayer. At decisive moments (his temptation in the desert, his selection of

The Lord is my shepherd, /
I shall not want;/ he makes me lie down in green pastures. / He leads me beside still waters; / he restores my soul. / He leads me in paths of righteousness for his name's sake. / Even though I walk through the valley of the shadow of death, / I fear no evil; / for you are with me; / your rod and your staff, they comfort me.

Ps 23

"Did you not know that I must be in my Father's house?"

Lk 2:49

"" To pray means to think lovingly about Jesus. Prayer is the soul's attention that is concentrated on Jesus. The more you love Jesus, the better you pray.

BL. CHARLES DE FOUCAULD
(1858–1916)

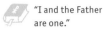 "I and the Father are one."

Jn 10:30

99 Jesus prays Psalm 22, which begins with the words: "My God, my God, why have you forsaken me?" (Ps 22:2). He takes to himself the whole suffering people of Israel, all of suffering humanity, the drama of God's darkness, and he makes God present in the very place where he seems definitively vanquished and absent.

JOSEPH CARDINAL RATZINGER / POPE BENEDICT XVI, Good Friday 2005

"But when you pray, go into your room and shut the door and pray to your Father who is in secret; and your Father who sees in secret will reward you."

Mt 6:6

"Therefore I tell you, whatever you ask in prayer, believe that you receive it, and you will."

Mk 11:24

the apostles, his death on the Cross) his prayer was especially intense. Often he withdrew into solitude to pray, especially at night. Being one with the Father in the Holy Spirit—that was the guiding principle of his earthly life. [2600–2605]

476 *How did Jesus pray as he was facing his death?*

When face to face with death, Jesus experienced the utmost depths of human fear. Yet he found the strength even in that hour to trust his heavenly Father: "Abba, Father, all things are possible to you; remove this chalice from me; yet not what I will, but what you will [be done]" (Mk 14:36). [2605–2606, 2620]

"Times of need teach us to pray." Almost everyone experiences that in his life. How did Jesus pray when he was threatened by death? What guided him in those hours was his absolute willingness to entrust himself to the love and care of his Father. Yet Jesus recited the most unfathomable prayer of all, which he took from the Jewish prayers for the dying: "My God, my God, why have you forsaken me?" (Mk 15:34, citing Ps 22:1). All the despair, all the laments, all the cries of mankind in all times, and yearning for God's helping hand are contained in this word of the Crucified. With the words, "Father, into your hands I commit my spirit" (Lk 23:46), he breathed forth his spirit. In them we hear his boundless trust in his Father, whose power knows the way to conquer death. Thus Jesus' prayer in the midst of dying already anticipates the Easter victory of his Resurrection. → 100

477 *What does it mean to learn from Jesus how to pray?*

Learning from Jesus how to pray means entering into his boundless trust, joining in his prayer, and being led by him, step by step, to the Father. [2607–2614, 2621]

The disciples, who lived in community with Jesus, learned to pray by listening to and imitating Jesus, whose whole life was prayer. Like him, they had to be watchful and strive for purity of heart, to give up everything for the coming of God's kingdom, to forgive their enemies, to trust boldly in God, and to love him above all things. By this example of devotion, Jesus invited his disciples to say to God Almighty, "Abba, dear Father". If we pray in the Spirit of Jesus, especially the Lord's Prayer, we walk in Jesus' shoes and can be sure that we will arrive unfailingly in the heart of the Father. → 495–496, 512

478 Why can we be confident that our prayer is heard by God?

Many people called on Jesus during his earthly life for healing, and their prayers were answered. Jesus, who rose from the dead, listens to our petitions and brings them to the Father. [2615–2616, 2621]

Even today we know the name of the synagogue official: Jairus was the name of the man who begged Jesus for help, and his prayer was answered. His little daughter was deathly ill. No one could help her. Jesus not only healed his little girl, he even raised her from the dead (Mk 5:21–43). Jesus worked a whole series of well-attested cures. He performed signs and miracles. The lame, the lepers, and the blind did not ask Jesus in vain. There are testimonies also of prayers answered by all the saints of the Church. Many Christians can tell stories of how they called to God and God heard their prayer. God, however, is not an automat. We must leave it up to him how he will answer our petitions.
→ 40, 51

479 What can we learn from the way in which Mary prayed?

To learn from Mary how to pray means to join in her prayer: "Let it be to me according to your word" (Lk 1:38). Prayer is ultimately self-giving in response to God's love. If we say Yes as Mary did, God has the opportunity to lead his life in our life. [2617–2618, 2622, 2674] → 84–85, 117

> "There are two parts to a prayer of petition: assurance that the prayer will be heard and absolute renunciation of an answer according to one's own plan.

KARL RAHNER
(1904-1984, German Jesuit and theologian)

> "He [Jesus] prays for us as our priest; he prays in us as our Head; we pray to him as our God. Let us therefore hear our voice in him and his voice in us.

ST. AUGUSTINE
(354–430)

> "If you would really pray to him for conversion, it would be granted to you.

ST. JOHN VIANNEY
(1786–1859)

AVE MARIA
(Latin = Hail, Mary): The first part of the most important and popular prayer after the Our Father is taken from the Bible (Lk 1:28; Lk 1:42). The second part, "...now and at the hour of our death", is an addition from the sixteenth century.

480 *What are the words of the "Hail Mary"?*

Hail, Mary,
full of grace,
the Lord is with you.
Blessed are you among women,
and blessed is the fruit of your womb, Jesus.
Holy Mary, Mother of God, pray for us sinners,
now and at the hour of our death. Amen.

In Latin:
Ave Maria, gratia plena.
Dominus tecum.
Benedicta tu in mulieribus,
et benedictus fructus ventris tui, Jesus.
Sancta Maria, Mater Dei,
ora pro nobis peccatoribus,
nunc et in hora mortis nostrae. Amen.

481 How do you pray the Rosary?

1. In the name of the Father ...
2. Apostles' Creed (see → 28)
3. Our Father
4. Three Hail Marys
5. "Glory be to the Father, and to the Son, and to the Holy Spirit, as it was in the beginning, is now and ever shall be, world without end. Amen."
6. Five decades, each with one Our Father, ten Hail Marys, and a Glory Be to the Father.

The complete Rosary consists of Joyful, Luminous, Sorrowful, and Glorious Mysteries.

The Joyful Mysteries (Monday, Saturday)
The Annunciation
The Visitation
The Nativity
The Presentation of the Child Jesus in the Temple
The Finding of the Child Jesus in the Temple

The Luminous Mysteries (Thursday)
The Baptism in the Jordan
The Wedding Feast at Cana
The Proclamation of the Kingdom of God and Repentance for Sin
The Transfiguration
The Institution of the Holy Eucharist

The Sorrowful Mysteries (Tuesday, Friday)
The Agony in the Garden
The Scourging at the Pillar
The Crowning with Thorns
The Carrying of the Cross
The Crucifixion

The Glorious Mysteries (Wednesday, Sunday)
The Resurrection
The Ascension
The Descent of the Holy Spirit
The Assumption of the Blessed Virgin Mary
The Crowning of the Blessed Virgin Mary as Queen of Heaven

99 The Rosary is my favorite prayer. A marvelous prayer! Marvelous in its simplicity and its depth ... Against the background of the words *Ave Maria* the principal events of the life of Jesus Christ pass before the eyes of the soul ... At the same time our heart can embrace in the decades of the Rosary all the events that make up the lives of individuals, families, nations, the Church, and all mankind: our personal concerns and those of our neighbor, especially those who are closest to us, who are dearest to us. Thus the simple prayer of the Rosary marks the rhythm of human life.

POPE JOHN PAUL II
(1920–2005), October 29, 1978

ROSARY

The name of a set of prayer beads and the name of a devotional prayer that originated in the twelfth century, particularly among the Cistercian and Carthusian monks, whose lay brothers did not participate in the Liturgy of the Hours and had in the Rosary their own form of prayer (the "Marian Psalter"). Later the Rosary was promoted by other religious orders, especially by the Dominicans. The Popes have recommended this prayer again and again, and for many people it is a beloved devotion.

Prayer in my opinion is nothing else than a close sharing between friends; it means taking time frequently to be alone with him who we know loves us.

ST. TERESA OF AVILA
(1515–1582)

Worship ... is not a luxury, but a priority. To seek Jesus must be the constant desire of believers, young people and adults, of the faithful and of their pastors.

POPE BENEDICT XVI,
August 28, 2005

482 What role did prayer play among the first Christians?

The first Christians prayed intensively. The early Church was moved by the Holy Spirit, who had come down upon the disciples and to whom they owed all their influence. "They held steadfastly to the apostles' teaching and fellowship, to the breaking of the bread and to the prayers" (Acts 2:42).

483 What are the names of the five main types of prayer?

The five main types of prayer are → BLESSING and adoration, prayer of petition, prayer of intercession, prayer of thanksgiving, and prayer of praise. [2626–2643]

484 What is a prayer of blessing?

A prayer of blessing is a prayer that calls down God's → BLESSING upon us. From God alone all blessings flow. His goodness, his closeness, his mercy—that is blessing. "May the Lord bless you" is the shortest prayer of blessing. [2626–2627]

Every Christian should call down God's blessing upon himself and upon other people. Parents can trace the Sign of the Cross on their child's forehead. People who love each other can bless one another. Furthermore a → PRIEST, by virtue of his office, blesses explicitly in the name of Jesus and on behalf of the Church. His request for blessings is made especially effective through Holy Orders and the prayer power of the whole Church.

485 Why should we adore God?

Every person who understands that he is God's creature will humbly recognize the Almighty and adore him. Christian adoration, however, sees not only the greatness, omnipotence, and → HOLINESS of God. It also kneels before the divine Love that became man in Jesus Christ.

Someone who really adores God kneels down before him or prostrates himself on the ground. This gives expression to the truth about the relation between man and God: He is great and we are little. At the same time, man is never greater than when he freely and devoutly kneels down before God. The unbeliever who is seeking God and is beginning to pray can find God in this way. → 353

486   *Why should we petition God?*

God, who knows us through and through, knows what we need. Nevertheless, God wants us to ask, to turn to him in times of need, to cry out, implore, lament, call upon him, indeed, even to struggle with him in prayer. [2629–2933]

Certainly God does not need our petitions in order to help us. It is for our own sake that we are supposed to offer prayers of petition. Someone who does not ask and does not want to ask shuts himself up in himself. Only a person who asks opens himself and turns to the Author of all good. Someone who asks goes back home to God. Thus the prayer of petition brings man into the right relationship to God, who respects our freedom.

Every day, at sunrise and sunset, believers renew their "adoration" or acknowledgment of the presence of God, Creator and Lord of the Universe. This recognition is full of gratitude that wells up from the depths of their heart and floods their entire being, for it is only by adoring and loving God above all things that human beings can totally fulfill themselves.

POPE BENEDICT XVI, August 7, 2005

What do Christians express by prayer postures?

Christians bring their life before God through the language of the body: They cast themselves down before God. They fold their hands in prayer or stretch them out (the Orante position). They genuflect (bend the knee) or kneel before the All-Holy God. They listen to the Gospel while standing. They meditate while seated.

 Standing in the presence of God expresses reverence (you stand up when a superior enters) and also vigilance and readiness (you are ready to set out on a journey immediately). If at the same time the hands are outstretched in praise of God (the Orante position), the person praying assumes the original gesture of praise.

 While **sitting** in God's presence, the Christian listens to what is happening interiorly; he ponders the Word in his heart (Lk 2:51) and meditates on it.

 By **kneeling**, a person makes himself small in the presence of God's greatness. He recognizes his dependence on God's grace.

 By **prostrating** himself, a person adores God.

 By **folding the hands,** a person overcomes distraction, "recollects himself" (gathers his thoughts) and unites himself to God. Folded hands are also the original gesture of petition.

487 *Why should we petition God for other people?*

As Abraham intervened by his prayer for the inhabitants of Sodom, as Jesus prayed for his disciples, and as the early Christian community looked "not only to [their] own interests, but also to the interests of others" (Phil 2:4), so too Christians always pray for

everyone—for people who are dear to their hearts, for people who are not close to them, and even for their enemies. [2634–2636, 2647]

The more a person learns to pray, the more profoundly he realizes that he has ties to a spiritual family through which the power of prayer is made effective. With all my concern for the people whom I love, I stand in the midst of the family of mankind and may receive strength from the prayers of others and may call down divine assistance for others. → 477

To intercede means to send someone an angel.

MARTIN LUTHER (1483–1546)

There must be people who pray even for those who never pray.

VICTOR HUGO (1802–1885, French writer)

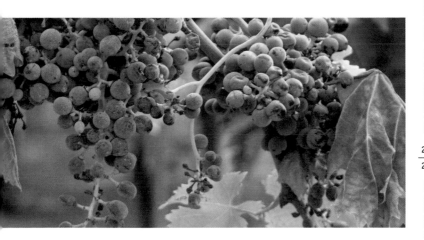

488 *Why should we thank God?*

Everything that we are and have comes from God. Paul says, "What have you that you did not receive?" (1 Cor 4:7). Being grateful to God, the giver of all good things, makes you happy. [2637–2638, 2648]

The greatest prayer of thanks is the "→ EUCHARIST" ("thanksgiving" in Greek) of Jesus, in which he takes bread and wine so as to offer in them to God all of creation, transformed. Whenever Christians give thanks, they are joining in Jesus' great prayer of thanksgiving. For we, too, are transformed and redeemed by Jesus, and so from the depths of our hearts we can be grateful and tell God this in a variety of ways.

Give thanks in all circumstances; for this is the will of God in Christ Jesus for you.

1 Thess 5:18

For what is past— thanks! For what is to come—yes!

DAG HAMMARSKJÖLD (1905–1961)

Continue steadfastly in prayer, being watchful in it with thanksgiving.

Col 4:2

Prayer does not change God, but it changes the person who prays.

SØREN KIERKEGAARD (1813–1855)

Above all, the Gospels sustain me during my hours of prayer; in them I find everything that my poor little soul needs. I constantly discover in them new insights, hidden, mysterious meanings.

ST. THÉRÈSE OF LISIEUX (1873–1897)

Prayer is nothing other than attention in its purest form.

SIMONE WEIL (1909–1943, French political activist, philosopher, and mystic)

Seven times a day I praise you for your righteous ordinances.

Ps 119:164

489 *What does it mean to praise God?*

God needs no applause. But we need to express spontaneously our delight in God and the rejoicing in our hearts. We praise God because he exists and because he is good. We thereby join even now in the eternal praise of the angels and saints in heaven. [2639–2642] → 48

≪≫ CHAPTER TWO ≪≫
The Sources of Prayer

490 *Is it enough to pray when you feel like praying?*

No. Someone who prays only when he feels like it does not take God seriously and will leave off praying. Prayer thrives on faithfulness. [2650]

491 *Can you learn to pray from the Bible?*

The → BIBLE is like a wellspring of prayer. To pray with the Word of God means to use the words and events of the Bible for one's own prayer. "To be ignorant of Scripture is to be ignorant of Christ" (St. Jerome). [2652–2653]

Sacred Scripture, especially the Psalms and the → NEW TESTAMENT, are a valuable treasury; in it we find the most beautiful and most powerful prayers of the Judeo-Christian world. Reciting these prayers unites us with millions of people from all times and cultures who have prayed, but above all with Christ himself, who is present in all these prayers.

492 *Does my personal prayer have something to do with the prayer of the Church?*

In the Church's public worship, in her Liturgy of the Hours and in Holy Mass, common prayers are recited that come from Sacred Scripture or from the Tradition of the Church. They unite the individual with the praying community of the Church. [2655–2658, 2662]

Christian prayer is not a private matter, but it is very personal. Personal prayer becomes purified, expands, and is strengthened when it regularly flows into the prayer of the whole Church. It is a great and beautiful sign when believers throughout the earth are united at the same time in the same prayers and thereby sing one hymn of praise to God. → 188

493 What are the characteristics of Christian prayer?

Christian prayer is prayer in the attitude of faith, hope, and charity. It is persevering and resigns itself to the will of God. [2656–2658, 2662]

Someone who prays as a Christian steps at that moment out of himself and enters into an attitude of trusting faith in the one God and Lord; at the same time he places all his hope in God—that HE will hear, understand, accept, and perfect him. St. John Bosco once said, "To know the will of God, three things are required: prayer, waiting, taking counsel." Finally, Christian prayer is always an expression of love, which comes from Christ's love and seeks the divine love.

494 How can my everyday routine be a school of prayer?

Everything that happens, every encounter can become the occasion for a prayer. For the more deeply we live in union with God, the deeper we understand the world around us. [2659–2660]

Someone who already seeks union with Jesus in the morning can be a blessing to the people he meets, even his opponents and enemies. Over the course of the day he casts all his cares on the Lord. He has more peace within himself and radiates it. He makes his judgments and decisions by asking himself how Jesus would act at that moment. He overcomes fear by staying close to God. In desperate situations he is not without support. He carries the peace of heaven within him and thereby brings it into the world. He is full of gratitude and joy for the beautiful things, but also endures the difficult things that he encounters. This attentiveness to God is possible even at work.

> You are great, O Lord, and greatly to be praised.... And man, so small a part of your creation, wants to praise you.... You yourself encourage him to delight in your praise, for you have made us for yourself, and our heart is restless until it rests in you.
>
> ST. AUGUSTINE (354–430)

> I waited patiently for the Lord; he inclined to me and heard my cry.
>
> Ps 40:1

> My secret is quite simple: I pray. And through my prayer I become one with the love of Christ and see that praying is loving him, that praying is living with him, and that means making his words come true.... For me, praying means being one with the will of Jesus twenty-four hours a day, living for him, through him, and with him.
>
> BL. TERESA OF CALCUTTA (1910–1997)

495 Can we be sure that our prayers are heard?

Our prayers, which we offer in Jesus' name, go to the place where Jesus' prayers also went: to the heart of our heavenly Father. [2664–2669, 2680–2681]

We can be sure of this if we trust Jesus. For Jesus has opened again for us the way to heaven, which had been barred by sin. Since Jesus is the way to God, Christians conclude their prayers with the phrase, "we ask this through Jesus Christ, our Lord." → 477

496 Why do we need the Holy Spirit when we pray?

The →BIBLE says, "We do not know how to pray as we ought, but the Spirit himself intercedes for us with sighs too deep for words" (Rom 8:26).

Praying *to* God *is* possible only *with* God. It is not primarily our accomplishment that our prayer actually reaches God. We Christians have received the Spirit of Jesus, who wholeheartedly yearned to be one with the Father: to be loving at all times, to listen to each other with complete attention, to understand each other thoroughly, to want wholeheartedly what the other person wants. This holy Spirit of Jesus is in us, and he is speaking through us when we pray. Basically prayer means that from the depths of my heart, God speaks to God. The Holy Spirit helps our spirit to pray. Hence we should say again and again, "Come, Holy Spirit, come and help me to pray." → 120

497 Why does it help to turn to the saints when we pray?

Saints are people who are aflame with the Holy Spirit; they keep God's fire burning in the Church. Even during their earthly life, the saints prayed ardently, in a way that was contagious. When we are close to them, it is easy to pray. Of course, we never worship saints; we are allowed, though, to call on them in heaven, so that they may present petitions for us at the throne of God. [2683–2684]

The Holy Spirit is the Spirit of Jesus Christ, the Spirit who unites the Father with the Son in Love.

POPE BENEDICT XVI,
Vigil of Pentecost 2006

Come, O Holy Spirit, come;
And from Thy heavenly Home
Shed a ray of Light divine ...

Sequence for Pentecost

Likewise the Spirit helps us in our weakness.

Rom 8:26a

> If you are seeking God but do not know how you should begin, learn to pray and make the effort to pray every day.
>
> BL. TERESA OF CALCUTTA (1910–1997)

> The more generous you are toward God, the more generous you will find that he is toward you.
>
> ST. IGNATIUS LOYOLA (1491–1556)

> Not all saints have the same sort of holiness. There are those who could never have lived with other saints. Not all have the same path. But all arrive at God.
>
> ST. JOHN VIANNEY (1786–1859)

SPIRITUALITY
Forms of piety in the Church, which in many cases developed out of the Spirit-filled way of life of the saints. Thus we speak about Benedictine, Franciscan, or Dominican spirituality.

Around the great saints developed particular schools of → SPIRITUALITY, which like the colors of the spectrum all point to the pure light of God. They all start with a fundamental element of the faith, so as to lead—in each case by a different gate—to the center of the faith and devotion to God. Thus Franciscan spirituality starts with poverty of spirit, Benedictine spirituality with the praise of God, and Ignatian spirituality with discernment and vocation. A spirituality to which someone feels attracted, depending on his personal character, is always a school of prayer.

498 *Can you pray anywhere?*

Yes, you can pray anywhere. Nevertheless a Catholic will always look also for those places where God "dwells" in a special way. Above all these are Catholic churches, where our Lord is present in the → TABERNACLE under the appearance of bread. [2691, 2696]

It is very important for us to pray everywhere: in school, on the subway, during a party, in the midst of our friends. The whole world has to be drenched with → BLESSINGS. But it is also important for us to visit sacred places, where God waits for us, so to speak, so that we can rest in his presence, be strengthened, replenished, and sent forth by him. A genuine Christian is never just sightseeing when he visits a church. He lingers a moment in silence, adores God, and renews his friendship and love for him. → 218

◇ CHAPTER THREE ◇
The Way of Prayer

499 *When should a person pray?*

From the earliest times Christians have prayed at least in the morning, at meals, and in the evening. Someone who does not pray regularly will soon not pray at all. [2697–2698, 2720]

Anyone who loves another person and all day long never gives that person a sign of his love does not really love him. So it is with God, too. Anyone who truly seeks him will keep sending him signals of his longing for his company and friendship. Get up in the morning and give the day to God, asking for his → BLESSING and to "be there" in all your meetings and needs. Thank him, especially at mealtimes. At the end of the day, place everything into his hands, ask him for forgiveness, and pray for peace for yourself and others. A great day—full of signs of life that reach God. → 188

500 *Are there various ways to pray?*

Yes, there is vocal prayer, meditation, and contemplative prayer. All three ways of prayer presuppose recollecting one's mind and heart. [2699, 2721]

501 *What is vocal prayer?*

In the first place, prayer is lifting the heart to God. And yet Jesus himself taught his disciples to pray with words. With the *Our Father* he left us the perfect

vocal prayer as his testament to show how we should pray. [2700–2704, 2722]

While praying we should not try to think pious thoughts. We should *express* what is in our hearts and offer it to God as complaint, petition, praise, and thanks. Often it is the great vocal prayers—the Psalms and hymns of Sacred Scripture, the Our Father, the Hail Mary—that direct us to the true substance of prayer and lead to a kind of free, interior prayer. → 511–527

502 *What is the essence of meditation?*

The essence of meditation is a prayerful seeking that starts with a sacred text or a sacred image and explores the will, the signs, and the presence of God. [2705–2708]

We cannot "read" sacred images and texts the way we read things in the newspaper that do not immediately concern us. Instead, we should meditate on them; in other words I should lift my heart to God and tell him that I am now quite open to what God wants to say to me through what I have read or seen. Besides Sacred Scripture, there are many texts that lead to God and are suitable for meditative prayer. → 16

→ If you do not know how to pray, ask him to teach you, and ask your heavenly Mother to pray with you and for you.

POPE BENEDICT XVI
to the young people of the Netherlands, November 21, 2005

” There are many paths of prayer. Some people follow only one, while others walk along all of them. There are moments of a lively certainty: Christ is there, he is speaking inside us. In other moments he is the silent one, a distant stranger … . For everyone prayer remains, in its infinite variations, a passageway to a life that does not come from ourselves but from somewhere else.

BROTHER ROGER SCHUTZ

” Much knowledge is not what satisfies the soul and gives it contentment, but rather interior meditation on things and savoring them.

ST. IGNATIUS LOYOLA
(1491–1556)

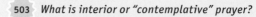

> Keep your soul in peace. Let God work in you. Welcome thoughts that raise your heart to God. Open wide the window of your soul.

ST. IGNATIUS LOYOLA
(1491–1556)

> I look at him, and he looks at me.

A peasant to St. John Vianney (1786–1859), when asked about his prayer

MEDITATION
(from Latin *meditare* = to think over, consider): Meditation is a spiritual exercise practiced in various religions and cultures in which man is supposed to find his way to himself (and to God). Christianity recognizes and treasures a variety of meditative practices, but rejects those practices that promise union with God or with the divine as the result of a particular technique of meditation.

Zzzzzz....

503 *What is interior or "contemplative" prayer?*

Contemplative prayer is love, silence, listening, and being in the presence of God. [2709–2719, 2724]

For interior prayer one needs time, resolve, and above all a pure heart. It is the humble, poor devotion of a creature that drops all masks, believes in love, and seeks God from the heart. Interior prayer is often called the prayer of the heart and → CONTEMPLATION. → 463

504 *What can a Christian accomplish through meditation?*

In → MEDITATION a Christian seeks silence so as to experience intimacy with God and to find peace in his presence. He hopes for the sensible experience of his presence, which is an undeserved *gift of grace*; he does not expect it, however, as the product of a particular technique of meditation.

→ MEDITATION can be an important aid to faith that strengthens and matures the human person. Nevertheless, techniques of meditation that promise to bring about an experience of God, or even the soul's union with God, are deceptive. On account of such false promises, many people believe that God has abandoned them just because they do not perceive him. But God cannot be compelled to show up by particular methods. He communicates himself to us whenever and however he wishes.

505 *Why is prayer sometimes a struggle?*

The spiritual masters of all times have described growth in faith and in love for God as a spiritual, life-and-death combat. The battlefield is man's interior life. The Christian's weapon is prayer. We can allow ourselves be defeated by our selfishness and lose ourselves over worthless things — or we can win God. [2725–2752]

Often someone who wants to pray must first conquer his lack of will power. Even the Desert Fathers were acquainted with spiritual sluggishness ("acedia"). Reluctance to seek God is a big problem in the spiritual life. The spirit of the times sees no point in praying, and our full calendars leave no room for it. Then there is the battle against the tempter, who will try anything to keep a person from devoting himself to God. If God did not want us to find our way to him in prayer, we would not win the battle.

506 Is prayer not just a sort of conversation with yourself?

The distinctive feature about prayer is precisely the fact that one goes from Me to You, from self-centeredness to radical openness. Someone who is really praying can experience the fact that God speaks—and that often he does not speak as we expect and would like.

Those who are experienced in prayer report that a person very often comes out of a prayer session different from the way he went in. Sometimes expectations are met: you are sad and find consolation; you lack confidence and receive new strength. It can also happen, though, that you would like to forget pressures but are made even more uneasy; that you would like to be left in peace and instead receive an assignment. A real encounter with God—the kind that occurs again and again in prayer—can shatter our preconceptions about both God and prayer.

507 What happens if you find that prayer does not help?

Prayer does not seek superficial success but rather the will of God and intimacy with him. God's apparent silence is itself an invitation to take a step farther—in total devotion, boundless faith, endless expectation. Anyone who prays must allow God the complete freedom to speak whenever he wants, to grant whatever he wants, and to give himself however he wants. [2735–2737]

Often we say: I have prayed, but it did not help at all. Maybe we are not praying intensely enough. The

---

> We should have a holy boldness, because God helps the courageous and is not a respecter of persons.

ST. TERESA OF AVILA
(1515–1582)

Fight the good fight of the faith.

1 Tim 6:12

> Here God and the devil struggle, and the battlefield is the human heart.

FYODOR M. DOSTOYEVSKY
(1821–1881), *The Brothers Karamazov*

> As long as we live, we fight, and as long as we are fighting, that is a sign that we are not defeated and that the good Spirit dwells within us. And if death does not meet you as the victor, he should find you a warrior.

ST. AUGUSTINE (354–430)

> Praying means listening more than speaking. Meditation means being looked at more than looking.

CARLO CARRETTO
(1910-1988, Italian writer, mystic, and "Little Brother of Jesus")

saintly Curé of Ars once asked a brother priest who was complaining about his lack of success, "You have prayed, you have sighed ... but have you fasted, too? Have you kept vigil?" It could also be that we are asking God for the wrong things. St. Teresa of Avila once said, "Do not pray for lighter burdens; pray for a stronger back." → 40, 49

508 *What happens if you do not feel anything when you pray or even experience reluctance to pray?*

Distractions during prayer, the feeling of interior emptiness and dryness, indeed, even an aversion to prayer are experienced by everyone who prays. Then to persevere faithfully is itself already a prayer. [2729–2733]

Even St. Thérèse of Lisieux for a long time could not sense God's love at all. Shortly before her death she was visited one night by her sister Céline. She noticed that Thérèse's hands were clasped together. "What are you doing? You should try to sleep", Céline said. "I cannot. I am suffering too much. But I am praying", Thérèse replied. "And what do you say to Jesus?" "I do not say anything to him. I love him."

509 *Isn't praying a flight from reality?*

Someone who prays does not flee from reality; rather, he opens his eyes for reality as a whole. From Almighty God himself he receives the strength to cope with reality.

→ the same insistence as a poor man on the street would ask for alms.

ST. PHILIPP NERI (1515–1595, the "Apostle of Rome" and founder of the Oratorians)

Prayer is like going to a gas station where we get free fuel for our long journeys and extreme challenges. Praying does not lead out of reality but, rather, deeper into it. Praying does not take time away from other things but, rather, doubles the remaining time and fills it with intrinsic meaning. → 356

510 *Is it possible to pray always?*

Prayer is always possible. Prayer is vitally necessary. Prayer and life cannot be separated.
[2742–2745, 2757]

You cannot keep God content with a few words in the morning or evening. Our life must become prayer, and our prayers must become life. Every Christian life story is also a story of prayer, one long attempt to achieve ever greater union with God. Because many Christians experience a heartfelt longing to be with

" Thus Christian spirituality ... is not a ... flight from or rejection of the world, nor can it be reduced to mere temporal activity. Imbued by the Spirit ..., it is a spirituality of the transfiguration of the world and of hope in the coming of God's kingdom.

POPE JOHN PAUL II (1920–2005), December 2, 1998

God constantly, they turn to the so-called "Jesus prayer", which has been an age-old custom particularly in the Eastern Churches. The person who prays it tries to integrate a simple formula—the most well-known formula is *"Lord Jesus Christ, Son of God, have mercy on me, a sinner"*—into his daily routine in such a way that it becomes a constant prayer.

❧ SECTION TWO ❧
The Lord's Prayer: The Our Father

511 *What are the words of the Our Father?*

**Our Father, who art in heaven,
hallowed be thy name,
thy kingdom come,
thy will be done
on earth as it is in heaven.
Give us this day our daily bread,
and forgive us our trespasses,
as we forgive those who trespass against us;
and lead us not into temptation,
but deliver us from evil.
For thine is the kingdom and the power and the glory
forever. Amen.**

In Latin:
*Pater noster, qui es in caelis;
sanctificetur nomen tuum; adveniat regnum tuum,
fiat voluntas tua, sicut in caelo et in terra.
Panem nostrum quotidianum da nobis hodie;
et dimitte nobis debita nostra,
sicut et nos dimittimus debitoribus nostris;
et ne nos inducas in tentationem;
sed libera nos a malo.
Quia tuum est regnum, et potestas, et gloria
in saecula. Amen.*

The Our Father is the only prayer that Jesus himself taught his disciples (Mt 6:9–13; Lk 11:2–4). That is why the Our Father is also called "the Lord's Prayer". Christians of all Christian denominations pray it daily, both in the liturgy and privately. The conclusion, "For thine is the kingdom ... " is mentioned as early as the

"Teaching of the Twelve Apostles" (Didache, ca. A.D. 150), and so it can be added to the Our Father.

512 How did the Our Father come about?

The Our Father came about at the request of one of Jesus' disciples, who saw his Master praying and wanted to learn from Jesus himself how to pray correctly. → 477

513 What structure does the Our Father have?

The Our Father consists of seven petitions to our merciful Father in heaven. The first three petitions relate to God and the right way of serving him. The last four petitions present our basic human needs to our Father in heaven. [2803–2806, 2857]

514 What position does the Our Father hold among prayers?

The Our Father is "the most perfect prayer" (St. Thomas Aquinas) and the "summary of the whole Gospel" (Tertullian). [2761–2772, 2774, 2776]

The Our Father is more than a prayer—it is a path that leads directly into the heart of our Father. The early Christians recited this original prayer of the Church, which is entrusted to every Christian at Baptism, three times a day. We, too, should not let a day pass without trying to recite the Lord's Prayer with our lips, to take it to heart, and to make it come true in our lives.

515 Where do we get the confidence to call God "Father"?

We can be so bold as to address God as Father because Jesus has called us to a close relationship with himself and made us children of God. In communion with him, "who is in the bosom of the Father" (Jn 1:18), we are privileged to cry, "Abba, Father!" [2777–2778, 2797–2800] → 37

[Jesus] was praying in a certain place, and when he ceased, one of his disciples said to him, "Lord, teach us to pray, as John taught his disciples."

Lk 11:1

Let us pray therefore, dearest brethren, as God, the Master, has taught us. It is an intimate and fervent prayer, when we pray to God with what is his, when we make Christ's prayer ascend to his ears. May the Father recognize again the words of his Son when we recite a prayer ... Consider that we stand in the sight of God.

ST. CYPRIAN OF CARTHAGE (200–258)

516 *How can people say "Father" to God if they have been tormented or abandoned by their earthly father/their earthly parents?*

Human fathers and mothers often distort the image of a kind, fatherly God. Our Father in heaven, however, is not the same as our experiences of human parents. We must purify our image of God from all inadequate ideas so as to be able to encounter him with unconditional trust. [2779]

Even individuals who have been raped by their own father can learn to pray the Our Father. Often it is their task in life to allow themselves to experience a love that was cruelly refused them by others but that nevertheless exists in a marvelous way, beyond all human imagining.

517 *How are we changed by the Our Father?*

The Our Father allows us to discover joyfully that we are children of one Father. Our common vocation is to praise our Father and to live together as though "of one heart and soul" (Acts 4:32). [2787–2791, 2801]

Because God the Father loves each of his children with the same exclusive love, as though we were the only object of his devotion, we too must get along together in a completely new way: peacefully, full of consideration and love, so that each one can *be* the awe-inspiring miracle that he actually is in God's sight.
→ 61, 280

518 *If the Father is "in heaven", where is that heaven?*

Heaven is wherever God is. The word "heaven" does not designate a place but, rather, indicates God's presence, which is not bound by space and time. [2794–2796, 2803]

We should not look for heaven above the clouds. Wherever we turn to God in his glory and to our

neighbor in his need; wherever we experience the joys of love; whenever we convert and allow ourselves to be reconciled with God, *heaven opens there.* "Not that God is where heaven is, but rather heaven is where God is" (Gerhard Ebeling). → 52

519 What does it mean to say, "Hallowed be thy name"?

To "hallow" or to treat God's name as something holy means to place him above everything else. [2807– 2815, 2858]

A "name" in Sacred Scripture indicates the true nature of a person. To hallow God's name means to do justice to his reality, to acknowledge him, to praise him, to give him due honor, and to live according to his commandments. → 31

520 What does it mean to say, "Thy kingdom come"?

When we pray, "Thy kingdom come", we call for Christ to come again, as he promised, and for God's reign, which has already begun here on earth, to prevail definitively. [2816–2821, 2859]

> In the Lord's Prayer we say all together, "Our Father". So says the emperor, the beggar, the slave, the master. They are all brothers, because they have one Father.
>
> ST. AUGUSTINE
> (354–430)

> Heaven on earth is wherever people are filled with love for God, for their fellowmen, and for themselves.
>
> ST. HILDEGARD OF BINGEN
> (1098–1179)

> Set your minds on things that are above, not on things that are on earth.
>
> Col 3:2

François Fénelon says, "To will everything that God wills, and to will it always, in all circumstances and without reservations: that is the kingdom of God which is entirely within." → 89,91

521 *What does it mean to say, "Thy will be done on earth as it is in heaven"?*

When we pray for the universal accomplishment of God's will, we pray that on earth and in our own heart it may become as it already is in heaven. [2822–2827, 2860]

As long as we continue to set our hearts on our own plans, our will, and our ideas, earth cannot become heaven. One person wants this, the other that. We find our happiness, however, when together we want what God wills. Praying means making room bit by bit for God's will on this earth. → 49–50, 52

522 *What does it mean to say, "Give us this day our daily bread"?*

The petition about our daily bread makes us people who await *everything* from the goodness of our heavenly Father, including the material and spiritual goods that are vitally necessary. No Christian can pronounce this petition without thinking about his real responsibility for those in the world who lack the basic necessities of life. [2828–2834, 2861]

523 *Why does man not live on bread alone?*

"Man shall not live by bread alone, but by every word that proceeds from the mouth of God" (Mt 4:4, citing Deut 8:3). [2835]

This passage of Scripture reminds us that men have a spiritual hunger that cannot be satisfied by material means. One can die for lack of bread, but one can also die because one has received bread alone. In a profound sense we are nourished by the one who has "the words of eternal life" (Jn 6:68) and a food that does not perish (Jn 6:27): the Holy → EUCHARIST.

> There is hunger for ordinary bread, but there is also hunger for love, kindness, and mutual respect—and that is the great poverty from which people today suffer so much.

BL. TERESA OF CALCUTTA
(1910–1997)

[God] desires all men to be saved and to come to the knowledge of the truth.

1 Tim 2:4

> Complete self-renunciation means accepting with a smile whatever HE gives and whatever HE takes away.... Giving whatever is demanded—even if it is your good name or your health—that is self-renunciation, and then you are free.

BL. TERESA OF CALCUTTA
(1910–1997)

If any one says, "I love God," and hates his brother, he is a liar; for he who does not love his brother whom he has seen, cannot love God whom he has not seen.

1 Jn 4:20

"Be merciful, even as your Father is merciful."

Lk 6:36

" Someone who is not tempted is not tested; someone who is not tested makes no progress.

ST. AUGUSTINE
(354–430)

Be sober, be watchful. Your adversary the devil prowls around like a roaring lion, seeking some one to devour.

1 Pet 5:8

We know that we are of God, and the whole world is in the power of the Evil One.

1 Jn 5:19

" The devil's most cunning trick is to convince us that he does not exist.

CHARLES BAUDELAIRE
(1821–1867, French poet)

524 *What does it mean to say, "Forgive us our trespasses, as we forgive those who trespass against us"?*

Merciful forgiveness—the mercy that we show to others and the mercy that we ourselves seek—is indivisible. If we ourselves are not merciful and do not forgive one another, God's mercy will not reach our hearts. [2838–2845, 2862]

Many people have a lifelong struggle with their inability to forgive. The deep blockade of being unreconciled is resolved only by looking to God, who adopted us "while we were yet sinners" (Rom 5:8). Because we have a kind Father, forgiveness and reconciliation in life are possible. → 227, 314

525 *What does it mean to say, "Lead us not into temptation"?*

Because every day and every hour we are in danger of falling into sin and saying No to God, we beg God not to leave us defenseless in the power of temptation. [2846–2849]

Jesus, who was tempted himself, knows that we are weak human beings, who have little strength of our own with which to oppose the evil one. He graciously gives us the petition from the Our Father, which teaches us to trust in God's assistance in the hour of trial.

526 *What does it mean to say, "Deliver us from evil"?*

"Evil" in the Our Father does not mean a negative spiritual force or energy, but rather Evil in person, whom Sacred Scripture knows by the name of "the tempter", "the father of lies", Satan, or the devil. [2850–2854, 2864]

No one can deny that evil in the world is devastating in its power, that we are surrounded by devilish suggestions, that there are often demonic processes at work in history. Only Sacred Scripture calls things by their name: "For we are not contending against flesh and blood, but against the principalities, against

the powers, against the world rulers of this present darkness" (Eph 6:12). The petition from the Our Father "deliver us from evil" brings all the misery of this world before God and begs God Almighty to free us from all evils.

527 *Why do we end the Our Father with "Amen"?*

Christians and Jews alike from ancient times have concluded all their prayers with "Amen", thereby saying, "Yes, so be it!" [2855–2856, 2865]

When a person says "Amen" to his words, "Amen" to his life and his destiny, "Amen" to the joy that awaits him, then heaven and earth come together and we are at the goal: with the love that created us in the beginning.

→ 165

EMBOLISM
(from Greek, *emballein* = insert): a clause added to the Our Father when it is recited at Mass: *Deliver us, Lord, we pray, from every evil, graciously grant peace in our days, that, by the help of your mercy, we may be always free from sin and safe from all distress, as we await the blessed hope and the coming of our Savior, Jesus Christ.*

The Amen of our faith is not death, but life.

MICHAEL CARDINAL FAULHABER
(1869–1952)

Subject Index

The numbers in this index refer to the numbers of the individual questions. A number printed in bold gives the main reference; other numbers indicate further discussion.

Definitions

The definitions of these terms can be found on the following pages:

Abbreviations of the biblical books

Gen	Genesis	**Song**	Song of Solomon	**Acts**	The Acts of the Apostles
Ex	Exodus	**Wis**	Wisdom	**Rom**	Romans
Lev	Levitucus	**Sir**	Sirach/Ecclesiasticus	**1 Cor**	1. Corinthians
Num	Numbers	**Is**	Isaiah	**2 Cor**	2. Corinthians
Dtn	Deuteronomy	**Jer**	Jeremiah	**Gal**	Galatians
Josh	Joshua	**Lam**	Lamentations	**Eph**	Ephesians
Judg	Judges	**Bar**	Baruch	**Phil**	Philippians
Ruth	Ruth	**Ezek**	Ezekiel	**Col**	Colossians
1 Sam	1 Samuel	**Dan**	Daniel	**1 Thess**	1. Thessalonians
2 Sam	2 Samuel	**Hos**	Hosea	**2 Thess**	2. Thessalonians
1 Kings	1 Kings	**Joel**	Joel	**1 Tim**	1. Timothy
2 Kings	2 Kings	**Am**	Amos	**2 Tim**	2. Timothy
1 Chron	1 Chronicles	**Obad**	Obadiah	**Tit**	Titus
2 Chron	2 Chronicles	**Jona**	Jonah	**Phlm**	Philemon
Ezra	Ezra	**Mic**	Micah	**Heb**	Hebrew
Neh	Nehemiah	**Nahum**	Nahum	**Jas**	James
Tob	Tobit	**Hab**	Habakkuk	**1 Pet**	1. Peter
Jud	Judith	**Zeph**	Zephania	**2 Pet**	2. Peter
Esther	Esther	**Hag**	Haggai	**1 Jn**	1. John
1 Mac	1 Maccabees	**Zech**	Zechariah	**2 Jn**	2. John
2 Mac	2 Maccabees	**Mal**	Malachi	**3 Jn**	3. John
Job	Job	**Mt**	Matthew	**Jude**	Jude
Ps	Psalms	**Mk**	Mark	**Rev**	Revelation/Apocalypse
Prov	Proverbs	**Lk**	Luke		
Eccles	Ecclesiastes	**Jn**	John		

Abbreviations

The documents of the Second Vatican Council and other sources have been cited using the following abbreviations:

CCC   Catechism of the Catholic Church

CIC   *Codex Iuris Canonici,* Code of Canon Law of the Catholic Church

CiV   Pope Benedict XVI, Encyclical *Caritas in veritate*

DH   Second Vatican Council, Declaration on Religious Liberty *Dignitatis humanae*

DV   Second Vatican Council, Dogmatic Constitution on Divine Revelation *Dei Verbum*

GS   Second Vatican Council, Pastoral Constitution on the Church in the Modern World *Gaudium et Spes*

LE   Pope John Paul II, Encyclical *Laborem exercens*

LG   Second Vatican Council, Dogmatic Constitution on the Church *Lumen Gentium*

PP   Pope Paul VI, Encyclical *Populorum progressio*

Acknowledgments

The German, Austrian, and Swiss bishops' conferences thank the following persons who assisted in the development of the German edition and the international editions of this work: Dr. Johannes zu Eltz (Frankfurt), Michaela Heereman (Meerbusch), Bernhard Meuser (München) and Dr. Christian Schmitt (Münster). Important advice was given by Prof. Dr. Dr. Michael Langer (Oberaudorf), Dr. Manfred Lütz (Bonn), Prof. Dr. Edgar Korherr (Graz), Otto Neubauer (Vienna), Regens Martin Straub (Augsburg) und Dr. Hubert-Philipp Weber (Vienna)

They also wish to thank all the youth collaborators: Agnes, Alexander, Amelie, Anne-Sophie, Angelika, Antonia, Assunta, Carl, Claudius, Clemens, Coco, Constantin, Damian, Daniela, Dario, Dominik, Donata, Esther, Felicitas, Felix, Felix, Gina, Giuliano, Huberta, Ida, Isabel, Ivo, Johanna, Johannes, Josef-Erwein, Karl, Katharina, Kristina, Lioba, Lukas, Marie-Sophie, Marie, Marie, Mariella, Matern, Monika, Nico, Nicolo, Niki, Niko, Philippa, Pia, Rebekka, Regina, Robert, Rudolph, Sophie, Stephanie, Tassilo, Theresa, Theresa, Theresa, Theresa, Teresa, Uta, Valerie, Victoria

Photographs
Paul Badde 34, 65, 66, 74, 130, 170, 264, 275; Nikolaus Behr 160, 163, 253, 285; Anne-Sophie Boeselager 98; Damian Boeselager 110, 153, 206, 246; Ilona Boeselager 138, 205; Gary Huber 151; Ildikó Ketteler 44; Kloster Magdenau 91, 164; Josef Kressierer 144, 145; Michael Langer 216; Caroline Lasson 180; Alexander Lengerke 19, 32, 52, 55, 57, 87, 88, 104, 113, 114, 118, 175, 192, 196, 210, 250, 256; Marie-Sophie Lobkowicz 15, 28, 30; Philippa Loë 184; Felix Löwenstein 12, 24, 68, 77, 78, 188, 238, 301; 245; Jerko Malinar (www.cross-press.net) 66, 249, 260; Nightfever (www.nightfever.de) 149, 267, 272, 273; Christiane Pottgießer 287; Bernhard Rindt 108, 125; Luc Serafin 38, 40, 43, 47, 84, 85, 100, 121, 157, 203, 219, 226, 230, 239, 259, 278, 279, 280, 283; Sxc.hu 150, 168, 194, 213; Wieslaw Smetek 62,63

Personal notes